PUBLISHING

C000090147

ONLINE
RESOURCES
INCLUDED

THIS COMPLETE TEXT COMES WITH FREE ONLINE ACCESS SO THAT YOU CAN STUDY ANYTIME, ANYWHERE

IN ADDITION TO THE CONTENTS OF THE TEXT, EN-gage ALSO ENABLES YOU TO BENEFIT FROM EXTRA ONLINE TESTING AND OTHER USEFUL STUDY MATERIALS:

- An online version of the Text which allows you to click in and out of the expandable content and view the answers to the Test Your Understanding exercises
- Fixed Online Tests with instant answers
- Test History and Reports to allow you to track and compare your results
- Interim and Final Assessment Questions and Answers

And you can access all of these extra resources anytime, anywhere using your EN-gage account.

How to access your online resources

If you are a Kaplan Financial student	You will already have an EN-gage account and these extra resources will be available to you online. You do not need to register again, as this process was completed when you enrolled. If you are having problems accessing online materials, please ask your course administrator.
If you purchased through Kaplan Flexible Learning or via the Kaplan Publishing website	You will automatically receive an e-mail invitation to EN-gage online. Please register your details using this e-mail to gain access to your content. If you do not receive the e-mail or book content, please contact Kaplan Flexible Learning.
If you are already a registered EN-gage user	Go to www.EN-gage.co.uk and log in. Select the 'add a book' feature and enter the ISBN number of this book and the unique pass key at the bottom of this card. Then click 'finished' or 'add another book'. You may add as many books as you have purchased from this screen.
If you are a new EN-gage user	Register at www.EN-gage.co.uk and click on the link contained in the e-mail we sent you to activate your account. Then select the 'add a book' feature, enter the ISBN number of this book and the unique pass key at the bottom of this card. Then click 'finished' or 'add another book'.

Your Code and Information

This code can only be used once for the registration of one book online. This registration will expire when the final sittings for the examinations covered by this book have taken place. Please allow one hour from the time you submitted your book details for us to process your request.

ajXl-rgTw-oAhZ-BPae

For technical support, please visit www.EN-gage.co.uk

ACCA

Paper F3 (INT)

Financial accounting

Complete Text

British library cataloguing-in-publication data

A catalogue record for this book is available from the British Library.

Published by:
Kaplan Publishing UK
Unit 2 The Business Centre
Molly Millars Lane
Wokingham
Berkshire
RG41 2QZ

ISBN 978 1 84710 723 7

© Kaplan Financial Limited, 2009

The text in this material and any others made available by any Kaplan Group company does not amount to advice on a particular matter and should not be taken as such. No reliance should be placed on the content as the basis for any investment or other decision or in connection with any advice given to third parties. Please consult your appropriate professional adviser as necessary. Kaplan Publishing Limited and all other Kaplan group companies expressly disclaim all liability to any person in respect of any losses or other claims, whether direct, indirect, incidental, consequential or otherwise arising in relation to the use of such materials.

Printed in the UK by CPI William Clowes Beccles NR34 7TL

Acknowledgements

We are grateful to the Association of Chartered Certified Accountants and the Chartered Institute of Management Accountants for permisssion to reproduce past examination questions. The answers have been prepared by Kaplan Publishing.

All rights reserved. No part of this publication may be reproduced, stored in a retrieval system, or transmitted, in any form or by any means, electronic, mechanical, photocopying, recording or otherwise, without the prior written permission of Kaplan Publishing.

KAPLAN PUBLISHING

Contents

KAPLAN PUBLISHING

Paper Introduction

How to Use the Materials

These Kaplan Publishing learning materials have been carefully designed to make your learning experience as easy as possible and to give you the best chances of success in your examinations.

The product range contains a number of features to help you in the study process. They include:

(1) Detailed study guide and syllabus objectives

(2) Description of the examination

(3) Study skills and revision guidance

(4) Complete text or essential text

(5) Question practice

The sections on the study guide, the syllabus objectives, the examination and study skills should all be read before you commence your studies. They are designed to familiarise you with the nature and content of the examination and give you tips on how to best to approach your learning.

The **complete text or essential text** comprises the main learning materials and gives guidance as to the importance of topics and where other related resources can be found. Each chapter includes:

- The **learning objectives** contained in each chapter, which have been carefully mapped to the examining body's own syllabus learning objectives or outcomes. You should use these to check you have a clear understanding of all the topics on which you might be assessed in the examination.

- The **chapter diagram** provides a visual reference for the content in the chapter, giving an overview of the topics and how they link together.

- The **content** for each topic area commences with a brief explanation or definition to put the topic into context before covering the topic in detail. You should follow your studying of the content with a review of the illustration/s. These are worked examples which will help you to understand better how to apply the content for the topic.

- **Test your understanding** sections provide an opportunity to assess your understanding of the key topics by applying what you have learned to short questions. Answers can be found at the back of each chapter.

- **Summary diagrams** complete each chapter to show the important links between topics and the overall content of the paper. These diagrams should be used to check that you have covered and understood the core topics before moving on.

- **Question practice** is provided at the back of each text.

Icon Explanations

Definition - Key definitions that you will need to learn from the core content.

Key Point - Identifies topics that are key to success and are often examined.

Expandable Text - Expandable text provides you with additional information about a topic area and may help you gain a better understanding of the core content. Essential text users can access this additional content on-line (read it where you need further guidance or skip over when you are happy with the topic)

Illustration - Worked examples help you understand the core content better.

Test Your Understanding - Exercises for you to complete to ensure that you have understood the topics just learned.

Tricky topic - When reviewing these areas care should be taken and all illustrations and test your understanding exercises should be completed to ensure that the topic is understood.

On-line subscribers

Our on-line resources are designed to increase the flexibility of your learning materials and provide you with immediate feedback on how your studies are progressing. Ask your local customer services staff if you are not already a subscriber and wish to join.

If you are subscribed to our on-line resources you will find:

(1) On-line referenceware: reproduces your Complete or Essential Text on-line, giving you anytime, anywhere access.

(2) On-line testing: provides you with additional on-line objective testing so you can practice what you have learned further.

(3) On-line performance management: immediate access to youron-line testing results. Review your performance by key topics and chart your achievement through the course relative to your peer group.

Paper introduction

Paper background

The aim of ACCA Paper F3 (INT), Financial Accounting, is to develop knowledge and understanding of the underlying principles and concepts relating to financial accounting and technical proficiency in the use of double-entry accounting techniques including the preparation of basic financial statements.

Objectives of the syllabus

- Explain the context and purpose of financial reporting.
- Define the qualitative characteristics of financial information and the fundamental bases of accounting.
- Demonstrate the use of double entry and accounting systems.
- Record transactions and events.
- Prepare a trial balance (including identifying and correcting errors).
- Prepare basic financial statements for incorporated and unincorporated entities.

Core areas of the syllabus

- The context and purpose of financial reporting
- The qualitative characteristics of financial information and the fundamental bases of accounting
- The use of double entry and accounting systems
- Recording transactions and events
- Preparing a trial balance
- Preparing basic financial statements

Syllabus objectives

We have reproduced the ACCA's syllabus below, showing where the objectives are explored within this book. Within the chapters, we have broken down the extensive information found in the syllabus into easily digestible and relevant sections, called Content Objectives. These correspond to the objectives at the beginning of each chapter.

KAPLAN PUBLISHING

Syllabus learning objective	Chapter reference

A THE CONTEXT AND PURPOSE OF FINANCIAL REPORTING

1 The reasons for and objectives of financial reporting

(a) Define financial reporting – recording, analysing and summarising financial data.[1]	1
(b) Identify and define types of business entity – sole trader, partnership, limited liability company.[1]	1
(c) Recognise the legal differences between a sole trader,partnership and a limited liability company.[1]	1
(d) Identify the advantages and disadvantages of operating as a limited liability company, sole trader or partnership.[1]	16 & 17
(e) Understand the nature, principles and scope of financial reporting.[1]	1

2 Users' and stakeholders' needs

(a) Identify the users of financial statements and state and differentiate between their information needs.[1]	1

3 The main elements of financial reports

(a) Understand and identify the purpose of each of the main financial statements.[1]	2
(b) Define and identify assets, liabilities, equity, revenue and expenses.[1]	2 & 20

4 The regulatory framework

(a) Understand the role of the regulatory system including the roles of the International Accounting Standards Committee Foundation (IASCF), the International Accounting Standards Board (IASB), the Standards Advisory Council (SAC) and the International Financial Reporting Interpretations Committee (IFRIC).[1]	20
(b) Understand the role of International Financial Reporting Standards.[1]	20

B THE QUALITATIVE CHARACTERISTICS OF FINANCIAL INFORMATION AND THE FUNDAMENTAL BASES OF ACCOUNTING

1 The qualitative characteristics of financial reporting

(a) Define, understand and apply accounting concepts and qualitative characteristics:[1] 2 & 20

    (i) fair presentation

    (ii) going concern

    (iii) accruals

    (iv) consistency

    (v) materiality

    (vi) relevance

    (vii) reliability

    (viii)faithful representation

    (ix) substance over form

    (x) neutrality

    (xi) prudence

    (xii) completeness

    (xiii)comparability

    (xiv)understandability

    (xv) Business entity concept.

(b) Understand the balance between qualitative characteristics.[1] 20

2 Alternative bases used in the preparation of financial information

(a) Identify and explain the main characteristics of alternative valuation bases e.g. historical cost, replacement cost, net realisable value, economic value.[1] 20

(b) Understand the advantages and disadvantages of historical cost accounting.[1] 20

(c) Understand the provision of International Financial Reporting Standards governing financial statements regarding changes in accounting policies.[1] 18

(d) Identify the appropriate accounting treatment if a company changes a material accounting policy.[1] 18

C THE USE OF DOUBLE ENTRY AND ACCOUNTING SYSTEMS

1 Double entry bookkeeping principles including the maintenance of accounting records and sources of information

(a) Identify and explain the function of the main data sources in an accounting system.[1] — 10

(b) Outline the contents and purpose of different types of business documentation, including: quotation, sales order, purchase order, goods received note, goods despatched note, invoice, statement, credit note, debit note, remittance advice, receipt.[1] — 10

(c) Understand and apply the concept of double entry accounting and the duality concept.[1] — 3

(d) Understand and apply the accounting equation.[1] — 3

(e) Understand how the accounting system contributes to providing useful accounting information and complies with organisational policies and deadlines.[1] — 1

(f) Identify the main types of business transactions, e.g. sales, purchases, payments, receipts.[1] — 2, 3 & 10

2 Ledger accounts, books of prime entry and journals

(a) Identify the main types of ledger accounts and books of prime entry, and understand their nature and function.[1] — 3

(b) Understand and illustrate the uses of journals and the posting of journal entries into ledger accounts.[1] — 3

(c) Identify correct journals from given narrative.[1] — 3

(d) Illustrate how to balance and close a ledger account.[1] — 3

3 Accounting systems and the impact of information technology on financial reporting

(a) Understand the basic function and form of accounting records in a typical manual system.[1] — 14

(b) Understand the basic function and form of accounting records in a typical computerised system.[1] — 14

(c) Compare manual and computerised accounting systems.[1] — 14

(d) Identify advantages and disadvantages of computerised accounting systems.[1] — 14

(e) Understand the uses of integrated accounting software packages.[1] — 14

D RECORDING TRANSACTIONS AND EVENTS

1 Sales and purchases

(a) Record sale and purchase transactions in ledger accounts and in day books.[1] — 3 & 10

(b) Understand and record sales and purchase returns.[1] — 3

(c) Understand the general principles of the operation of a sales tax.[1] — 5

(d) Calculate sales tax on transactions and record the consequent accounting entries.[1] — 5

(e) Account for discounts allowed and discounts received.[1] — 3

2 Cash

(a) Record cash transactions in ledger accounts.[1] — 2, 10

(b) Understand the need for a record of petty cash transactions.[1] — 10

(c) Describe the features and operation of a petty cash imprest system.[1] — 10

(d) Account for petty cash using imprest and non-imprest methods.[1] — 10

(e) Understand the importance of and identify controls and security over the petty cash system.[1] — 10

3 Inventory

(a) Recognise the need for adjustments for inventory in preparing financial statements.[1] — 4

(b) Record opening and closing inventory.[1] — 4

(c) Identify the alternative methods of valuing inventory.[1] — 4

(d) Understand and apply the IASB requirements for valuing inventories.[1] — 4

(e) Recognise which costs should be included in valuing inventories.[1] — 4

(f) Understand the use of continuous and period end inventory records.[1] — 4

(g) Calculate the value of closing inventory using FIFO (first in, first out) and AVCO (average cost).[1] — 4

(h) Understand the impact of accounting concepts on the valuation of inventory.[1] — 4

(i) Identify the impact of inventory valuation methods on profit and on assets.[1] — 4

KAPLAN PUBLISHING

4 Tangible non-current assets

(a) Define non-current assets.[1] — 2 & 8

(b) Recognise the difference between current and non-current assets.[1] — 2 & 17

(c) Explain the difference between capital and revenue items. [1] — 8

(d) Classify expenditure as capital or revenue expenditure.[1] — 8

(e) Prepare ledger entries to record the acquisition and disposal of non-current assets.[1] — 8

(f) Calculate and record profits or losses on disposal of non-current assets in the income statement, including part exchange transactions. [1] — 8

(g) Record the revaluation of a non-current asset in ledger accounts, the statement of comprehensive income and in the statement of financial position.[1] — 8

(h) Calculate the profit or loss on disposal of a revalued asset.[1] — 8

(i) Illustrate how non-current asset balances and movements are disclosed in the company financial statements.[1] — 8

(j) Explain the purpose and function of an asset register.[1] — 8

5 Depreciation

(a) Understand and explain the purpose of depreciation.[1] — 8

(b) Calculate the charge for depreciation using straight line and reducing balance methods.[1] — 8

(c) Identify the circumstances where different methods of depreciation would be appropriate.[1] — 8

(d) Illustrate how depreciation expense and accumulated depreciation are recorded in ledger accounts.[1] — 8

(e) Calculate depreciation on a revalued non-current asset including the transfer of excess depreciation between the revaluation reserve and retained earnings.[1] — 8

(f) Calculate the adjustments to depreciation necessary if changes are made in the estimated useful life and/or residual value of a non-current asset.[2] — 8

(g) Record depreciation in the income statement and statement of financial position.[1] — 8

6 Intangible non-current assets and amortisation

(a) Recognise the difference between tangible and intangible non-current assets.[1] — 18

(b) Identify types of intangible assets.[1] — 18

(c) Identify the definition and treatment of 'research costs' and 'development costs' in accordance with International Financial Reporting Standards.[1]   18

(d) Calculate amounts to be capitalised as development expenditure or to be expensed from given information.[1]   18

(e) Explain the purpose of amortisation.[1]   18

(f) Calculate and account for the charge for amortisation.[1]   18

7 Accruals and prepayments

(a) Understand how the matching concept applies to accruals and prepayments.[1]   6

(b) Identify and calculate the adjustments needed for accruals and prepayments in preparing financial statements.[1]   6

(c) Illustrate the process of adjusting for accruals and prepayments in preparing financial statements.[1]   6

(d) Prepare the journal entries and ledger entries for the creation of an accrual or prepayment.[1]   6

(e) Understand and identify the impact on profit and net assets of accruals and prepayments.[1]   6

8 Receivables and payables

(a) Explain and identify examples of receivables and payables.[1]   2

(b) Identify the benefits and costs of offering credit facilities to customers.[1]   7

(c) Understand the purpose of an aged receivables analysis.[1]   7

(d) Understand the purpose of credit limits.[1]   7

(e) Prepare the bookkeeping entries to write off a bad (irrecoverable) debt.[1]   7

(f) Record a bad (irrecoverable) debt recovered.[1]   7

(g) Identify the impact of bad (irrecoverable) debts on the income statement and on the statement of financial position.[1]   7

(h) Prepare the bookkeeping entries to create and adjust an allowance for receivables.[1]   7

(i) Illustrate how to include movements in the allowance for receivables in the income statement and how the closing balance of the allowance should appear in the statement of financial position.[1]   7

(j) Account for contras between trade receivables and payables.[1]   10

KAPLAN PUBLISHING

(k) Prepare, reconcile and understand the purpose of supplier statements.[1] 10

(l) Classify items as current or non-current liabilities in the statement of financial position.[1] 2

9 Provisions and contingencies

(a) Understand the definition of 'provision', 'contingent liability' and 'contingent asset'.[1] 18

(b) Distinguish between and classify items as provisions, contingent liabilities or contingent assets.[1] 18

(c) Identify and illustrate the different methods of accounting for provisions, contingent liabilities and contingent assets.[1] 18

(d) Calculate provisions and changes in provisions.[1] 18

(e) Account for the movement in provisions.[1] 18

(f) Report provisions in the final accounts.[1] 18

10 Capital structure and finance costs

(a) Understand the capital structure of a limited liability company including: [1] 17

   (i) ordinary shares

   (ii) preference shares (redeemable and irredeemable)

   (iii) loan notes.

(b) Record movements in the share capital and share premium accounts.[1] 17

(c) Identify and record the other reserves which may appear in the company statement of financial position.[1] 17

(d) Define a bonus (capitalisation) issue and its advantages and disadvantages.[1] 17

(e) Define a rights issue and its advantages and disadvantages.[1] 17

(f) Record and show the effects of a bonus (capitalisation) issue in the statement of financial position.[1] 17

(g) Record and show the effects of a rights issue in the statement of financial position.[1] 17

(h) Record dividends in ledger accounts and the financial statements. [1] 17

(i) Calculate and record finance costs in ledger accounts and the financial statements.[1] 17

(j) Identify the components of the statement of changes in equity.[1] 17

KAPLAN PUBLISHING

KAPLAN PUBLISHING

(e) Calculate the figures needed for the statement of cash flows including:[1]

    (i)   cash flows from operating activities

    (ii) cash flows from investing activities

    (iii) cash flows from financing activities.

    19

(f) Calculate the cash flow from operating activities using the indirect and direct method[1]

    19

(g) Prepare extracts from statement of cash flows from given information.[1]

    19

(h) Identify the treatment of given transactions in a company's statement of cash flows.[1]

    19

6 Incomplete records

(a) Understand and apply techniques used in incomplete record situations:[1]

    15

    (i)   use of accounting equation

    (ii) use of ledger accounts to calculate missing figures

    (iii) use of cash and/or bank summaries

    (iv) use of profit percentages to calculate missing figures.

The superscript numbers in square brackets indicate the intellectual depth at which the subject area could be assessed within the examination. Level 1 (knowledge and comprehension) broadly equates with the Knowledge module, Level 2 (application and analysis) with the Skills module and Level 3 (synthesis and evaluation) to the Professional level. However, lower level skills can continue to be assessed as you progress through each module and level.

The examination

Examination format

The syllabus is assessed by a two-hour paper or computer-based examination. Questions will assess all parts of the syllabus and will contain both computational and noncomputational elements:

	Number of marks
Forty 2-mark questions	80
Ten 1-mark questions	10
	90

Total time allowed: 2 hours

Paper-based examination tips

Spend the first few minutes of the examination reading the paper.

Divide the time you spend on questions in proportion to the marks on offer. One suggestion **for this exam** is to allocate 1 and 1/3 minutes to each mark available, so a 2 mark question should be completed in approximately 2 minutes 40 seconds.

Multiple-choice questions: Read the questions carefully and work through any calculations required. If you don't know the answer, eliminate those options you know are incorrect and see if the answer becomes more obvious. Guess your final answer rather than leave it blank if necessary.

Computer-based examination (CBE) – tips

Be sure you understand how to use the software before you start the exam. If in doubt, ask the assessment centre staff to explain it to you.

Questions are **displayed on the screen** and answers are entered using keyboard and mouse. At the end of the exam, you are given a certificate showing the result you have achieved.

Do not attempt a CBE until you have **completed all study material** relating to it. **Do not skip any of the material** in the syllabus.

Read each question very carefully.

Double-check your answer before committing yourself to it.

Answer every question – if you do not know an answer, you don't lose anything by guessing. Think carefully before you **guess.**

With a multiple-choice question, eliminate first those answers that you know are wrong. Then choose the most appropriate answer from those that are left.

Remember that only **one answer to a multiple-choice question can be right.** After you have eliminated the ones that you know to be wrong, if you are still unsure, guess. But only do so after you have double-checked that you have only eliminated answers that are definitely wrong.

Don't panic if you realise you've answered a question incorrectly.Getting one question wrong will not mean the difference between passing and failing.

Study skills and revision guidance

This section aims to give guidance on how to study for your ACCA exams and to give ideas on how to improve your existing study techniques.

Preparing to study

Set your objectives

Before starting to study decide what you want to achieve - the type of pass you wish to obtain. This will decide the level of commitment and time you need to dedicate to your studies.

Devise a study plan

Determine which times of the week you will study.

Split these times into sessions of at least one hour for study of new material. Any shorter periods could be used for revision or practice.

Put the times you plan to study onto a study plan for the weeks from now until the exam and set yourself targets for each period of study – in your sessions make sure you cover the course, course assignments and revision.

If you are studying for more than one paper at a time, try to vary your subjects as this can help you to keep interested and see subjects as part of wider knowledge.

When working through your course, compare your progress with your plan and, if necessary, re-plan your work (perhaps including extra sessions) or, if you are ahead, do some extra revision/practice questions.

Effective studying

Active reading

You are not expected to learn the text by rote, rather, you must understand what you are reading and be able to use it to pass the exam and develop good practice. A good technique to use is SQ3Rs – Survey, Question, Read, Recall, Review:

(1) **Survey** the chapter – look at the headings and read the introduction, summary and objectives, so as to get an overview of what the chapter deals with.

(2) **Question** – whilst undertaking the survey, ask yourself the questions that you hope the chapter will answer for you.

(3) **Read** through the chapter thoroughly, answering the questions and making sure you can meet the objectives. Attempt the exercises and activities in the text, and work through all the examples.

(4) **Recall** – at the end of each section and at the end of the chapter, try to recall the main ideas of the section/chapter without referring to the text. This is best done after a short break of a couple of minutes after the reading stage.

(5) **Review** – check that your recall notes are correct.

You may also find it helpful to re-read the chapter to try to see the topic(s) it deals with as a whole.

Note-taking

Taking notes is a useful way of learning, but do not simply copy out the text. The notes must:

- be in your own words
- be concise
- cover the key points
- be well-organised
- be modified as you study further chapters in this text or in related ones.

Trying to summarise a chapter without referring to the text can be a useful way of determining which areas you know and which you don't.

Three ways of taking notes:

Summarise the key points of a chapter.

Make linear notes – a list of headings, divided up with subheadings listing the key points. If you use linear notes, you can use different colours to highlight key points and keep topic areas together. Use plenty of space to make your notes easy to use.

Try a diagrammatic form – the most common of which is a mind-map. To make a mind-map, put the main heading in the centre of the paper and put a circle around it. Then draw short lines radiating from this to the main sub-headings, which again have circles around them. Then continue the process from the sub-headings to sub-sub-headings, advantages, disadvantages, etc.

KAPLAN PUBLISHING

Highlighting and underlining

You may find it useful to underline or highlight key points in your study text – but do be selective. You may also wish to make notes in the margins.

Revision

The best approach to revision is to revise the course as you work through it. Also try to leave four to six weeks before the exam for final revision. Make sure you cover the whole syllabus and pay special attention to those areas where your knowledge is weak. Here are some recommendations:

Read through the text and your notes again and condense your notes into key phrases. It may help to put key revision points onto index cards to look at when you have a few minutes to spare.

Review any assignments you have completed and look at where you lost marks – put more work into those areas where you were weak.

Practise exam standard questions under timed conditions. If you are short of time, list the points that you would cover in your answer and then read the model answer, but do try to complete at least a few questions under exam conditions.

Also practise producing answer plans and comparing them to the model answer.

If you are stuck on a topic find somebody (a tutor) to explain it to you.

Read good newspapers and professional journals, especially ACCA's Student Accountant – this can give you an advantage in the exam.

Ensure you **know the structure of the exam** – how many questions and of what type you will be expected to answer. During your revision attempt all the different styles of questions you may be asked.

Further reading

You can find further reading and technical articles under the student section of ACCA's website.

A Students's Guide to IFRS by Clare Finch, Kaplan Publishing UK 2007.

KAPLAN PUBLISHING

Introduction to accounting

Chapter learning objectives

Upon completion of this chapter you will be able to:

- define accounting
- explain the different types of business entity:
  - sole trader
  - partnership
  - limited liability company
- explain who users of the financial statements are and their information needs
- explain the nature, principles and scope of accounting
- explain how the accounting system contributes to providing useful information and complies with organisational policies and deadlines.

1 Definition of accounting

Analysing data is also an important feature of accounting. Financial statements are prepared so that we can examine and evaluate all information, in order to make key decisions.

2 Types of business entity

A business can be organised in one of several ways:

- Sole trader – a business owned and operated by one person.
- Partnership – a business owned and operated by two or more people.
- Company – a business owned by many people and operated by many (though not necessarily the same) people.

KAPLAN PUBLISHING

Sole trader

The simplest form of business is the sole trader. This is owned and managed by one person, although there might be any number of employees. A sole trader is fully and personally liable for any losses that the business might make.

Partnership

A partnership is a business owned jointly by a number of partners. The partners are jointly and severally liable for any losses that the business might make. Traditionally the big accounting firms have been partnerships, although some are converting their status to limited liability companies.

Companies

Companies are owned by shareholders. There can be one shareholder or many thousands of shareholders. Shareholders are also known as members. Each shareholder owns part of the company. As a group, they elect the directors who run the business. Directors often own shares in their companies, but not all shareholders are directors.

Companies are almost always limited companies. This means that the shareholders will not be personally liable for any losses the company incurs. Their liability is limited to the nominal value of the shares that they own. Their shares may become worthless, but they will not be forced to make good the losses.

This limited liability is achieved by treating the company as a completely separate legal entity.

For all three types of entity, the money put up by the individual, the partners or the shareholders, is referred to as the business capital. In the case of a company, this capital is divided into shares.

3 Users of the financial statements

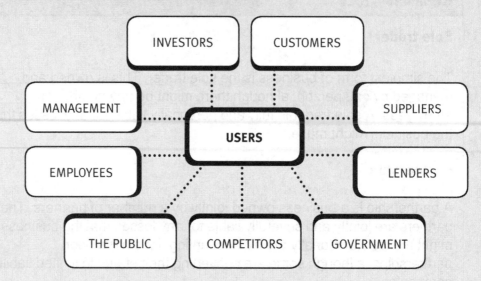

Different user groups are interested in a company's financial statements for different reasons:

- **Management** need detailed information in order to control their business and plan for the future. Budgets will be based upon past performance and future plans. These budgets will then be compared with actual results. Information will also be needed about the profitability of individual departments and products. Management information must be very up to date and is normally produced on a monthly basis.

- **Investors** and potential investors are interested in their potential profits and the security of their investment. Future profits may be estimated from the target company's past performance as shown in the income statement. The security of their investment will be revealed by the financial strength and solvency of the company as shown in the statement of financial position. The largest and most sophisticated groups of investors are the institutional investors, such as pension funds and unit trusts.

- **Employees** and trade union representatives need to know if an employer can offer secure employment and possible pay rises. They will also have a keen interest in the salaries and benefits enjoyed by senior management. Information about divisional profitability will also be useful if a part of the business is threatened with closure.

- **Lenders** need to know if they will be repaid. This will depend on the solvency of the company, which should be revealed by the statement of financial position. Long-term loans may also be backed by 'security' given by the business over specific assets. The value of these assets will be indicated in the statement of financial position.

- **Government** agencies need to know how the economy is performing in order to plan financial and industrial policies. The tax authorities also use financial statements as a basis for assessing the amount of tax payable by a business.

KAPLAN PUBLISHING

- **Suppliers** need to know if they will be paid. New suppliers may also require reassurance about the financial health of a business before agreeing to supply goods.

- **Customers** need to know that a company can continue to supply them into the future. This is especially true if the customer is dependent on a company for specialised supplies.

- **Competitors** wish to compare their own performance against that of other companies and learn as much as possible about their rivals in order to help develop strategic plans.

- **The public** may wish to assess the effect of the company on the economy, local environment and local community. Companies may contribute to their local economy and community through providing employment and patronising local suppliers. Some companies also run corporate responsibility programmes through which they support the environment, economy and community by, for example supporting recycling schemes.

Test your understanding 1

Which of the following users do you think require the most detailed financial information to be made available to them?

A Competitors

B Management of the business

C Trade unions

D Investors

4 Types of accounting

```
                    ┌──────────────────────────┐
                    │       ACCOUNTING         │
                    └──────────────────────────┘
```

Financial accounting
- Production of summary financial statements for external users.

- Prepared annually (six-monthly or quarterly in some countries).
- Generally required by law.
- Reflects past performance and current position.

- Information calculated and presented in accordance with international accounting standards.

Management accounting
- Production of detailed accounts, used by management to control the business and plan for the future.
- Normally prepared monthly, often on a rolling basis.
- Not mandatory.

- Includes budgets and forecasts of future activities, as well as reflecting past performance.

- Information computed and presented in order to be relevant to managers.

Expandable text

Financial accounting

Financial accounting is concerned with the production of financial statements for external users. These are a report on the directors' stewardship of the funds entrusted to them by the shareholders.

Investors need to be able to choose which companies to invest in and compare their investments. In order to facilitate comparison, financial accounts are prepared using accepted accounting conventions and standards. International Accounting Standards (IASs) and International Financial Reporting Standards (IFRSs) help to reduce the differences in the way that companies draw up their financial statements in different countries.

The financial statements are public documents, and therefore they will not reveal details about, for example, individual products' profitability.

Management accounting

Management require much more detailed and up-to-date information in order to control the business and plan for the future. They need to be able to cost-out products and production methods, assess profitability and so on. In order to facilitate this, management accounts present information in any way which may be useful to management, for example by operating unit or product line.

Management accounting is an integral part of management activity concerned with identifying, presenting and interpreting information used for:

- formulating strategy

- planning and controlling activities

- decision making

- optimising the use of resources.

5 How an accounting system contributes to providing useful information

The main features of an accounting system and how it helps in providing information to the business are as follows:

- In a computerised system all information about the business transactions can be quickly accessed. This will help in decision making.

- It provides details of transactions of the business in the relevant accounts.

- When the accounts are closed off the balances for each outstanding account are determined. This will give the value of assets and liabilities in the business.

- It gives a summary of outstanding balances.

- This summary can then be used for the preparation of financial statements.

- Normally the financial statements are prepared at regular intervals. The accounting system will allow the business to obtain the data and also prepare the financial statements to determine the profitability, liquidity, risks, etc. applicable to the business for a particular period. For internal reporting purposes this could be monthly, whilst for external reporting purposes this is usually yearly.

Chapter summary

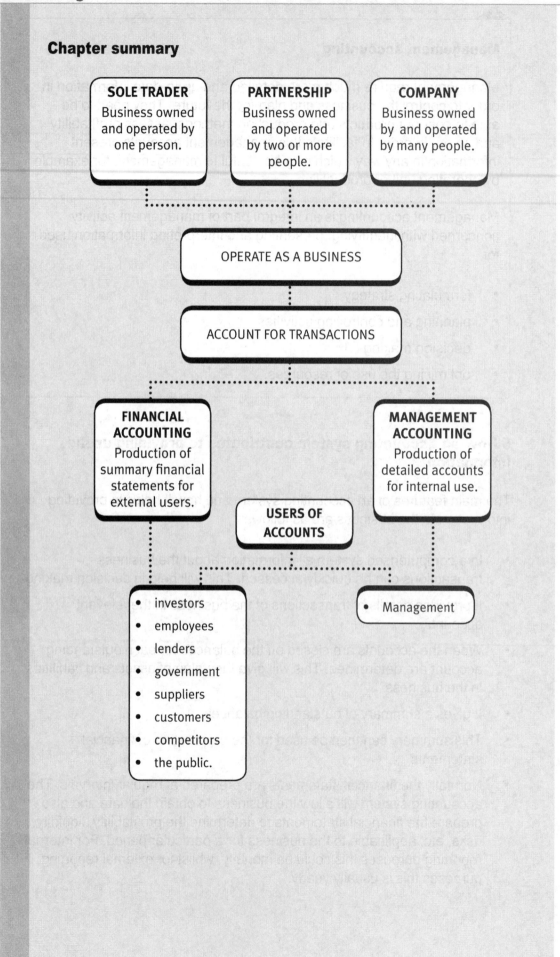

Test your understanding answers

Test your understanding 1

B Management

They need detailed information in order to control their business and make informed decisions about the future. Management information must be very up to date and is normally produced on a monthly basis.

Other parties will need far less detail:

- Competitors will be monitoring what the competition are currently planning and working on, but they will not be making the key decisions themselves.

- Trade unions will only require information which relates to their job role. They will only be particularly interested in disputes.

- Investors are interested in profitability and the security of their investment.

KAPLAN PUBLISHING

Statement of financial position and income statement

Chapter learning objectives

Upon completion of this chapter you will be able to:

- explain the main elements of financial statements:
  - statement of financial position
  - income statement
- explain the purpose of each of the main statements
- list the main types of business transactions
- explain how the accounting equation and business entity convention underpin the statement of financial position
- define assets and liabilities
- identify examples of receivables and payables
- explain how and why assets and liabilities are disclosed in the statement of financial position.
- draft a simple statement of financial position in vertical format
- explain the matching convention and how it applies to revenue and expenses
- explain how and why revenue and expenses are disclosed in the income statement
- illustrate how the statement of financial position and income statement are interrelated
- draft a simple income statement in vertical format

- identify the two sides of each transaction (duality concept)
- determine the accounting equation after each transaction.

1 Financial statements

There are **two** key elements to the financial statements of a sole trader business:

- **Statement of financial position**, showing the financial position of a business at a point in time, and
- **Income statement**, showing the financial performance of a business over a period of time.

The financial statements show the effects of business transactions. The main types are:

- sales of goods (either for cash or on credit)

If a sale is made for cash, then cash in the business will increase and a sales transaction will have also been created. The cash will be recorded in the statement of financial position and the sale will be recorded in the income statement.

If a sale is made on credit, then the payment for the goods has not been made immediately. Therefore we are still owed for these items. The sale will still be recorded in the income statement, however a receivable will be recorded in the statement of financial position.

- purchase of inventory for resale (either for cash or on credit)

If we buy inventory for cash, then we are spendng money. This decrease in cash will be recorded in the statement of financial position. The increase in inventory that we now own will also be recorded as an asset in the statement of financial position.

If we buy inventory on credit, then we will owe the supplier for these goods. This is called a payable. Therefore inventory will increase and also a payable will be created. Both of these are entered onto the statment of financial position.

- purchase of non-current assets

If we buy a non-current asset (eg: a motor vehicle) then we are spending cash, so this will decrease. However, we have now gained a new asset, and both of these entires are recorded in the statement of financial position.

- payment of expenses such as utilities

Making this payment will reduce our cash balance and this will affect our statement of financial position. We will have created an expense which we have made the payment for, untilities. This expense belongs on the income statement.

- introduction of new capital to the business

If the owner of the business introduces funds into the business, this is called capital. We have increased the capital within the business and also increased our cash or bank balances. Both of these entires are recorded on the statement of financial position.

- withdrawal of funds from the business by the owner.

If the owner then withdraws some of these funds back out of the business again, this is known as drawings. The capital will reduce and also the amount of funds within the bank account will too. Both of these are recorded on the statement of financial position.

The business entity concept

- The business entity concept states that financial accounting information relates only to the activities of the business entity and not to the activities of its owner.
- The business entity is treated as **separate** from its owners.

Expandable text

A company is both legally and for accounting purposes a separate entity distinct from its owners, the shareholders. On the other hand, the business of a sole trader is not a legal entity distinct from its proprietor; however, for accounting purposes, the business is regarded as being a separate entity and accounts are drawn up for the business separately from the sole trader's own personal financial dealings.

The entity concept is essential in order to be able to account for the business as a separate economic unit. Flows of money between the business and the proprietors are also separately identified from other money flows.

The correct terms for these cash movements are:

Cash movement from/to proprietors	Sole trader, partnership	Company
In	Either 'loans from proprietors' or 'increase in capital'	Share issue proceeds
Out	Either 'drawings' or 'reduction in capital'	

The key link between the owner and the business is the amount stated as capital which is the amount the business owes to the proprietor.

KAPLAN PUBLISHING

2 Statement of financial position

The vertical format of the statement of financial position is shown below:

Note: this format relates to a sole trader only. The company format is looked at later within chapter 17.

W Xang Statement of financial position as at 31 December 20X6		
	$	$
Non-current assets:		
Motor van		2,400
Current assets:		
Inventory	2,390	
Receivables	1,840	
Cash at bank	1,704	
Cash in hand	56	
	———	
		5,990
		———
		8,390
		———
Capital account:		
Balance at 1 January 20X6	4,200	
Add: Net profit for year	3,450	
Increase in capital	1,000	
	———	
	8,650	
Less: Drawings for year	(2,960)	
	———	
		5,690
Non-current liabilities:		1,000
Current liabilities:		
Payables		1,700
		———
		8,930
		———

- The top half of the statement of financial position shows the assets of the business.

- The bottom half of the statement of financial position shows the capital and liabilities of the business.

3 Income statement

The format of the income statement is shown below:

Mr W Xang Income statement for the year ended 31 December 20X6

	$	$
Sales revenue		33,700
Cost of sales		
Opening inventory	3,200	
Purchases	24,490	
	———	
	27,690	
Less: Closing inventory	(2,390)	
	———	
		(25,300)
		———
Gross profit		8,400
Wages	3,385	
Rent	1,200	
Sundry expenses	365	
	———	
		(4,950)
		———
Net profit		3,450
		———

- **Income** is increases in economic benefits during the period in the form of inflows or enhancements of assets or decreases of liabilities that result in increases in equity, other than those relating to contributions from equity participants.

- **Expenses** are decreases in economic benefits during the period in the form of outflows or depletions of assets or increases of liabilities that result in decreases in equity, other than those relating to distributions to equity participants.

- The income statement shows the performance of the business over a period of time, in this case for a full year.

- The income statement is prepared following the accruals concept. This means that income and expenses are recorded in the income statement as they are earned/incurred regardless of whether cash has been received/paid.

- The sales revenue shows the income from goods sold in the year, regardless of whether those goods have been paid for.

- The cost of buying the goods sold must be deducted from the revenue. It is important that the cost of any goods remaining unsold is not included here.

- The current year's sales will include goods bought in the previous year, so this **opening inventory** must be added to the current year's purchases.

- Some of this year's purchases will be unsold at 31 December 20X6 and this **closing inventory** must be deducted from purchases to be set off against next year's sales.

- The income statement is split into two parts, the first part gives gross profit and the second part, net profit.

- Gross profit divided by sales revenue gives the **gross profit margin** which illustrates the profitability of the business at a trading level.

- We must distinguish between wages and drawings. Wages relate to payments to third parties (employees) and represent a deduction or charge in arriving at net profit. Amounts paid to the proprietor (even if he calls them 'salary'!) must be treated as drawings.

4 Relationship between the statement of financial position and income statement

The link between the statement of financial position and income statement is shown below:

- The statement of financial position are not isolated statements; they are linked over time with the income statement.

- As the business records a profit in the income statement, that profit is added to the capital section of the statement of financial position, along with any capital introduced. Cash taken out of the business by the proprietor, called drawings, is deducted.

5 The accounting equation

> ASSETS = PROPRIETOR'S CAPITAL + LIABILITIES

> ASSETS – LIABILITIES = PROPRIETOR'S CAPITAL

The accounting equation

The statement of financial position shows the position of a business at one point in time. A statement of financial position will always satisfy the accounting equation as shown above.

- Each and every transaction that the business makes or enters into has two aspects to it and has a double effect on the business and the accounting equation. This is known as the duality concept.

- The accounting equation is a simple expression of the fact that at any point in time the assets of the business will be equal to its liabilities plus the capital of the business.

- It follows that assets less liabilities equal the capital of the business. Assets less liabilities are known as net assets.

Assets and liabilities

Assets are resources an entity controls as a result of past events and from which future economic benefits are expected to flow to the entity. Some examples are:

- inventory, e.g. goods manufactured or purchased for resale
- receivables, e.g. money owed by credit customers, prepaid expenses
- cash
- non-current assets
- and is available for use in the business.

A **liability** is an entity's present obligation arising from a past event, the settlement of which will result in an outflow of economic benefits from the entity. This is something owed by the business to someone else, such as:

- payables, e.g. amounts owed to credit suppliers, accrued expenses
- loans.

Equity is defined as the residual interest in the entity's assets after deducting its liabilities. You will become more familiar with this term when you come to look at Company accounts in chapter 17.

KAPLAN PUBLISHING

Capital is a type of liability. This is the amount that is due to the owner(s) of the business. It will increase each year by any new capital injected into the business and by the profit made by the business. It will decrease by any amounts withdrawn from the business by the owner(s).

Disclosure of assets and liabilities in the statement of financial position

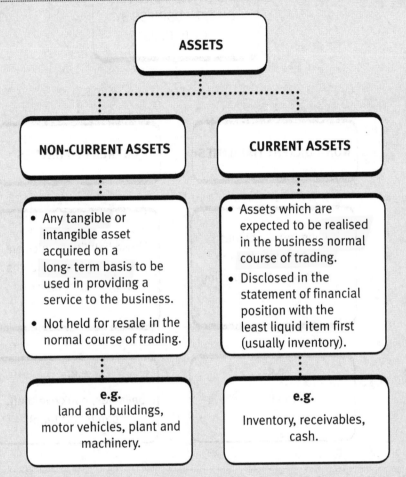

ASSETS

NON-CURRENT ASSETS

CURRENT ASSETS

- Any tangible or intangible asset acquired on a long- term basis to be used in providing a service to the business.
- Not held for resale in the normal course of trading.

- Assets which are expected to be realised in the business normal course of trading.
- Disclosed in the statement of financial position with the least liquid item first (usually inventory).

e.g.
land and buildings, motor vehicles, plant and machinery.

e.g.
Inventory, receivables, cash.

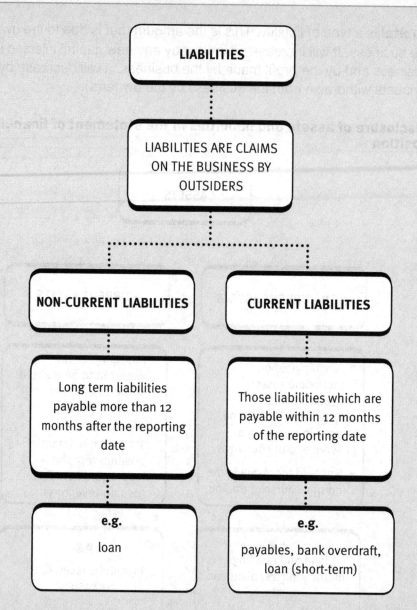

LIABILITIES

LIABILITIES ARE CLAIMS ON THE BUSINESS BY OUTSIDERS

NON-CURRENT LIABILITIES

Long term liabilities payable more than 12 months after the reporting date

e.g.

loan

CURRENT LIABILITIES

Those liabilities which are payable within 12 months of the reporting date

e.g.

payables, bank overdraft, loan (short-term)

Test your understanding 1

Classify the following items into current and non-current assets and liabilities:

- land and buildings *non current asset.*
- receivables *current asset.*
- cash *current asset*
- loan repayable in two years' time *non current liability*
- payables *current liability.*
- delivery van. *non current asset*

Illustration 1– The accounting equation

This illustration involves a series of transactions using the dual effect of transactions and then the accounting equation to build up a set of financial statements. The transactions are as follows:

Day 1 Avon commences business introducing $1,000 cash.

Day 2 Buys a motor car for $400 cash.

Day 3 Buys inventory for $200 cash.

Day 4 Sells all the goods bought on Day 3 for $300 cash.

Day 5 Buys inventory for $400 on credit.

Using the accounting equation, we will draw up a statement of financial position at the end of each day's transactions.

Expandable text

Solution

Day 1: Avon commences business introducing $1,000 cash

The dual effect of this transaction is:

(a) the business has $1,000 of cash

(b) the business owes the owner $1,000 – this is capital.

Statement of financial position Day 1

Assets	$	Capital and liabilities	$
Cash	1,000	Capital	1,000
	1,000		1,000

Day 2: Buys a motor car for $400 cash

The dual effect of this transaction is:

(a) the business has an asset of $400
(b) the business has spent $400 in cash

This transaction changes the form in which the assets are held.

Statement of financial position Day 2

	$		$
Assets		Capital and liabilities	
Cash	600	Capital	1,000
Car	400		
	1,000		1,000

Note that the acquiring of an asset must lead to one of the following:

- reducing another asset by a corresponding amount (as above)
- incurring a corresponding liability (Day 5)
- increasing the capital contributed by the proprietor (Day 1).

Day 3: Buys inventory for $200 cash

The dual effect of this transaction is:

(a) the business has $200 of inventory
(b) the business has spent $200 in cash.

Again this is merely a change in the form in which the assets are held. $200 is withdrawn from cash and invested in inventory.

Statement of financial position Day 3

	$		$
Assets		Capital and liabilities	
Motor car	400	Capital	1,000
Inventory	200		
Cash:			
($600 – $200)	400		
	1,000		1,000

Day 4: Sells all the goods bought on day 3 for $300 cash

This is an important new development. It is true that one asset (inventory) is being replaced by another (cash), but the amounts do not correspond.

	$
Cash acquired (sale proceeds)	300
Asset relinquished (inventory)	200
	___
Difference (= profit)	100
	___

Thus total assets have increased by $100. Since there are no liabilities involved, if the fundamental equation is to remain valid the capital must increase by $100.

Profit is the difference between purchase price and sale proceeds and it belongs to the proprietor(s) of the business. It is an increase in the capital of the business.

The dual effect of this transaction is:

(a) The business has received $300 of cash.

(b) The business has reduced inventory by $200 and made a profit of $100.

Statement of financial position Day 4

Assets	$	Capital and liabilities	$
Motor car	400	Capital	1,000
Cash: ($400 + $300)	700	Add: Profit	100
	___		___
	1,100		1,100
	___		___

Day 5: Buys inventory for $400 on credit

The dual effect of this transaction is:

(a) The business has $400 of inventory.

(b) The business has a liability to the supplier of $400.

Assets can be increased by a corresponding increase in liabilities as follows:

Statement of financial position Day 5

Assets	$	Capital and liabilities	$
Motor car	400	Capital	1,000
Inventory	400	Add: Profit	100
Cash	700	Payables	400
	1,500		1,500

Note that the payables are acting in effect as a source of finance for the business.

Test your understanding 2

Continuing from the illustration above, prepare the statement of financial position at the end of each day after accounting for the transactions below:

Day 6 Sells half of the goods bought on Day 5 on credit for $250.

Day 7 Pays $200 to his supplier.

Day 8 Receives $100 from a customer.

Day 9 Proprietor draws $75 in cash.

Day 10 Pays rent of $40 in cash.

Day 11 Receives a loan of $600 repayable in two years.

Day 12 Pays cash of $30 for insurance.

Your starting point is the statement of financial position at the end of Day 5, from the illustration above.

Once you have dealt with each of the transactions, prepare a **statement of financial position** at the end of Day 12 and an **income statement** for the first 12 days of trading.

Statement of comprehensive income

Later on in this textbook you will be introduced to the Statement of comprehensive income. This relates to a company and not to a sole trader.

Chapter summary

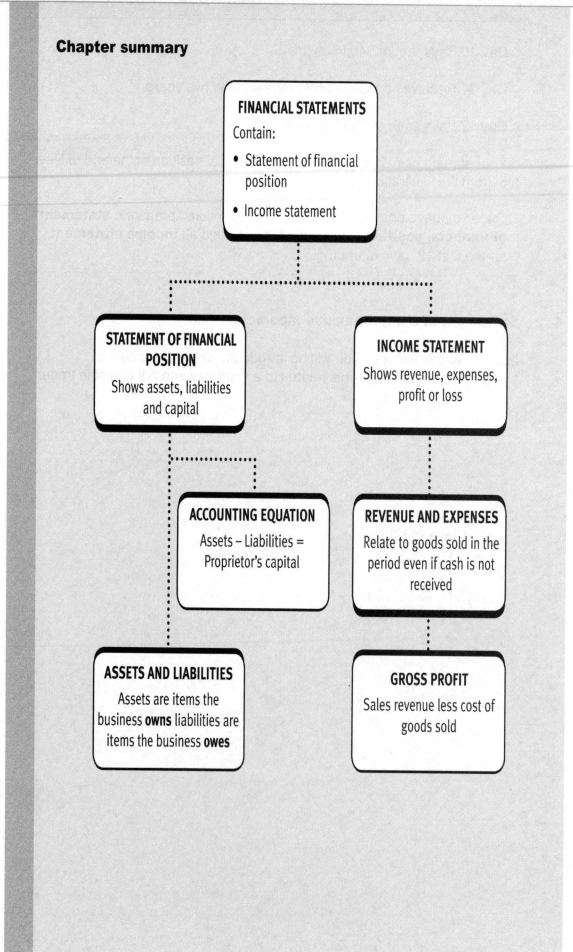

Test your understanding answers

Test your understanding 1

- Land and buildings – **non-current asset**.
- Receivables – **current asset**.
- Cash – **current asset**.
- Loan repayable in two years time – **non-current liability**.
- Payables – **current liability**.
- Delivery van – **non-current asset**.

Test your understanding 2

Day 6: Sells half of the goods bought on Day 5 on credit for $250

This transaction introduces two new concepts:

- **Sale on credit.** Essentially this is the same as a sale for cash, except that the asset increased is not cash, but receivables.

- Sale of **part** of the inventory. In practice this is the normal situation. The important accounting requirement is to separate:
  - inventory still held as an asset, from
  - cost of inventory sold.

Statement of financial position for Day 6

Assets	$	Capital and liabilities	$
Motor car	400	Capital introduced	1,000
Inventory	200	Add: Profit to date	
Receivables	250	($100 + $50)	150
Cash	700		
			1,150
		Payables	400
	1,550		1,550

Day 7: Pays $200 to his supplier

- The dual effect of this transaction is:
- (a) The business has paid out $200 in cash.
- (b) The business has reduced the payable (liability) by $200.

This is simply the reduction of one liability (payables) and one asset (cash) by a corresponding amount ($200).

KAPLAN PUBLISHING

Statement of financial position for Day 7

Assets		$	Capital and liabilities		$
Motor car		400	Capital		1,000
Inventory		200	Add: Profit to date		150
Receivables		250			
Cash ($700 – $200)		500			
					1,150
			Payables ($400 – $200)		200
		1,350			1,350

Day 8: Receives $100 from a customer

- The dual effect of this transaction is:
- (a) The business has received $100 in cash.
- (b) The receivables of the business have reduced by $100.

Statement of financial position for Day 8

Assets		$	Capital and liabilities		$
Motor car		400	Capital		1,000
Inventory		200	Add: Profit to date		150
Receivables ($250 – $100)		150			1,150
Cash ($500 + $100)		600	Payables		200
		1,350			1,350

Day 9: Proprietor draws $75 in cash

This shows on the statement of financial position as a reduction of capital, and as a reduction of cash.

Cash or other assets taken out of the business by the owner are called 'amounts withdrawn', or 'drawings'.

- The dual effect of this transaction is:

(a) The business has reduced cash by $75.

(b) The business has a drawings balance of $75 which reduces capital.

Statement of financial position for Day 9

Assets	$	Capital and liabilities	$
Motor car	400	Capital	1,000
Inventory	200	Add: Profit to date	150
Receivables	150		
Cash ($600 – $75)	525		1,150
		Less: Drawings	(75)
			1,075
		Payables	200
	1,275		1,275

Day 10: Pays rent of $40

This is an example of a business expense.

The dual effect of this transaction is:

(a) The business pays out $40 in cash.

(b) The business has a rent expense of $40 which reduces profit.

Statement of financial position for Day 10

Assets	$	Capital and liabilities	$
Motor car	400	Capital	1,000
Inventory	200	Add: Profit to date	
Receivables	150	($150 – $40)	110
Cash ($525 – $40)	485		
			1,110
		Less: Drawings	(75)
			1,035
		Payables	200
	1,235		1,235

Day 11: Receives a loan of $600 repayable in two years' time

The dual effect of this transaction is:

(a) The business receives $600 in cash.

(b) The business has a liability of $600.

Statement of financial position for Day 11

Assets		$	Capital and liabilities	$
Motor car		400	Capital introduced	1,000
Inventory		200	Add: Profit to date	110
Receivables		150		
Cash ($485 + $600)		1,085		
				1,110
			Less: Drawings	(75)
				1,035
			Loan	600
			Payables	200
		1,835		1,835

Day 12: Pays cash of $30 for insurance

The dual effect of this transaction is:

(a) the business pays out $30 in cash

(b) the business has an insurance expense of $30 which reduces profit.

Statement of financial position for Day 12

	$		$
Assets		**Capital and liabilities**	
Motor car	400	Capital introduced	1,000
Inventory	200	Add: Profit to date	
Receivables	150	($110 – $30)	80
Cash ($1,085 – $30)	1,055		
	1,805		
		Less: Drawings	(75)
			1,005
		Loan	600
		Payables	200
	1,805		1,805

This marks the end of the transactions. The financial statements for the 12 day period can now be considered.

Avon, income statement for the 12 days

			$	$
Sales revenue:	Cash			300
	Credit			250
				550
Cost of sales:	Purchases:	Cash	200	
		Credit	400	
			600	
Less: Closing inventory			(200)	
Cost of goods sold				(400)
Gross profit				150
Rent			40	
Insurance			30	
				(70)
Net profit				80

Avon, statement of financial position as at end of Day 12

		$	$
Non-current asset:	Motor car (at cost)		400
Current assets:	Inventory	200	
	Receivables	150	
	Cash	1,055	
			1,405
			1,805
Capital account:	Capital introduced	1,000	
	Net profit	80	
		1,080	
Less: Drawings		(75)	
			1,005
Non-current liability:	Loan		600
Current liabilities:	Payables		200
			1,805

3

Double entry bookkeeping

Chapter learning objectives

Upon completion of this chapter you will be able to:

- explain the concept of double entry and the duality concept
- explain the debit and credit principle
- explain the meaning of the balance on each type of account
- record cash transactions in ledger accounts
- record credit sale and purchase transactions in ledger accounts
- illustrate how to account for discounts
- explain sales and purchase returns and demonstrate their recording
- illustrate how to balance a ledger account
- extract the ledger balances into a trial balance
- identify the purpose of a trial balance
- prepare a simple income statement and statement of financial position from a trial balance
- explain and illustrate the process of closing the ledger accounts in the accounting records when the financial statements have been completed.

1 The duality concept and double entry bookkeeping

- Each transaction that a business enters into affects the financial statements in two ways, e.g.

  A business buys a non-current asset for cash.

  The two effects on the financial statements are:

  (1) There is an increase in non-current assets.

  (2) There is a decrease in cash.

- To follow the rules of double entry bookkeeping, each time a transaction is recorded, both effects must be taken into account.

- These two effects are equal and opposite such that the accounting equation will always prove correct:

$$\text{Assets} - \text{Liabilities} = \text{Capital}$$

- Traditionally, one effect is referred to as the debit side (abbreviated to Dr) and the other as the credit side of the entry (abbreviated to Cr).

2 Ledger accounts, debits and credits

- Transactions are recorded in the relevant ledger accounts. There is a ledger account for each asset, liability, revenue and expense item.

- Each account has two sides – the debit and credit sides:

Debit (Dr)	**Credit (Cr)**

Name of account e.g. cash, sales

Date	Narrative	$	Date	Narrative	$

- The duality concept means that each transaction will affect two ledger accounts.

- One account will be debited and the other credited.

- Whether an entry is to the debit or credit side of an account depends on the type of account and the transaction:

Debit	Credit
Increase in:	Increase in:
Expense (Income statement)	Liability (Statement of financial position)
Asset (Statement of financial position)	Income (Income statement)
Drawings (Statement of financial position)	Capital (Statement of financial position)

Summary of steps to record a transaction

(1) Identify the two items that are affected.

(2) Consider whether they are being increased or decreased.

(3) Decide whether each account should be debited or credited.

(4) Check that a debit entry and a credit entry have been made and they are both for the same amount.

Recording cash transactions

Cash transactions are those where payment is made or received immediately.

Cheque payments or receipts are classed as cash transactions

Double entry involves the bank ledger:

- a debit entry is where funds are received
- a credit entry is where funds are paid out.

Test your understanding 1

Recording cash transactions

Show the following transactions in ledger accounts: (Tip: the ledger accounts you need are Bank, Rent, Drawings, and Sales)

(1) Kamran pays $80 for rent by cheque. CR

(2) Kamran sells goods for $230 cash which he banks. DR

(3) He then takes $70 out of the business for his personal living DR expenses.

(4) Kamran sells more goods for cash, receiving $3,400. DR

Test your understanding 2

Yusuf enters into the following transactions in his first month of trading:

(1) Buys goods for cash for $380. DR

(2) Pays $20 in sundry expenses. CR

(3) Makes $1,000 in sales. DR

(4) Receives a bank loan of $5,000. DR

(5) Pays $2,600 for fixtures and fittings. CR

What is the total entry to the credit side of the cash T account?

A $6,000

B $6,380

C $3,000

D $2,620

Recording credit sales and purchases

Credit sales and purchases are transactions where goods or services change hands immediately, but payment is not made or received until some time in the future.

Money that a business is owed is accounted for in the receivables ledger.

Money that a business owes is accounted for in the payables ledger.

Test your understanding 3

Norris notes down the following transactions that happened in June.

(1) Sell goods for cash for $60.

(2) Pay insurance premium by cheque – $400.

(3) Sell goods for $250 – the customer will pay in a month.

(4) Pay $50 petrol for the delivery van.

(5) Buy $170 goods for resale on credit.

(6) Take $57 out of the business for living expenses.

(7) Buy another $40 goods for resale, paying cash.

(8) Buy a new computer for the business for $800.

Record these transactions using ledger accounts

Test your understanding 4

For each of the following individual transactions state the two ledger accounts affected, and whether the ledger account should be debited or credited:

(1) Ole purchases goods for $5,000, and pays by cheque. *Cr*

(2) Ole makes a sale to a customer for $500. The customer pays in 30 days' time. *Cr*

(3) Ole pays a telephone bill amounting to $40, and pays by cheque. *Cr*

(4) Ole receives bank interest income of $150. *Dr*

(5) Ole purchases stationery for $12 and pays cash. *Cr*

(6) Ole makes a sale to a customer for $400. The customer pays cash. *Dr*

3 Recording sales and purchases returns

- It is normal for customers to return unwanted goods to a business; equally the business will occasionally have cause to return unwanted goods to their supplier.

- The double entries arising will depend upon whether the returned goods were initially purchased on credit:

	Originally a credit transaction	Originally a cash transaction
Sales returns (returns inwards)	Dr Sales returns Cr Receivables	Dr Sales returns Cr Cash
Purchases returns (returns outwards)	Dr Payables Cr Purchases returns	Dr Cash Cr Purchases returns

Test your understanding 5

For each of the following, state the double entry required to record the transaction in the accounts:

(1) Alfie invests $10,000 of his life savings into his business bank account.

(2) He then buys goods from Isabel, a supplier for $1,000 and pays by cheque.

(3) A sale is made for $400 – the customer pays by cheque.

(4) Alfie makes a sale for $600 and the customer promises to pay in the future.

(5) Alfie then buys goods from his supplier, Kamen, for $500 on credit.

(6) Alife pays a telephone bill of $150 by cheque.

(7) The credit customer pays the balance on her account.

(8) Alfie pays Kamen $340.

(9) Bank interest of $30 is received.

(10) A cash customer returned $20 goods to Alfie for a refund.

(11) Alfie sent goods of $100 back to Kamen.

4 Accounting for discounts

Discounts may be given in the case of credit transactions for prompt payment:

- A business may give its customer a discount – known as **Discount allowed**.

- A business may receive a discount from a supplier – known as **Discount received**.

The correct double entries are:

Discount allowed

Dr Discount allowed (expense)   X

Cr Receivables   X

The expense is shown beneath gross profit in the income statement, alongside other expenses of the business.

Discount received

Dr Payables   X

Cr Discount received (income)   X

The income is shown beneath gross profit in the income statement.

Trade discounts

Trade discounts are given to try and increase the volume of sales being made by the supplier. By reducing the selling price, buying items in bulk then becomes more attractive. If you are able to source your products cheaper, you can then also sell them on to the consumer cheaper too. For example, if we were to buy over 1000 items, the supplier might be able to drop the price of those items by 5%.

Early settlement discounts

This type of discount encourages people to pay for items much quicker. If you pay for the goods within a set time limit, then you will receive a % discount. For example, a cash discount of 3% is offered to any customers who pay within 14 days.

Whilst offering this discount makes the cash flow in quicker, it is still a 'lost cost' to the business who offers such a discount.

Test your understanding 6

George owes a supplier, Herbie, $2,000 and is owed $3,400 by a customer, Iris. George offers a cash discount to his customers of 2.5% if they pay within 14 days and Herbie has offered George a cash discount of 3% for payment within ten days.

George pays Herbie within ten days and Iris takes advantage of the cash discount offered to her.

What ledger entries are required to record these discounts?

A	Dr	Payables	60	Dr	Discount allowed	85
	Cr	Discount received	60	Cr	Receivables	85
B	Dr	Discount allowed	60	Dr	Payables	85
	Cr	Receivables	60	Cr	Discount received	85
C	Dr	Payables	50	Dr	Discount allowed	102
	Cr	Discount received	50	Cr	Receivables	102
D	Dr	Discount allowed	50	Dr	Payables	102
	Cr	Receivables	50	Cr	Discount received	102

KAPLAN PUBLISHING

5 Balancing off a statement of financial position ledger account

Once the transactions for a period have been recorded, it will be necessary to find the balance on the ledger account:

(1) Total both sides of the T account and find the larger total.

(2) Put the larger total in the total box on the debit and credit side.

(3) Insert a balancing figure to the side of the T account which does not currently add up to the amount in the total box. Call this balancing figure 'balance c/f' (carried forward) or 'balance c/d' (carried down).

(4) Carry the balance down diagonally and call it 'balance b/f' (brought forward) or 'balance b/d' (brought down).

Test your understanding 7

Balance off the following account:

Cash

	$		$
Capital	10,000	Purchases	200
Sales	250	Rent	150
		Electricity	75

Test your understanding 8

Balance off the following account:

Bank

	$		$
Capital	10,000	Purchases	1,000
Sales	300	Rent	2,500
		Electricity	750
		New van	15,000

6 The trial balance

- Once all ledger accounts have been balanced off a trial balance is prepared.

- A trial balance is a list of the 'balance b/f' on the ledger accounts according to whether they are on the debit or credit side. Trial balance as at 31 December 2005

Trial balance as at 31 December 2005

Name of account	Dr $	Cr $
Sales		X
Purchases	X	
Receivables	X	
Payables		X
Capital		X
	X	X

What does the trial balance prove?

The trial balance will balance if for every debit entry made, an equal credit entry was made and the balances were correctly extracted and cast (added up!).

- The purpose of a trial balance is:

- to check that for every debit entry made, an equal credit entry has been made.

- as a first step in preparing the financial statements.

Note that a number of adjustments will be made after the trial balance is extracted. These adjustments do not therefore appear in the trial balance.

KAPLAN PUBLISHING

7 Closing off the ledger accounts

At the year end, the ledger accounts must be closed off in preparation for the recording of transactions in the next accounting period.

Statement of financial position ledger accounts

- Assets/liabilities at the end of a period = Assets/liabilities at start of the next period, e.g. the cash at bank at the end of one day will be the cash at bank at the start of the following day.

- Balancing the account will result in:
  - a balance c/f (being the asset/liability at the end of the accounting period)
  - a balance b/f (being the asset/liability at the start of the next accounting period).

7.2 Income statement ledger accounts

- At the end of a period any amounts that relate to that period are transferred out of the income and expenditure accounts into another ledger account called the income statement.

- This is done by closing the account.

- Do not show a balance c/f or balance b/f but instead put the balancing figure on the smallest side and label it 'income statement'.

Capital account

- At the start of the next accounting period the capital account will have an opening balance, i.e. a balance b/f equal to the amount that is owed to the owner at the start of that period.

- This amount is equal to what was owed to the owner at the start of the previous period, plus any capital that the owner introduced in the period, plus any profits earned in the period less any drawings taken out in the period.

- Therefore we transfer the balance on the income statement and the balance on the drawings account to the capital account at the end of the period so that it will have the correct opening balance at the start of the next.

Capital

	$			$
			Balance b/f	X
Loss for year	X		Profit for year	X
Drawings	X		Cash injections	X
Balance c/f	X			
	X			X
			Balance b/f	X

Test your understanding 9

Oddjob had $7,800 capital invested in his business at the start of the year. During the course of the year he took $3,100 cash out of the business for himself and also paid his wife, who did some secretarial work for the business, $500. The business' overall profit for the year was $8,900. Oddjob also paid $350 for a new personal suit using the business cheque book during the year.

What is the balance on the capital account at the end of the year?

A $12,750

B $13,250

C $13,600

D $13,100

8 Opening balances in the ledger accounts

- If a business has been in operation in the previous year, then at the beginning of any accounting period it will have assets and liabilities such as cash and non-current assets.

- Any opening amounts are shown in statement of financial position ledger accounts as opening balances.

- The opening balance on an asset account is a debit entry.

KAPLAN PUBLISHING

- The opening balance on a liability account is a credit entry.

- Transactions during the year are then entered as normal in the ledger account, and at the year end it is balanced off taking into account the opening balance.

Note: Income statement ledger accounts do not have an opening balance.

Test your understanding 10

Johnny had receivables of $4,500 at the start of 20X5. During the year to 31 December 20X5 he makes credit sales of $45,000 and receives cash of $46,500 from credit customers.

What is the balance on the receivables account at 31 December 20X5?

A $6,000Dr

B $6,000Cr

C $3,000Dr

D $3,000Cr

9 Preparation of financial statements

The process seen thus far is as follows:

Examination questions may draw on any particular stage of this process.

Test your understanding 11

Matthew set up a business and in the first nine days of trading the following transactions occurred:

1 January	Matthew introduces $10,000 capital by cheque.
2 January	Matthew buys supplies worth $4,000 and pays by cheque.
3 January	Matthew buys a delivery van for $2,000 and pays by cheque.
4 January	Matthew buys $1,000 of purchases on credit.
5 January	Matthew sells goods for $1,500 and receives a cheque of that amount.
6 January	Matthew sells all his remaining goods for $5,000 on credit.
7 January	Matthew pays $800 to his supplier by cheque.
8 January	Matthew pays rent of $200 by cheque.
9 January	Matthew draws $100 for living expenses from the business bank account.

Required:

(a) Complete the relevant ledger accounts.

(b) Extract a trial balance.

(c) Prepare the income statement for the first nine days.

(d) Prepare the Statement of financial position as at 9 January.

KAPLAN PUBLISHING

Chapter summary

```
┌─────────────────────────────────────┐
│         TRANSACTIONS OCCUR           │
└─────────────────────────────────────┘
```

```
┌─────────────────────────────────────┐
│        TWO EFFECTS RECORDED          │
│         IN LEDGER ACCOUNTS           │
│            Debit = credit            │
│  Dr = increase in │ Cr = increase in │
│      Expense      │     Liability    │
│       Asset       │      Income      │
│      Drawings     │      Capital     │
└─────────────────────────────────────┘
```

```
┌─────────────────────────────────────┐
│     LEDGER ACCOUNTS BALANCED OFF     │
```
1   Total both sides and find the larger total.
2   Put the larger total in both total boxes.
3   Insert a balancing figure as required in statement of financial position accounts, call this balancing figure 'Balance c/f'. For income and expense accounts, take this balancing figure to the profit and loss account T account.
4   For statement of financial position accounts, carry the balance down diagonally and call it 'balance b/f'.

```
┌─────────────────────────────────────┐
│            TRIAL BALANCE             │
```
Is extracted. Double entry has been correctly upheld as long as total debits = total credits.

```
┌─────────────────────────────────────┐
│   YEAR END ADJUSTMENTS AND LEDGER    │
│          ACCOUNTS CLOSED OFF         │
```
- statement of financial position accounts result in a balance c/f.
- income statement accounts are closed off to the income statement ledger account.
- the balance on the income statement and drawings ledger accounts are transferred to the capital account.

```
┌─────────────────────────────────────┐
│         FINANCIAL STATEMENTS         │
└─────────────────────────────────────┘
```

Test your understanding answers

Test your understanding 1

Bank

DR			CR
	$		$
Sales (2)	230	Rent (1)	80
Sales (4)	3,400	Drawings (3)	70

Sales

	$		$
		Bank (2)	230
		Bank (4)	3,400

Rent

	$		$
Bank (1)	80		

Drawings

	$		$
Bank (3)	70		

Test your understanding 2

The correct answer is C

Cash

	$		$
Sales	1,000	Purchases	380
Loan	5,000	Sundry expenses	20
		Fixtures and fittings	2,600

KAPLAN PUBLISHING

Test your understanding 3

DR **Bank** CR.

	$		$
Sales (1)	60	Insurance (2)	400
		Motor expenses (4)	50
		Drawings (6)	57
		Purchases (7)	40
		Non-current assets (8)	800

Sales

	$		$
		Bank (1)	60
		Receivables (3)	250

Insurance (expense)

	$		$
Bank (2)	400		

Receivables

	$		$
Sales (3)	250		

Motor expenses

	$		$
Bank (4)	50		

Purchases

	$		$
Payables (5)	170		
Cash (7)	40		

Payables

	$		$
		Purchases (5)	170

Drawings			
	$		$
Bank (6)	57		

Non-current asset (computer)			
	$		$
Bank (8)	800		

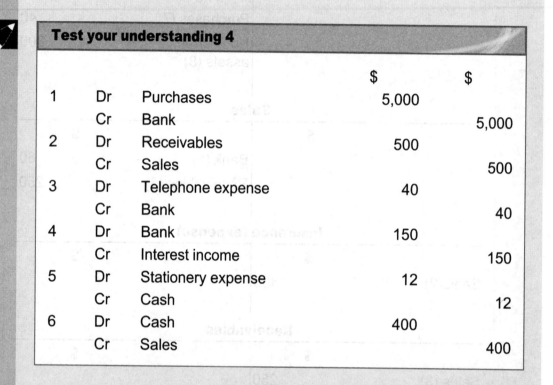

Test your understanding 4

			$	$
1	Dr	Purchases	5,000	
	Cr	Bank		5,000
2	Dr	Receivables	500	
	Cr	Sales		500
3	Dr	Telephone expense	40	
	Cr	Bank		40
4	Dr	Bank	150	
	Cr	Interest income		150
5	Dr	Stationery expense	12	
	Cr	Cash		12
6	Dr	Cash	400	
	Cr	Sales		400

KAPLAN PUBLISHING

Test your understanding 5

			$	$
1	Dr	Bank	10,000	
	Cr	Capital		10,000
2	Dr	Purchases	1,000	
	Cr	Bank		1,000
3	Dr	Bank	400	
	Cr	Sales		400
4	Dr	Receivables	600	
	Cr	Sales		600
5	Dr	Purchases	500	
	Cr	Payables		500
6	Dr	Telephone expense	150	
	Cr	Bank		150
7	Dr	Bank	600	
	Cr	Receivables		600
8	Dr	Payables	340	
	Cr	Bank		340
9	Dr	Bank	30	
	Cr	Interest income		30
10	Dr	Sales returns	20	
	Cr	Bank		20
11	Dr	Payables	100	
	Cr	Purchases returns		100

Test your understanding 6

The correct answer is A

Payables

	$		$
Cash (97% x 2,000)	1,940	Balance b/f	2,000
Discount received	60		
	2,000		2,000

Receivables

	$		$
Balance b/f	3,400	Cash (97.5% x 3,400)	3,315
		Discount allowed	85
	3,400		3,400

Discount received

	$		$
		Payables	60

Discount allowed

	$		$
Receivables	85		

KAPLAN PUBLISHING

Test your understanding 7

Cash

	$		$
Capital	10,000	Purchases	200
Sales	250	Rent	150
		Electricity	75
		Balance c/f	9,825
	———		———
	10,250		10,250
	———		———
Balance b/f	9,825		

Test your understanding 8

Bank

	$		$
Capital	10,000	Purchases	1,000
Sales	300	Rent	2,500
		Electricity	750
Balance c/f	8,950	New van	15,000
	———		———
	19,250		19,250
	———		———
		Balance b/f	8,950

Test your understanding 9

The correct answer is B.

Capital

	$		$
Drawings	3,100	Balance b/f	7,800
Drawings (suit)	350	Profit for the year	8,900
Balance c/f	13,250		
	16,700		16,700
		Balance b/f	13,250

Test your understanding 10

The correct answer is C.

Receivables

	$		$
Balance b/f	4,500		
Sales	45,000	Cash received	46,500
		Balance c/f	3,000
	49,500		49,500
Balance b/f	3,000		

KAPLAN PUBLISHING

Test your understanding 11

Bank

		$			$
1 Jan	Capital	10,000	2 Jan	Purchases	4,000
5 Jan	Sales	1,500	3 Jan	Delivery van	2,000
			7 Jan	Payables	800
			8 Jan	Rent	200
			9 Jan	Drawings	100
				Balance c/f	4,400
		11,500			
	Balance b/f	4,400			

Capital

		$			$
	Balance c/f	10,000	1 Jan	Bank	10,000
		10,000			10,000

Purchases

		$			$
2 Jan	Bank	4,000		P&L	5,000
4 Jan	Payables	1,000			
		5,000			5,000

Delivery van

		$		$
3 Jan	Bank	2,000	Balance c/f	5,000
		2,000		5,000
Balance b/f		2,000		

Payables

		$			$
7 Jan	Bank	800	4 Jan	Purchases	1,000
		200			
Balance c/f		1,000			1,000
			Balance b/f		2,000

Sales

	$			$
P&L	6,500	5 Jan	Bank	1,500
		6 Jan	Receivables	5,000
	6,500			6,500

Receivables

		$		$
7 Jan	Sales	5,000	Balance c/f	5,000
		5,000		5,000
Balance b/f		5,000		

Rent

		$		$
8 Jan	Bank	200	P&L	200
		200		200

Drawings

		$		$
9 Jan	Bank	100	Balance c/f	100
		100		100
	Balance b/f	100		

Trial balance as at 9 January

	Dr	Cr
	$	$
Bank	4,400	
Capital		10,000
Purchases	5,000	
Delivery van	2,000	
Payables		200
Sales		6,500
Receivables	5,000	
Rent	200	
Drawings	100	
	16,700	16,700

Income statement for the period ended 9 January

	$	$
Sales		6,500
Opening inventory	–	
Purchases	5000	
Closing inventory	–	
		5,000
Gross profit		1,500
Expenses		
Rent		200
		1,300
Net profit		

Statement of financial positionas at 9 January		
	$	$
Non current assets		
Delivery van		2,000
Current assets		
Inventory	–	
Receivables	5,000	
Bank	4,400	
	————	
		9,400
		————
		11,400
		————
Capital		10,000
Profit		1,300
Drawings		(100)
		————
		11,200
Current liabilities		
Payables		200
		————
		11,400
		————

KAPLAN PUBLISHING

4

Inventory

Chapter learning objectives

Upon completion of this chapter you will be able to:

- explain the need for adjustments for inventory in preparing financial statements

- illustrate income statements with opening and closing inventory

- explain and demonstrate how opening and closing inventory are recorded in the inventory account

- explain the IAS 2 requirements regarding the valuation of closing inventory

- define the cost and net realisable value of closing inventory

- discuss alternative methods of valuing inventory

- explain and demonstrate how to calculate the value of closing inventory from given movements in inventory levels, using FIFO (first in first out) and AVCO (average cost)

- assess the effect of using either FIFO or AVCO on both profit and asset value

- explain the IASB requirements for inventories

- explain the use of continuous and period-end inventory records.

1 Valuation of inventory

Inventory consists of:

- goods purchased for resale
- consumable stores (such as oil)
- raw materials and components (used in the production process)
- partly-finished goods (usually called **work in progress – WIP**)
- finished goods (which have been manufactured by the business).

Inventory is included in the statement of financial position at:

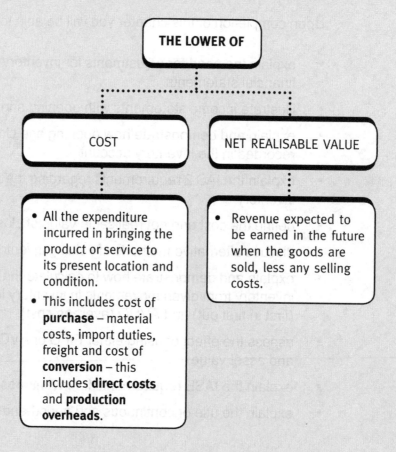

THE LOWER OF

COST

- All the expenditure incurred in bringing the product or service to its present location and condition.
- This includes cost of **purchase** – material costs, import duties, freight and cost of **conversion** – this includes **direct costs** and **production overheads**.

NET REALISABLE VALUE

- Revenue expected to be earned in the future when the goods are sold, less any selling costs.

Cost

Cost includes all the expenditure incurred in bringing the product or service to its present location and condition.

This includes:

- Cost of purchase – material costs, import duties, freight.
- Cost of conversion – this includes direct costs and production overheads.

Costs which must be **excluded** from the cost of inventory are:

- selling costs
- storage costs
- abnormal waste of materials, labour or other costs
- administrative overheads.

Example

Gordano is a small furniture manufacturing company. All of its timber is imported from Scandinavia and there are only three basic products - a company has 200 completed bookcases in inventory. For final accounts purposes, these will be stated at the lower of cost and net realisable value. How is 'cost' arrived at?

Solution

'Cost' will include several elements:

- Cost of purchase. First of all we must identify the timber used in the manufacture of bookcases (as opposed to dining tables and cupboards). The relevant costs will include the cost of the timber, the import duty and all the insurance and freight expenses associated with transporting the timber from Scandinavia to the factory.

- Cost of conversion. This will include costs which can be directly linked to the bookcases produced during the year. This includes labour costs 'booked' and sundry material costs (e.g. hinges and screws). Production overheads present particular problems. Costs such as factory heating and light, salaries of supervisors and depreciation of equipment are likely to relate to the three product ranges. These costs must be allocated to these product ranges on a reasonable basis. In particular, any percentage additions to cover overheads must be based on the normal level of production. If this proviso was not made, the inventory could be overvalued at the end of a period of low production, because there would be a smaller number of items over which to spread the overhead cost.

These groups of cost must relate to either:

- bookcases sold during the year, or
- bookcases in inventory at the year end (i.e. 200 bookcases).

NRV

The comparison between cost and NRV must be made item by item, not on the total inventory value. It may be acceptable to consider groups of items together if all are worth less than cost.

Expandable text

Inventory valuation

It can be a complicated procedure to arrive at the valuation placed on closing inventory, because:

- Initially the existence of the inventory, and the quantities thereof, have to be ascertained by means of an inventory count.

- Following on from this, a valuation has to be placed on the inventory which, as will be seen, may differ according to whatever accounting policy a company adopts.

The matching and prudence concept

- The concept of matching justifies the carrying forward of purchases not sold by the end of the accounting period, to leave the remaining purchases to be 'matched' with sales.

  When it comes to placing a value on the inventory carried forward, we have a further concept to consider: the prudence concept.

  If it weren't for this concept, we would carry forward inventory at its cost to the business. The prudence concept, however, requires the application of a degree of caution in making estimates under conditions of uncertainty.

In the context of the value of inventory, this means that if goods are expected to be sold below cost after the statement of financial position date (for example, because they are damaged or obsolete), account must be taken of the loss in order to prepare the statement of financial position.

The amount at which inventory should be stated in the statement of financial position is the lower of cost and net realisable value.

Keeping inventory records

A business may choose to keep inventory records on a continuous basis throughout the year or only count inventory at the period end.

In preparing the financial statements, the calculation of what is in closing inventory can be a major exercise for a business. The business may need to count its inventory at the statement of financial position date. A formal title for the sheets recording the inventory count is 'period-end inventory records'.

An alternative would be to have records which show the amount of inventory at any date, i.e. continuous inventory records. These records may take a variety of forms but, in essence, a record of each item of inventory would be maintained showing all the receipts and issues for that item.

The merits of continuous inventory records are as follows:

- There is better information for inventory control.

- Excessive build up of certain lines of inventory whilst having insufficient inventory of other lines is avoided.

- Less work is needed to calculate inventory at the end of the accounting period.

The merits of period-end inventory records are as follows:

- They are cheaper in most situations than the costs of maintaining continuous inventory records.

- Even if there is a continuous inventory record, there will still be a need to check the accuracy of the information recorded by having a physical check of some of the inventory lines.

2 Adjustments for inventory in the financial statements

- In order to be able to prepare a set of financial statements, inventory must be accounted for at the end of the period.

- Opening inventory must be included in cost of sales as these goods are available for sale along with purchases during the year.

- Closing inventory must be deducted from cost of sales as these goods are held at the period end and have not been sold.

Expandable text

In order to be able to prepare a set of financial statements, it is first necessary to learn how to account for any items of goods held at the end of the year, i.e. closing inventory. (In some countries inventory is referred to as 'stock'.)

Example

A trader starts in business and by the end of his first year he has purchased goods costing $21,000 and has made sales totalling $25,000. Goods which cost him $3,000 have not been sold by the end of the year.

What profit has he made in the year?

Solution

The unsold goods are referred to as closing inventory. This inventory is deducted from purchases in the income statement.

Gross profit is thus:

	$	$
Sales revenue		25,000
Purchases	21,000	
Less: Closing inventory	(3,000)	
	_____	
Cost of sales		(18,000)
		_____
Gross profit		7,000

Closing inventory of $3,000 will appear on the statement of financial position as an asset.

Illustration 1– Adjustments for inventory

Peter buys and sells washing machines. He has been trading for many years. On 1 January 20X7, his opening inventory is 30 washing machines which cost $9,500. He purchased 65 machines in the year amounting to $150,000 and on 31 December 20X7 he has 25 washing machines left in inventory with a cost of $7,500. Peter has sold 70 machines with a sales value of $215,000 in the year.

Calculate the gross profit for the year ended 31 December 20X7.

Expandable text

Solution

- Gross profit is sales revenue less cost of sales.
- We must match the 70 machines sold with the cost of those machines and exclude from cost of sales the machines that are left in inventory.
- Opening inventory must be included in cost of sales as some of the goods sold during the year come from the goods the trader started off with at the beginning of the year.
- We can calculate the gross profit as follows:

	$	$
Sales revenue		215,000
Opening inventory (at cost)	9,500	
Purchases (at cost)	150,000	
	159,500	
Less: Closing inventory (at cost)	(7,500)	
Cost of sales		(152,000)
Gross profit		63,000

3 Recording inventory in the ledger accounts

- Inventory is only recorded in the ledger accounts at the end of the accounting period.
- In the inventory ledger account the opening inventory will be the brought forward balance from the previous period. This must be transferred to the income statement ledger account with the following entry:

  Dr Income statement (Ledger account)

  Cr Inventory (Ledger account).

- The closing inventory is entered into the ledger accounts with the following entry:

  Dr Inventory (Ledger account)

  Cr Income statement (Ledger account).

- Once these entries have been completed, the income statement ledger account contains both opening and closing inventory and the inventory ledger account shows the closing inventory for the period to be shown in the statement of financial position.

Illustration 2 – Recording inventory in the ledger accounts

Continuing from previous Illustration, we will now see how the ledger accounts for inventory are prepared.

We will look at the ledger accounts at the following times:

(a) Immediately before extracting a trial balance at 31 December 20X7.

(b) Immediately after the year-end adjustments and closing off of the ledger accounts.

(a)Ledger accounts before extracting a trial balance

Inventory

20X7	$		$
1 Jan Balance b/f	9,500		

The inventory is an asset and therefore is a debit entry in the inventory account.

Purchases

20X7	$		$
Various suppliers	150,000		

Sales revenue

	$	20X7	$
		Various customers	215,000

- The balance of $9,500 in inventory account originated from last year's statement of financial position when it appeared as closing inventory. This figure remains unchanged in the inventory account until the very end of the year when closing inventory at 31 December 20X7 is considered.

- The closing inventory figure is not usually provided to us until after we have extracted the trial balance at 31 December 20X7.

- The purchases and sales figures have been built up over the year and represent the year's accumulated transactions.

- The trial balance will include opening inventory, purchases and sales revenue in respect of the inventory transactions.

KAPLAN PUBLISHING

(b) Ledger accounts reflecting the closing inventory

- Closing inventory for accounting purposes has been valued at $7,500.

Step 1

The income statement forms part of the double entry. At the year end the accumulated totals from the sales and purchases accounts must be transferred to it using the following journal entries:

Dr Sales revenue	$215,000
Cr Income statement	$215,000
Dr Income statement	$150,000
Cr Purchases	$150,000

These transfers are shown in the ledger accounts below.

Step 2

The opening inventory figure ($9,500) must also be transferred to the income statement account in order to arrive at cost of sales.

Dr Income statement $9,500 Cr Inventory $9,500

Step 3

The income statement cannot be completed (and hence gross profit calculated) until the closing inventory is included.

Dr Inventory $7,500 Cr Income statement $7,500

After summarising and balancing off, the ledger then becomes:

Inventory

20X7	$	20X7	$
1 Jan Balance b/f	9,500	31 Dec Income statement	9,500
31 Dec Income statement	7,500	31 Dec Balance c/f	7,500
	17,000		17,000
20X8			
1 Jan Balance b/f	7,500		

Purchases

20X7	$	20X7	$
Various dates		31 Dec	
Payables	150,000	Income statement	150,000

Sales revenue

20X7	$	20X7	$
31 Dec		Various dates	
Income statement	215,000	Receivables	215,000

Income statement ('T' account form)

20X7	$	20X7	$
31 Dec		31 Dec	
Purchases	150,000	Sales revenue	215,000
Inventory	9,500	Inventory	7,500
Gross profit c/f	63,000		
	222,500		222,500
		Gross profit b/f	63,000

Expandable text

Key points:

- The sales revenue and the purchases accounts are cleared out to and summarised in the income statement.

- Opening inventory is cleared out to the income statement and closing inventory is entered into the inventory account and the income statement.

- The balance on the inventory account remains at the end of the period and is listed in the statement of financial position under current assets as inventory.

- The first part of the income statement can be balanced at this stage to show the gross profit figure carried down and brought down.

- The above layout of the income statement is not particularly useful, but it assists the appreciation of the actual double entry processes and the realisation that the income statement is part of the double entry.

The more common layout of the first part of the income statement is:

	$	$
Sales revenue		215,000
Opening inventory	9,500	
Add: Purchases	150,000	
	159,500	
Less: Closing inventory	(7,500)	
Cost of sales		(152,000)
Gross profit		63,000

Test your understanding 1

The trading position of a simple cash-based business for its first week of trading was as follows:

	$
Capital introduced by the owner	1,000
Purchases for cash	800
Sales for cash	900

At the end of the week there were goods which had cost $300 left in inventory.

Write up the ledger accounts for the first week, including the income statement, and then prepare a vertical income statement together with a statement of financial position at the end of the first week.

Test your understanding 2

The business described in Test your understanding 1 now continues into its second week. Its transactions are as follows:

	$
Sales for cash	1,000
Purchases for cash	1,100

The goods left in inventory at the end of this second week originally cost $500.

Write up the ledger accounts for the second week, including the income statement, and then prepare a vertical income statement together with a statement of financial position at the end of the second week.

4 Drawings of inventory

It is not unusual for a sole trader to take inventory from their business for their own use. This type of transaction is a form of drawings.

The correct double entry to account for such drawings is:

Dr Drawings   cost of inventory taken
Cr Cost of sales   cost of inventory taken

The credit entry ensures that the cost of inventory taken is not included as part of the cost of inventory sold in the income statement.

Test your understanding 3

Cole's business sells three products X, Y and Z. The following information was available at the year end:

	X	Y	Z
	$	$	$
Cost	7	10	19
Net realisable value (NRV)	10	8	15
Units	100	200	300

What is the value of the closing inventory?

A $8,400

B $6,800

C $7,100

D $7,200

Test your understanding 4

In what circumstances might the NRV of inventories be lower than their cost?

5 Methods of calculating cost of inventory

Method	Key points	
Unit cost	This is the actual cost of purchasing identifiable units of inventory.	Only used when items of inventory are individually distinguishable and of high value
FIFO – first infirst out	For costing purposes, the first items of inventory received are assumed to be the first ones sold.	The cost of closing inventory is the cost of the younger inventory.
AVCO – Average cost	The cost of an item of inventory is calculated by taking the average of all inventory held.	The average cost can be calculated periodically or continuously.

Test your understanding 5

Sam started her business on 1 January and provides details of the following transactions:

Purchases

(1) January 5 units at $4/unit

(2) January 5 units at $5/unit

(3) January 5 units at $5.50/unit

She then sold 7 units for $10/unit on 5 January.

(a) Calculate the value of the closing inventory at the end of the first week of trading using the FIFO and the AVCO methods.

(b) Prepare the income statement for the first week of trading under both FIFO and AVCO.

Test your understanding 6

A business commenced on 1 January and purchases are made as follows:

Month	No of units	Unit price $	Value $
Jan	380	2.00	760
Feb	400	2.50	1,000
Mar	350	2.50	875
Apr	420	2.75	1,155
May	430	3.00	1,290
Jun	440	3.25	1,430
	2,420		6,510

In June, 1,420 articles were sold for $7,000.

What is the cost of closing inventory and gross profit for the period using the FIFO method:

	Closing inventory $	Gross profit $
A	2,690	3,180
B	2,310	2,800
C	3,077	3,567

Expandable text

The impact of valuation methods on profit and the statement of financial position.

Different valuation methods will result in different closing inventory values.

This will in turn impact both profit and statement of financial position asset value.

Similarly any incorrect valuation of inventory will impact the financial statements.

KAPLAN PUBLISHING

If inventory is overvalued then:

- assets are overstated in the statement of financial position
- profit is overstated in the income statement (as cost of sales is too low)

If inventory is undervalued then:

- assets are understated in the statement of financial position
- profit is understated in the income statement (as cost of sales is too high).

Test your understanding 7

IAS 2 Inventories defines the items that may be included in computing the value of an inventory of finished goods manufactured by a business.

Which one of the following lists consists only of items which may be included in the statement of financial position value of such inventories according to IAS 2?

A   Foreman's wages, carriage inwards, carriage outwards, raw materials.

B   Raw materials, carriage inwards, costs of storage of finished goods, plant depreciation.

C   Plant depreciation, carriage inwards, raw materials, foreman's wages.

D   Carriage outwards, raw materials, foreman's wages, plant depreciation.

Chapter summary

INVENTORY
Valued at the lower
of cost and NVR

ADJUSTMENTS FOR INVENTORY
Opening inventory must be
transferred to the income
statement, closing inventory must
be entered into the accounts at
the year end.

VALUATION OF INVENTORY
Methods used:
- Unit cost
- FIFO
- AVCO

IAS 2 INVENTORIES
Provides rules on valuation of
inventory as well as disclosure
requirements

**RECORD INVENTORY IN THE
LEDGER ACCOUNTS**
Closing inventory:
Dr Inventory a/c
Cr Income statement ledger
Drawings of Inventory:
Dr Drawings
Cr Cost of Sales

Test your understanding answers

First, the transactions are entered into the ledger accounts, and the accounts are balanced. Revenue and purchases are then transferred to the income statement ledger account.

Capital

	$		$
		Cash	1,000

Cash

	$		$
Capital	1,000	Purchases	800
Sales revenue	900	Balance c/f	1,100
	1,900		1,900
Balance b/f	1,100		

Sales revenue

	$		$
Income statement	900	Cash	900

Purchases

	$		$
Cash	800	Income statement	800

Next, the closing inventory must be accounted for in the inventory account and the income statement account. There is no opening inventory as this is the first week of trading for the business.

Inventory

	$		$
Income statement	300		

Income statement

	$		$
Purchases	800	Sales revenue	900
Gross profit c/f	400	Closing inventory	300
	1,200		1,200
		Gross profit b/f	400

The income statement is prepared in the vertical format by rearranging the income statement ledger account

Income Statement for Week 1

	$	$
Sales Revenue		900
Cost of goods sold:		
Purchases	800	
Less: Closing inventory	(300)	
		(500)
Gross Profit		400

The statement of financial position is prepared by listing the balances brought down from the ledger accounts.

Statement of financial position as at Week 1

Inventory	300
Cash	1,100
	1,400
Capital	1,000
Profit for the week	400
	1,400

KAPLAN PUBLISHING

First, the ledger accounts must be written up. You must remember that there are opening balances on the statement of financial position accounts (cash and capital) but the income statement accounts have no opening balances as they were transferred to the income statement in Week 1.

Cash

	$		$
Balance b/f	1,100	Purchases	1,100
Sales Revenue	1,000	Balance c/f	1,000
	2,100		2,100
Balance b/f	1,000		

Sales revenue

	$		$
Income statement	1,000	Cash	1,000

Purchases

	$		$
Cash	1,100	Income statement	1,100

Income statement

	$		$
Purchases	1,100	Sales revenue	1,000

The opening inventory must be transferred to the income statement, and the closing inventory entered into the ledger accounts (inventory and income statement) leaving the balance carried forward which will be included in the statement of financial position.

Inventory

	$		$
Balance b/f	300	Income statement	300
Income statement	500		

Income statement

	$		$
Purchases	1,100	Sales revenue	1,000
Opening inventory	300	Closing inventory	500
Gross profit c/f	100		
	1,500		1,500
		Gross profit b/f	100

Income statement for week 2

	$	$
Sales revenue		1,000
Cost of goods sold:		
Opening inventory	300	
Purchases	1,100	
	1,400	
Less: Closing inventory	(500)	
		(900)
Gross profit		100

Statement of financial position as at week 2

	$
Inventory	500
Cash	1,000
	1,500
Capital at start of Week 2	1,400
Profit for Week 2	100
	1,500

Test your understanding 3

The correct answer is B

X	$7	(cost) x 100	=	$700
Y	$8	(NRV) x 200	=	$1,600
Z	$15	(NRV) x 300	=	$4,500
				_____
Total				$6,800

Test your understanding 4

NRV may be relevant in special cases, such as where goods are slow-moving, damaged or obsolete. However, most items of inventory will be stated at cost.

Test your understanding 5

Units purchased (5 x 3) = 15

Units sold = 7
_____

Closing inventory = 8

(a) FIFO

3 units @ $5 = $15.00

5 units @ $5.50 = $27.50

        _____

        $42.50

AVCO Average cost per unit: ((5 x $4) + (5 x $5) + (5 x $5.50))/15 = $4.83

Closing inventory = 8 x $4.83 = $38.64

(b) FIFO

	$	$
Sales (7 x $10)		70
Cost of sales		
Purchases (5 x $4) + (5 x $5) + (5 x $5.50)	72.50	
Less: Closing inventory	(42.50)	
		(30)
Profit		40

	$	$
Sales (7 x $10)		70
Cost of sales		
Purchases (5 x $4) + (5 x $5) + (5 x $5.50)	72.50	
Less: Closing inventory	(38.64)	
		(33.86)
Profit		36.14

Test your understanding 6

- The correct answer is C
- Inventory valuation (inventory in hand 2,420 – 1,420 = 1,000 units)
- FIFO – inventory valued at latest purchase prices

		$
440	articles at $3.25	1,430
430	articles at $3.00	1,290
130	articles at $2.75	357
_____		_____
1,000		3,077

Calculation of gross profit:

	$	$
Sales revenue		7,000
Purchases	6,510	
Less:		
Closing inventory	(3,077)	
	_____	
Cost of goods sold		(3,433)
		_____
Gross profit		3,567

Test your understanding 7

The correct answer is C

The other three answers contain items which cannot be included in inventory according to IAS 2.

5

Sales tax

Chapter learning objectives

Upon completion of this chapter you will be able to:

- explain the general principles of the operation of a sales tax
- calculate sales tax on transactions correctly
- enter sales tax on sales and purchases into the ledger accounts.

1 Principles of sales tax

- Sales tax is a form of indirect taxation.

- A business that is registered for sales tax is essentially a collection agent for the government.

- Sales tax is charged on purchases (input tax) and sales (output tax).

- Sales tax is excluded from the reported sales and purchases of the business.

- Periodically the business pays the sales tax to the tax authorities.

- If output tax exceeds input tax, the business pays the excess to the tax authorities.

- If input tax exceeds output tax, the business is repaid the excess by the tax authorities.

- Sales tax is sometimes called value added tax (VAT) or goods and services tax.

- Sales tax is charged on most goods and services.

2 Calculation of sales tax

- It is common for a rate of 17.5% sales tax to be charged on the selling price.

- The following is therefore true:

Proforma

Net selling price (tax exclusive price)	100.0%
Sales tax	17.5%
Gross selling price (tax inclusive price)	117.5%

- The net selling price is the amount that the business wishes to achieve.
- The gross selling price is the price charged to customers.
- The difference is paid to the tax authorities.

Note: Whilst in the UK the Vat /sales tax rate is 17.5%, as this is an International based syllabus the Vat/sales tax % you are given may be any percentage. You should be prepared to apply any % to the proforma above.

Illustration 1 – Calculation of sales tax

Calculation of sales tax

Orlando sells the following goods:

(1) to Bruno at a tax inclusive price of $470.

(2) to Cosmo at a tax exclusive price of $700.

How much sales tax is Orlando collecting on behalf of the government?

Expandable Text

Solution

Sales tax can be calculated using the relevant percentage depending on whether the price is tax inclusive or exclusive.

Sales to Bruno (sales price tax inclusive) (17.5%/117.5%) x $470 = $70

Sales to Cosmo (sales price tax exclusive) (17.5%/100%) x $700 = $122.50

Total sales tax collected: $70 + $122.50 = $192.50

Test your understanding 1

Lorenzo purchases goods for $170,625 (including sales tax) and sells goods for $230,500 (including sales tax).

What amount of sales tax is ultimately payable to the tax authorities?

A $8,918

B $14,926

C $4,471

D $10,479

The sales tax rate is 17.5%.

3 Accounting entries for sales tax

The usual bookkeeping entries for purchases and sales are only slightly amended by sales tax, the main addition being the introduction of a sales tax account, which is a receivable or payable account with the tax authorities.

Sales tax paid on purchases (input tax)

Dr Purchases cost excluding sales tax (net cost)

Dr Sales tax Sales tax

Cr Payables/cash cost including sales tax (gross cost)

- The purchases account does not include sales tax because it is not an expense – it will be recovered.

- The payables account does include sales tax, as the supplier must be paid the full amount due.

Sales tax charged on sales (output tax)

Dr Receivables/cash — sales price including sales tax (gross selling price)

Cr Sales tax — sales price excluding sales (net selling price)

Cr Sales tax — Sales tax

- The sales account does not include sales tax because it is not income – it will have to be paid to the tax authorities.

- The receivables account does include sales tax, as the customer must pay the full amount due.

Payment of sales (output) tax

Dr Sales tax amount paid

Cr Cash amount paid

- If output tax exceeds input tax, a payment must be made to the tax authorities.

Receipt of sales (output) tax

Dr Cash amount received

Cr Sales tax amount received

- If input tax exceeds output tax, there will be a receipt from the tax authorities.

Test your understanding 2

		Net	Sales tax	Total
		$	$	$
Purchases	(all on credit)	180,000	31,500	211,500
Sales	(all on credit)	260,000	45,500	305,500

Record these transactions in the ledger accounts.

Test your understanding 3

Valerie's business is registered for sales tax purposes. During the quarter ending 31 March 20X6, she made the following sales, all of which were subject to sales tax at 17.5%:

$10,000 excluding sales tax

$7,402 including sales tax

$6,745 excluding sales tax

$11,632 including sales tax.

She also made the following purchases all of which were subject to sales tax at 17.5%:

$15,000 excluding sales tax

$12,455 including sales tax

$11,338 including sales tax

$9,870 including sales tax.

What is the balance on the sales tax account on 31 March 20X6?

A $7,639 Dr
B $1,875 Dr
C $7,639 Cr
D $1,875 Cr

Chapter summary

Principles of sales tax

- It is charged on purchases and sales.
- It is excluded from the reported sales and purchases of the business.
- The business is a collection agent for the government.
- It is paid periodically to the tax authorities (or it is repaid to the business if taxable purchases exceed sales).

Accounting entries for sales tax

- Sales and purchases ledger accounts are net of sales tax.
- Receivables and payables ledger accounts are inclusive of sales tax as the business collects the sales tax from customers and pays it to suppliers.
- The sales tax account is a payable (or receivable) account in the statement of financial position.

Test your understanding answers

Test your understanding 1

The correct answer is A

	$
Output tax:	
Sales (including sales tax)	230,500
Sales tax (17.5/117.5)	34,330
Input tax:	
Purchases (including sales tax)	170,625
Sales tax (17.5/117.5)	25,412
Payable to tax authorities:	
Output tax – Input tax (34,330 – 25,412)	8,918

Test your understanding 2

Sales			
	$		$
		Receivables	260,000
			260,000

Note that sales are recorded excluding sales tax, as this is not income for the business.

Purchases

	$		$
Payables	180,000		
	———		
	180,000		
	———		

Note that purchases are recorded net of sales tax, as this is not a cost to the business.

Receivables

	$		$
Sales/Sales tax	305,500		
	———		
	305,500		
	———		

Receivables are recorded including sales tax (the gross amount) as the customer must pay to the business the cost of the goods plus the sales tax.

Payables

	$		$
		Purchases/Sales tax	211,500
			———
			211,500
			———

As with receivables, the payables must be recorded inclusive of sales tax, as the business needs to pay its suppliers the gross amount.

Sales tax account(a personal account with tax authorities)

	$		$
Payables	31,500	Receivables	45,500
Balance c/f	14,000		
			45,500
	45,500		
		Balance b/f	14,000

Note: As the balance on the sales tax account represents a normal trade liability it is included in accounts payable on the statement of financial position.

Test your understanding 3

The correct answer is B

Sales tax

Purchases:	$	Sales:	$
15,000 x 17.5%	2,625	10,000 x 17.5%	1,750
12,455 x 17.5/117.5	1,855	7,402 x 17.5/117.5	1,102
11,338 x 17.5/117.5	1,689	6,745 x 17.5%	1,180
9,870 x 17.5/117.5	1,470	11,632 x 17.5/117.5	1,732
		Balance b/f	1,875
	7,639		7,639
Balance b/f	1,875		

6

Accruals and prepayments

Chapter learning objectives

Upon completion of this chapter you will be able to:

- explain the need for adjustments for accruals and prepayments in preparing financial statements
- illustrate the process of adjusting for accruals and prepayments in preparing financial statements.

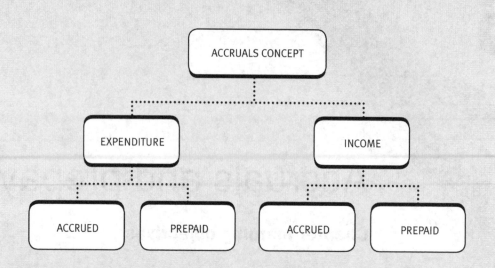

1 Accruals basis of accounting

The accruals basis of accounting means that to calculate the profit for the period, we must include all the income and expenditure relating to the period, whether or not the cash has been received or paid or an invoice received.

Profit is therefore:

Income earned	X
Expenditure incurred	(X)
	___
Profit	X

Expandable text

The accruals concept is identified as an important accounting concept by IAS 1 Presentation of Financial Statements. The concept is that income and expenses should be matched together and dealt with in the income statement for the period to which they relate, regardless of the period in which the cash was actually received or paid. Therefore all of the expenses involved in making the sales for a period should be matched with the sales income and dealt with in the period in which the sales themselves are accounted for.

Sales revenue

The sales revenue for an accounting period is included in the income statement when the sales are made. This means that, when a sale is made on credit, it is recognised in the income statement when the agreement is made and the invoice is sent to the customer rather than waiting until the cash for the sale is received. This is done by setting up a receivable in the statement of financial position for the amount of cash that is due from the sale (debit receivables and credit sales revenue).

Purchases

Similarly purchases are matched to the period in which they were made by accounting for all credit purchases when they took place and setting up a payable in the statement of financial position for the amount due (debit purchases and credit payables).

Cost of sales

The major cost involved in making sales in a period is the actual cost of the goods that are being sold. As we saw in a previous chapter, we need to adjust for opening and closing inventory to ensure that the sales made in the period are matched with the actual costs of those goods. Any goods unsold are carried forward to the next period so that they are accounted for when they are actually sold.

Expenses

The expenses of the period that the business has incurred in making its sales, such as rent, electricity and telephone, must also be matched with the sales for the period. This means that the actual expense incurred in the period should be included in the income statement rather than simply the amount of the expense that has been paid in cash.

2 Accrued expenditure

An accrual arises where expenses of the business, relating to the year, have not been paid by the year end.

In this case, it is necessary to record the extra expense relevant to the year and create a corresponding statement of financial position liability (called an accrual):

Dr Expense account X

Cr Accrual   X

An accrual will therefore reduce profit in the income statement.

Illustration 1 – Accrued expenditure

Accrued expenditure

A business' electricity charges amount to $12,000 pa. In the year to 31 December 20X5, $9,000 has been paid. The electricity for the final quarter is paid in January 20X6.

What year-end accrual is required and what is the electricity expense for the year?

Show the relevant entries in the ledger accounts.

Expandable text

Solution

- The total expense charged to the income statement in respect of electricity should be $12,000.

- The year-end accrual is the $3,000 expense that has not been paid in cash.

- The double entry required is:

- Dr Electricity expense $3,000

- Cr Accruals $3,000

Ledger accounts and accrued expenses

Method 1: know the accrual

Electricity expense

	$		$
Cash	9,000	Income statement (ß)	12,000
Accrual c/f	3,000		
	———		———
	12,000		12,000
	———		———
		Accrual b/f	3,000

Method 2: know the income statement charge

Electricity expense

	$		$
Cash	9,000	Income statement	12,000
Accrual c/f	3,000		
	12,000		12,000
		Accrual b/f	3,000

Test your understanding 1

John Simnel's business has an accounting year end of 31 December 20X1. He rents factory space at a rental cost of $5,000 per quarter, payable in arrears.

During the year to 31 December 20X1 his cash payments of rent have been as follows:

- 31 March (for the quarter to 31 March 20X1) $5,000
- 29 June (for the quarter to 30 June 20X1) $5,000
- 2 October (for the quarter to 30 September 20X1) $5,000

The final payment due on 31 December 20X1 for the quarter to that date was not paid until 4 January 20X2.

Show the ledger accounts required to record the above transactions.

Accrued expenditure will reduce profit in the Income statement and will also create a current liability on the Statement of financial position.

For example, if we were to put through an accrual of $500 for telephone expenses. The double entry would be:

Dr Telephone expenses $500

Cr Accruals $500

The additional telephone expense would reduce profits by $500. The additional accrual would increase our current liabilities by $500.

3 Prepaid expenditure

A prepayment arises where some of the following year's expenses have been paid in the current year.

In this case, it is necessary to remove that part of the expense which is not relevant to this year and create a corresponding statement of financial position asset (called a prepayment):

Dr Prepayment   X

Cr Expense account   X

A prepayment will therefore increase profit in the income statement.

Illustration 2– Prepaid expenditure

The annual insurance charge for a business is $24,000 pa. $30,000 was paid on 1 January 20X5 in respect of future insurance charges.

What is the year-end prepayment and what is the insurance expense for the year?

Show the relevant entries in the ledger accounts.

Expandable text

Solution

- The total expense charged to the income statement in respect of insurance should be $24,000.
- The year-end prepayment is the $6,000 that has been paid in respect of 20X6.

The double entry required is:

Dr Prepayment $6,000

Cr Insurance expense $6,000

Insurance – expense

	$		$
Cash	30,000	Income statement	24,000
		Prepayments c/f	6,000
	30,000		30,000

Test your understanding 2

Tubby Wadlow pays the rental expense on his market stall in advance. He starts business on 1 January 20X5 and on that date pays $1,200 in respect of the first quarter's rent. During his first year of trade he also pays the following amounts:

- 3 March (in respect of the quarter ended 30 June) $1,200
- 14 June (in respect of the quarter ended 30 September) $1,200
- 25 September (in respect of the quarter $1,400
- ended 31 December)
- 13 December (in respect of the first quarter of 20X6) $1,400

Show these transactions in the rental expense account.

Prepaid expenditure increases profit on the Income statement and also creates a current asset to be included on the Statement of financial position.

For example, if we were to put a prepayment of $1000 in our financial statments for insurance, the double entry would be:

Dr Prepayments $1000

Cr Insurance expense $1000

The prepayments side would increase our current assets by the $1000. The insurance expense would decrease by the $1000, and hence increase our overall profits.

Proforma expense T account

Expense

	$		$
Balance b/f (opening prepaid expense)	X	Balance b/f (opening accrued expense)	X
Bank (total paid during the year)	X	Income statement (total expense for the year)	X
Balance c/f (closing accrued expense)	X	Balance c/f (closing prepaid expense)	X
	X		X
Balance b/f (opening prepaid expense)	X	Balance b/f (opening accrued expense)	X

Test your understanding 3

On 1 January 20X5, Willy Mossop owed $2,000 in respect of the previous year's electricity. Willy made the following payments during the year ended 31 December 20X5:

- 6 February $2,800
- 8 May $3,000
- 5 August $2,750
- 10 November $3,100

At 31 December 20X5, Willy calculated that he owed $1,800 in respect of electricity for the last part of the year.

What is the electricity charge to the income statement?

A $1,800

B $11,450

C $11,650

D $13,450

4 Accrued income

Accrued income arises where income has been earned in the accounting period but has not yet been received.

In this case, it is necessary to record the extra income in the income statement and create a corresponding asset in the statement of financial position (called accrued income):

Dr Accrued income (SFP) X

Cr Income (IS) X

Accrued income creates an additional current asset on our Statement of financial position. It also creates additional income on our Income statement, and hence this will increase overall profits.

Illustration 3– Accrued income

Accrued income

A business earns bank interest income of $300 per month. $3,000 bank interest income has been received in the year to 31 December 20X5.

What is the year-end asset and what is the bank interest income for the year?

Show the relevant entries in the ledger accounts.

Expandable text

Solution

- The total amount credited to the income statement in respect of interest should be $3,600 (12 x $300).

- The year-end accrued income asset is the $600 that has not yet been received.

The double entry required is:

Dr Accrued income (SFP) $600

Cr Bank interest income (IS) $600

Bank interest income			
	$		$
Income statement	3,600	Bank	3,000
		Accrued income c/f	600
	3,600		3,600
Accrued income b/f	600		

5 Prepaid income

Prepaid income arises where income has been received in the accounting period but which relates to the next accounting period.

In this case, it is necessary to remove the income not relating to the year from the income statement and create a corresponding liability in the statement of financial position (called prepaid income):

Dr Income (IS)   X

Cr Prepaid Income (SFP)   X

Illustration 4 – Prepaid income

Prepaid income

A business rents out a property at an income of $4,000 per month. $64,000 has been received in the year ended 31 December 20X5.

What is the year-end liability and what is the rental income for the year?

Show the relevant entries in the ledger accounts.

KAPLAN PUBLISHING

Solution

- The total amount credited to the income statement in respect of rent should be $48,000 (12 x $4,000).

- The year-end prepaid income liability is the $16,000 ($64,000 – $48,000) that has been received in respect of next year.

The double entry required is:

Dr Rental income $16,000

Cr Prepaid income (SFP) $16,000

Rental income

	$		$
Income statement	48,000	Cash	64,000
	———		———
Prepaid income c/f	16,000		64,000
	———		———
	64,000	Prepaid income b/f	16,000

Prepaid income reduces income on the Income statement and hence reduces overall profits too. It also creates a current liability on our Statement of financial position.

Proforma income T account

Income

	$		$
Balance b/f (opening accrued income)	X	Balance b/f (opening prepaid income)	X
Income statement (total revenue for the year)	X	Cash (total received during the year)	X
Balance c/f (closing prepaid income)	X	Balance c/f (closing accrued income)	X
	X		X
Balance b/f (opening accrued income)	X	Balance b/f (opening prepaid income)	X

Test your understanding 4

Accrued and prepaid income

Libby Farquar receives income from two rental units as follows:

	Unit 1		Unit 2	
Period	$	Received	$	Received
1.10.X4 – 31.12.X4	2,100	30.9.X4	1,300	2.1.X5
1.1.X5 – 31.3.X5	2,150	27.12.X4	1,300	4.4.X5
1.4.X5 – 30.6.X5	2,150	25.3.X5	1,300	1.7.X5
1.7.X5 – 30.9.X5	2,200	21.6.X5	1,400	6.10.X5
1.10.X5 – 31.12.X5	2,200	21.9.X5	1,400	2.1.X6
1.1.X6 – 31.3.X6	2,200	29.12.X5	1,400	4.4.X6

What is Libby's rental income in the income statement for the year ended 31 December 20X5?

A $5,400

B $8,700

C $14,000

D $14,100

Chapter summary

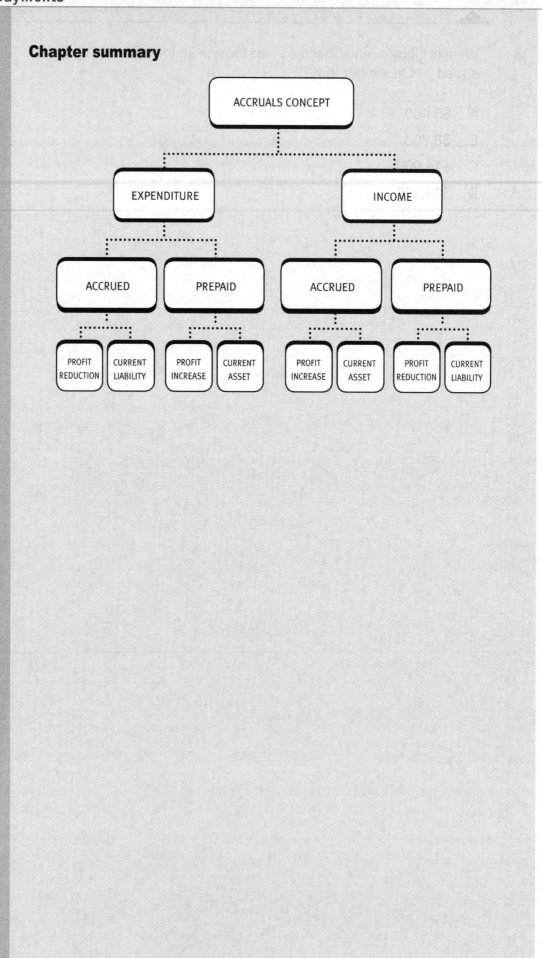

Test your understanding answers

Test your understanding 1

Rental expense

	$		$
31 March cash	5,000		
29 June cash	5,000		
2 October cash	5,000		
Accrual c/f	5,000	Income statement	20,000
	20,000		20,000
		Accrual b/f	5,000

Test your understanding 2

Rental expense

	$		$
1 January cash	1,200		
3 March cash	1,200		
14 June cash	1,200		
25 September cash	1,400	Income statement	5,000
13 December cash	1,400	Prepayment c/f	1,400
	6,400		6,400
Prepayment b/f	1,400		

Test your understanding 3

The correct answer is B

Electricity expense

	$		$
6 February cash	2,800	Accrual b/f	2,000
8 May cash	3,000		
5 August cash	2,750		
10 November cash	3,100	Income statement	11,450
Accrual c/f	1,800		
	13,450		13,450
		Accrual b/f	1,800

Test your understanding 4

The correct answer is D

Rental income (Unit 1)

	$		$
		Prepaid income b/f	2,150
		25.3.X5 cash	2,150
		21.6.X5 cash	2,200
Income statement	8,700	21.9.X5 cash	2,200
Prepaid income c/f	2,200	29.12.X5 cash	2,200
	10,900		10,900
		Prepaid income b/f	2,200

KAPLAN PUBLISHING

Rental income (Unit 2)

	$			$
Accrued income b/f	1,300	2.1.X5 cash		1,300
		4.4.X5 cash		1,300
		1.7.X5 cash		1,300
Income statement	5,400	6.10.X5 cash		1,400
		Accrued income c/f		1,400
	6,700			6,700
Accrued income b/f	1,400			

Total income: $8,700 + $5,400 = $14,100

Irrecoverable debts and allowances for receivables

Chapter learning objectives

Upon completion of this chapter you will be able to:

- identify the benefits and costs of offering credit facilities to customers
- explain the purpose of an aged receivables analysis
- explain the purpose of credit limits
- prepare the bookkeeping entries to write off an irrecoverable debt
- record an irrecoverable debt recovered
- identify the impact of irrecoverable debts on the income statement and statement of financial position
- prepare the bookkeeping entries to create and adjust an allowance for receivables
- illustrate how to include movements in the allowance for receivables in the income statement and how the closing balance of the allowance should appear in the statement of financial position.

1 The provision of credit facilities

The majority of businesses will sell to their customers on credit and state a defined time within which they must pay (a credit period). The main benefits and costs of doing so are as follows:

Expandable Text

Benefits

- The business may be able to enter new markets.
- There is a possibility of increased sales.
- Customer loyalty may be encouraged.

Costs

- Can be costly in terms of lost interest since the business is accepting payment later.
- Cash flow of the business may deteriorate.
- There is a potential risk of irrecoverable debts.

Aged receivables analysis

Where credit facilities are offered, it is normal for a business to maintain an aged receivables analysis.

- Analysis is usually a list, ordered by name, showing how much each customer owes and how old their debts are.
- The credit control function of a business uses the analysis to keep track of outstanding debts and follow up any that are overdue.
- Timely collection of debts improves cash flow and reduces the risk of them becoming irrecoverable.

Credit limits

It is also normal for a business to set a credit limit for each customer. This is the maximum amount of credit that the business is willing to provide.

The use of credit limits may:

- reduce risk to business of irrecoverable debts by limiting the amount sold on credit
- help build up the trust of a new customer
- be part of the credit control strategy of a business.

2 Irrecoverable debts

In this exam you must be prepared to see both the terms 'bad' and 'irrecoverable' debts being used frequently.

- The accruals concept dictates that when a sale is made, it is recognised in the accounts, regardless of whether or not the cash has been received.
- If sales are made on credit, there may be problems collecting the amounts owing from customers.
- Some customers may refuse to pay their debt or be declared bankrupt and unable to pay the amounts owing.
- Some customers may be in financial difficulties or may dispute the amount owed and there may be some doubt as to whether their debt will be paid.
- If it is highly unlikely that the amount owed by a customer will be received, then this debt is known as an irrecoverable debt. As it will probably never be received, it is written off by writing it out of the ledger accounts completely.

- If there is some doubt whether a customer can or will pay his debt, an allowance for receivables is created. These debts are not yet irrecoverable. However the creation of an **allowance for receivables** means that the possible loss is accounted for immediately, in line with the concept of prudence. The amount of the original debt will still remain in the ledger account just in case the customer does eventually pay.

Expandable text

Receivables and irrecoverable debts

If a sale is for cash, the customer pays for the goods immediately the sale is made. If the sale is on credit terms the customer will probably take the goods with him or arrange to have them delivered but he will not pay for the goods at that time. Instead, the customer will be given or sent an invoice detailing the goods and their price and the normal payment terms. This will tell the customer when he is expected to pay for those goods.

Under the accruals concept, a sale is included in the ledger accounts at the time that it is made.

For a cash sale, this will be when the cash or cheque is paid by the customer and the double entry will be:

Dr Cash

Cr Sales revenue

For a sale on credit, the sale is made at the time that the invoice is sent to the customer and therefore the accounting entries are made at that time as follows:

Dr Receivables

Cr Sales revenue

When the customer eventually settles the invoice the double entry will be:

Dr Cash account

Cr Receivables

This then clears out the balance on the customer's account.

3 Accounting for irrecoverable debts

An **irrecoverable debt** is a debt which is, or is considered to be, uncollectable.

With such debts it is prudent to remove them from the accounts and to charge the amount as an expense for irrecoverable debts to the income statement. The original sale remains in the accounts as this did actually take place.

The double entry required to achieve this is:

   Dr Irrecoverable debts expense

   Cr Receivables

Test your understanding 1

Araf & Co have total accounts receivable at the end of their accounting period of $45,000. Of these it is discovered that one, Mr Xiun who owes $790, has been declared bankrupt, and another who gave his name as Mr Jones has totally disappeared owing Araf & Co $1,240.

Calculate the effect in the financial statements of writing off these debts as irrecoverable.

4 Accounting for irrecoverable debts recovered

There is a possible situation where a debt is written off as irrecoverable in one accounting period, perhaps because the customer has been declared bankrupt, and the money, or part of the money, due is then unexpectedly received in a subsequent accounting period.

When a debt is written off the double entry is:

   Dr Irrecoverable debts expense

   Cr Receivables (removing the debt from the accounts)

When cash is received from a customer the normal double entry is:

   Dr Cash

   Cr Receivables

When an irrecoverable debt is recovered, the credit entry (above) cannot be taken to receivables as the debt has already been taken out of the receivables balance.

Instead the accounting entry is:

Dr Cash

Cr Irrecoverable debts expense

Some businesses may wish to keep a separate 'irrecoverable debts recovered' account to separate the actual cost of irrecoverable debts in the period.

Test your understanding 2

Celia Jones had receivables of $3,655 at 31 December 20X7. At that date she wrote off a debt from Lenny Smith of $699. During the year to 31 December 20X8 Celia made credit sales of $17,832 and received cash from her customers totalling $16,936. She also received the $699 from Lenny Smith that had already been written off in 20X7.

What is the final balance on the receivables account at 31 December 20X7 and 20X8?

	20X7 $	20X8 $
A	2,956	3,852
B	2,956	3,153
C	3,655	4,551
D	3,655	3,852

5 Allowance for receivables

There may be some debts in the accounts where there is some cause for concern but they are not yet definitely irrecoverable.

It is prudent to recognise the possible expense of not collecting the debt in the income statement, but the receivable must remain in the accounts in case the customer does in fact pay up.

An allowance is set up which is a credit balance. This is netted off against trade receivables in the statement of financial position to give a net figure for receivables that are probably recoverable.

There are two types of allowance that may appear in the organisation's accounts:

- There will be some specific debts where the customer is known to be in financial difficulties, is disputing their invoice, or is refusing to pay for some other reason (bad service for example), and therefore the amount owing may not be recoverable. The allowance for such a debt is known as a **specific allowance**.

- The past experience and history of a business will indicate that not all of its trade receivables will be recoverable in full. It may not be possible to identify the amount that will not be paid but an estimate may be made that a certain percentage of customers are likely not to pay. An additional allowance will be made for these items, often known as a **general allowance**.

6 Accounting for the allowance for receivables

An allowance for receivables is set up with the following journal:

Dr Irrecoverable debts expense

Cr Allowance for receivables

If there is already an allowance for receivables in the accounts (opening allowance), only the movement in the allowance is charged to the income statement (closing allowance less opening allowance).

As the allowance can increase or decrease, there may be a debit or a credit in the irrecoverable debts account so the above journal may be reversed.

When calculating and accounting for a movement in the allowance for receivables, the following steps should be taken:

(1) Write off irrecoverable debts.

(2) Calculate the receivables balance as adjusted for the write-offs.

(3) Ascertain the specific allowance for receivables required.

(4) Deduct the debt specifically provided for from the receivables balance (be sure to deduct the full amount of debt rather than the amount of specific allowance).

(5) Multiply the remaining receivables balance by the general allowance percentage to give the general allowance required.

%(closing receivables – irrecoverable debts – debts specifically allowed for).

(6) Add the specific and general allowances required together.

(7) Compare to the brought forward allowance.

(8) Account for the change in allowance.

Test your understanding 3

On 31 December 20X1 Jake Williams had receivables of $10,000. From past experience Jake estimated that the equivalent of 3% of these customers were likely never to pay their debts and he therefore wished to make an allowance for this amount.

During 20X2 Jake made sales on credit totalling $100,000 and received cash from his customers of $94,000. He still considered that the equivalent of 3% of the closing receivables may never pay and should be allowed for.

During 20X3 Jake made sales of $95,000 and collected $96,000 from his receivables. At 31 December 20X3 Jake still considered that the equivalent of 3% of his receivables should be allowed for.

Calculate the allowance for receivables and the irrecoverable debt expense as well as the closing balance of receivables for each of the years 20X1, 20X2, 20X3.

Test your understanding 4

John Stamp has opening balances at 1 January 20X6 on his trade receivables account and allowance for receivables account of $68,000 and $3,400 respectively. During the year to 31 December 20X6 John Stamp makes credit sales of $354,000 and receives cash from his receivables of $340,000.

At 31 December 20X6 John Stamp reviews his receivables listing and acknowledges that he is unlikely ever to receive debts totalling $2,000. These are to be written off as irrecoverable. Past experience indicates that John should also make an allowance equivalent to 5% of his remaining receivables after writing off the irrecoverable debts.

What is the amount charged to John's income statement for irrecoverable debt expense in the year ended 31 December 20X6?

A $2,700

B $6,100

C $2,600

D $6,000

What will the effect be of Irrecoverable debts on both the Income Statement and the Statement of financial position?

Chapter summary

IRRECOVERABLE DEBTS

- Amounts that the business will not receive from its customers
- May be due to bankruptcy, fraud or disputes

ALLOWANCE FOR RECEIVABLES

- There may be some doubt as to the collectability of some of the business' receivables balances
- An allowance is made to recognise the possible expense of not receiving the cash

ACCOUNTING FOR IRRECOVERABLE DEBTS

To recognise the expense in the income statement:

Dr   Irrecoverable debts expense

Cr   Receivables

ACCOUNTING FOR THE ALLOWANCE FOR RECEIVABLES

To record an increase or setting up the allowance:

Dr   Irrecoverable debts expense

Cr   Allowance for receivables

The journal entry is reversed if the allowance is reduced

ACCOUNTING FOR IRRECOVERABLE DEBTS RECOVERED

The debt has been taken out of receivables, the journal is:

Dr Cash

Cr Debt

FINANCIAL STATEMENTS

STATEMENT OF FINANCIAL POSITION

Receivables	X
Allowance for receivables	(X)
Net receivables	X

INCOME STATEMENT

Charge for irrecoverable debts

=

Irrecoverable debts written off

+/−

Change in allowance for receivables

Test your understanding answers

Test your understanding 1

As the two debts are considered to be irrecoverable, they must be removed from receivables:

Receivables

	$		$
Balance at period end	45,000	Irrecoverable debts	
		– Mr Xiun	790
		Irrecoverable debts	
		– Mr Jones	1,240
		Balance c/f	42,970
	45,000		45,000
	———		———
Balance b/f	42,970		

Irrecoverable debts expense

	$		$
Receivables			
– Mr Xiun	790		
Receivables			
– Mr Jones	1,240		
		Income statement	2,030
	2,030		2,030
	———		———

Note that the sales revenue account has not been altered and the original sales to Mr Xiun and Mr Jones remain. This is because these sales actually took place and it is only after the sale that the expense of not being able to collect these debts has occurred.

Test your understanding 2

The correct answer is A

20X7 Receivables

	$		$
31 Dec	3,655	Irrecoverable debts	
		– Lenny Smith	699
		Balance c/f	2,956
	3,655		3,655
Balance b/f	2,956		

20X7 Irrecoverable debts expense

	$		$
Receivables		Income statement	699
– Lenny Smith	699		
	699		699

20X8 Receivables

	$		$
Balance b/f	2,956		
Sales	17,832	Cash received	16,936
		Balance c/f	3,852
	20,788		20,788
Balance b/f	3,852		

20X8 Irrecoverable debts expense

	$		$
Income statement	699	Cash	699
	699		699

KAPLAN PUBLISHING

Test your understanding 3

20X1 Receivables

	$		$
At 31 December	10,000	Balance c/f	10,000
	10,000		10,000
Balance b/f	10,000		

Allowance required: $10,000 x 3%
= $300

Allowance for receivables

	$		$
Balance c/f	300	31 Dec	
		Irrecoverable debts	300
	300		300
		Balance b/f	300

Irrecoverable debts expense

	$		$
31 Dec		31 Dec	
Allowance for receivables	300	Income statement	300
	300		300

Statement of financial position presentation

	$	$
Current assets		
Receivables		10,000
Less: Allowance for receivables		(300)
		9,700

20X2 Receivables

	$		$
Balance b/f	10,000		
Sales	100,000	Cash	94,000
		Balance c/f	16,000
	110,000		110,000
Balance b/f	16,000		

Allowance required: $16,000 x 3% = $480

Allowance for receivables

	$		$
		Balance b/f	300
Balance b/f	480	31 Dec	
		increase in allowance	180
	480		480
		Balance b/f	480

Irrecoverable debts expense

	$		$
31 Dec		31 Dec	
Allowance for receivables	180	Income statement	180
	180		180

Statement of financial position presentation

	$	$
Current assets		
Receivables	16,000	
Less: Allowance for receivables	(480)	
		15,520

20X3 Receivables

	$		$
Balance b/f	16,000		
Sales	95,000	Cash	96,000
		Balance c/f	15,000
	111,000		
Balance b/f	15,000		111,000

Allowance required: $15,000 x 3% = $450

Allowance for receivables

	$		$
31 Dec		Balance b/f	480
decrease in	30		
allowance			
Balance c/f	450		
	480		480
		Balance b/f	450

Irrecoverable debts expense

	$		$
31 Dec		31 Dec	
Income statement	30	Allowance for	30
		receivables	
	30		30

Statement of financial position presentation

	$	$
Current assets		
Receivables	15,000	
Less: Allowance for	(450)	
receivables		
		14,550

Test your understanding 4

The correct answer is C

Receivables

20X6	$	20X6	$
1 Jan Balance b/f	68,000	31 Dec cash	340,000
31 Dec			
Sales revenue	354,000	31 Dec	
		Irrecoverable debts	2,000
		31 Dec	
		Balance c/f	80,000
	422,000		422,000
20X7			
1 Jan Balance b/f	80,000		

Irrecoverable debts expense

20X6	$	20X6	$
31 Dec Receivables	2,000		
31 Dec Allowance		31 Dec	
for receivables	600	Income statement	2,600
	2,600		2,600

Allowance for receivables

20X6	$	20X6	$
		1 Jan Balance b/f	3,400
31 Dec Balance c/f	4,000	31 Dec	
		Irrecoverable debts	600
	4,000		4,000
		20X7	
		1 Jan Balance b/f	4,000

Note that only the one irrecoverable debts expense account is used both to write off irrecoverable debts and to increase or decrease the allowance for receivables. There is no need to use separate accounts for each type of expense.

Working – Allowance for receivables

5% x $80,000 = $4,000

$4000 - b/f 3,400 = movement of 600

The **Statement of financial position** will show a receivables balance of 80,000. Underneath this separately the allowance for receivables c/f balance of 4,000 will be deducted to give a sub-total of $76,000.

The **Income statement** will show the $2,600 as an expense. This expense will cause a decrease in overall profits.

KAPLAN PUBLISHING

Non-current assets

Chapter learning objectives

Upon completion of this chapter you will be able to:

- define non-current assets
- distinguish between capital and revenue expenditure
- explain the function and purpose of an asset register
- explain and illustrate the ledger entries to record the acquisition of non-current assets
- define and explain the purpose of depreciation
- explain the straight-line and reducing balance methods of depreciation and make necessary calculations
- explain and illustrate how depreciation expense and accumulated depreciation are recorded in ledger accounts
- explain and illustrate how depreciation is presented in the income statement and statement of financial position
- explain the relevance of consistency and subjectivity in accounting for depreciation
- make the necessary adjustments if changes are made in the estimated useful life/residual value of a non-current asset
- explain and illustrate the ledger entries to record the disposal of non-current assets for cash
- explain and illustrate the ledger entries to record the disposal of non-current assets through part exchange
- explain and illustrate the inclusion of profits or losses on disposal in the income statement

- explain and record the revaluation of a non-current asset in ledger accounts and in the statement of financial position

- explain the impact of a revaluation on accounting for depreciation and disposal of a non-current asset

- explain and illustrate how non-current asset balances and movements are disclosed in company financial statements.

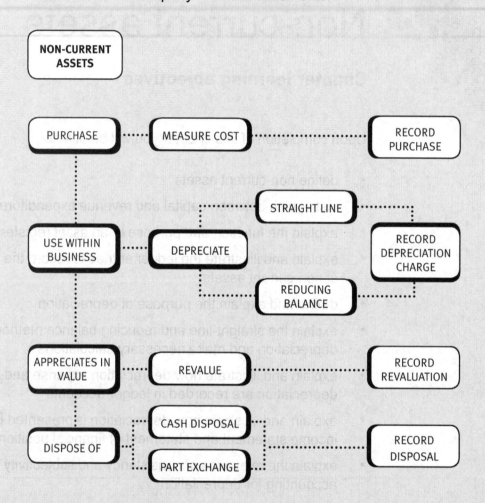

1 Non-current assets

Non-current assets are distinguished from current assets by the following characteristics: they:

- are long-term in nature

- are not normally acquired for resale

- are could be tangible or intangible

- are used to generate income directly or indirectly for a business

- are not normally liquid assets (i.e. not easily and quickly converted into cash without a significant loss in value).

2 Capital and revenue expenditure

It follows that a business' expenditure may be classified as one of two types:

CAPITAL EXPENDITURE
- Expenditure on the acquisition of non-current assets required for use in the business, not for resale.
- Expenditure on existing non-current assets aimed at increasing their earning capacity.

REVENUE EXPENDITURE
- Expenditure on current assets.
- Expenditure relating to running the business (such as administration costs).
- Expenditure on maintaining the earning capacity of non-current assets e.g. repairs and renewals.

Capital expenditure is long-term in nature as the business intends to receive the benefits of the expenditure over a long period of time.

Revenue expenditure relates to the current accounting period and is used to generate revenue in the business.

3 Non-current asset registers

Non-current asset registers are, as the name suggests, a record of the non-current assets held by a business. These form part of the internal control system of an organisation.

Expandable text

Details held on such a register may include:

- cost
- date of purchase
- description of asset
- serial/reference number
- location of asset
- depreciation method
- expected useful life
- net book value.

4 Acquisition of a non-current asset

A non-current asset register is maintained in order to control non-current assets and keep track of what is owned and where it is kept.

It is periodically reconciled to the non-current asset accounts maintained in the general ledger.

- The cost of a non-current asset is any amount incurred to acquire the asset and bring it into working condition

Includes	Excludes
Capital expenditure such as - purchase price - delivery costs - legal fees - subsequent expenditure which enhances the asset	Revenue expenditure such as: - repairs - renewals - repainting

- The correct double entry to record the purchase is:

  Dr Non-current asset X

  Cr Bank/Cash/Payables X

- A separate cost account should be kept for each category of non-current asset, e.g. motor vehicles, fixtures and fittings.

Expandable text

Subsequent expenditure on the non-current asset can only be recorded as part of the cost (or capitalised), if it enhances the benefits of the asset, i.e. increases the revenues capable of being generated by the asset.

An example of subsequent expenditure which meets this criterion, and so can be capitalised, is an extension to a shop building which provides extra selling space.

An example of subsequent expenditure which does not meet this criterion is repair work. Any repair costs must be debited to the income statement, i.e. expensed.

Test your understanding 1

Acquisition of a non-current asset

Bilbo Baggins started a business providing limousine taxi services on 1 January 20X5. In the year to 31 December he incurred the following costs:

	$
Office premises	250,000
Legal fees associated with purchase of office	10,000
Cost of materials and labour to paint office in Bilbo's favourite colour, purple	300
Mercedes E series estate cars	116,000
Number plates for cars	210
Delivery charge for cars	180
Road licence fee for cars	480
Drivers' wages for first year of operation	60,000
Blank taxi receipts printed with Bilbo Baggins' business name and number	450

What amounts should be capitalised as 'Land and buildings' and 'Motor vehicles'?

	Land and buildings	Motor vehicles
A	260,000	116,390
B	250,000	116,870
C	250,300	116,390
D	260,300	116,870

5 Depreciation

- IAS 16 defines depreciation as 'the measure of the cost or revalued amount of the economic benefits of the tangible non-current asset that has been consumed during the period'.

- In simple terms, depreciation is a mechanism to reflect the cost of using a non-current asset.

- Depreciation matches the cost of using a non-current asset to the revenues generated by that asset over its useful life.

- Depreciation must also be matched to the pattern of use of the asset. This must be regularly reviewed and may be changed if the method no longer matches the useage of the asset.

- This is achieved by recording a depreciation charge each year, the effect of which is twofold ('the dual effect'):

  - Reduce the statement of financial position value of the non-current asset by cumulative depreciation to reflect the wearing out.

  - Record the depreciation charge as an expense in the income statement to match to the revenue generated by the non-current asset.

Expandable text

Depreciation may arise from:

- use

- physical wear and tear

- passing of time, e.g. a ten-year lease on a property

- obsolescence through technology and market changes, e.g. plant and machinery of a specialised nature

- depletion, e.g. the extraction of a mineral from a quarry.

The purpose of depreciation is not to show the asset at its current value in the statement of financial position, nor is it intended to provide a fund for the replacement of the asset. It is simply a method of allocating the cost of the asset over the periods estimated to benefit from its use (the useful life).

Land normally has an unlimited life and so does not require depreciation, but buildings should be depreciated.

Depreciation of an asset begins when it is available for use.

KAPLAN PUBLISHING

6 Methods of calculating depreciation

STRAIGHT LINE

Depreciation charge is the same each year and so assumes that the benefit is consumed evenly.

Useful for assets which provide equal benefit each year, e.g. machinery.

REDUCING BALANCE

A reducing amount of depreciation is charged each year and so assumes that more benefit is consumed in earlier years.

Useful for assets which provide more benefit in earlier years, e.g. cars, IT equipment.

Straight-line method

Depreciation charge = (Cost – Residual value)/Useful life

Or X% x cost

Residual value: the estimated disposal value of the asset at the end of its useful life.

Useful life: the estimated number of years during which the business will use the asset.

Expandable text

The residual value may be a second-hand value or scrap value. It is unlikely to be a significant amount and is often zero.

The useful life does not necessarily equal the physical life of the asset. For example many businesses use a three-year useful life for computers. This does not mean that a computer can no longer be used after three years; it means that the business is likely to replace the computer after three years due to technological advancement.

> Straight-line depreciation is often expressed as a percentage of original cost, so that straight-line depreciation over four years would alternatively be described as straight-line depreciation at 25% pa.

Reducing balance method

Depreciation charge = X % x Net book value (NBV)

NBV: original cost of the non-current asset less accumulated depreciation on the asset to date.

Assets bought/sold in the period

If a non-current asset is bought or sold in the period, there are two ways in which the depreciation could be accounted for:

- provide a full year's depreciation in the year of acquisition and none in the year of disposal

- monthly or pro-rata depreciation, based on the exact number of months that the asset has been owned.

Illustration 1 – Reducing balance method

Dev, a trader, purchased an item of plant for $1,000 on 1 August 20X1 which he depreciates on the reducing balance at 20% pa. What is the depreciation charge for each of the first five years if the accounting year end is 31 July?

Expandable text

Solution

Year	Depreciation charge % x NBV	Depreciation charge $	Cumulative depreciation $
1	20% x $1,000	200	200
2	20% x $(1,000 – 200)	160	360
3	20% x $(1,000 – 360)	128	488
4	20% x $(1,000 – 488)	102	590
5	20% x $(1,000 – 590)	82	672

Test your understanding 2

Karen has been running a successful nursery school 'Little Monkeys' since 20X1. She bought the following assets as the nursery grew:

- a new oven for the nursery kitchen at a cost of $2,000 (purchased 1 December 20X4).

- a minibus to take the children on trips for $18,000 (purchased 1 June 20X4).

She depreciates the oven at 10% straight line and the minibus at 25% reducing balance. A full year's depreciation is charged in the year of purchase and none in the year of disposal.

What is the total depreciation charge for the year ended 31 October 20X6?

A $2,531

B $2,700

C $4,231

D $2,731

Test your understanding 3

The following information relates to Bangers & Smash, a car repair business:

	Machine 1	Machine 2
Cost	$12,000	$8,000
Purchase date	1 August 20X5	1 October 20X6
Depreciation method	20% straight line pro rata	10% reducing balance pro rata

What is the total depreciation charge for the years ended 31 December 20X5 and 20X6?

	20X5 $	20X6 $
A	2,400	2,600
B	1,000	2,600
C	2,400	3,200
D	1,000	3,200

7 Accounting for depreciation

Whichever method is used to calculate depreciation, the accounting remains the same:

Dr Depreciation expense (IS) X

Cr Accumulated depreciation (SFP) X

- The depreciation expense account is an income statement account and therefore is not cumulative.

- The accumulated depreciation account is a statement of financial position account and as the name suggests is cumulative, i.e. reflects all depreciation to date.

- On the statement of financial position it is shown as a reduction against the cost of non-current assets:

	$
Cost	X
Accumulated depreciation	(X)
	___
NBV	X

Illustration 2– Accounting for depreciation

Santa runs a large toy shop in Windsor. In the year ended 31 August 20X5, she bought the following fixed assets:

- A new cash register for $5,000. This was purchased on 1 December 20X4, in time for the Christmas rush, and was to be depreciated at 10% straight line.

- A new delivery van, purchased on 31 March 20X5, at a cost of $22,000. The van is to be depreciated at 15% reducing balance.

Santa charges depreciation on a monthly basis.

- What is the depreciation charge for the year ended 31st August 20X5?

- Show the relevant ledger accounts and statement of financial position presentation at that date.

Solution

Cash register Depreciation charge: 10% x $5,000 x 9/12

= $375

Delivery van Depreciation charge: 15% x $22,000 x 5/12

= $1,375

Cost (cash register)

	$		$
Cost	5,000	Balance c/f	5,000
	5,000		5,000
Balance b/f	5,000		

Cost (delivery van)

	$		$
Cost	22,000	Balance c/f	22,000
	22,000		22,000
Balance b/f	22,000		

Accumulated depreciation (cash register)

	$		$
Balance c/f	375	Depreciation expense 20X5	375
	375		375
		Balance b/f	375

Accumulated depreciation (delivery van)

	$		$
Balance c/f	1,375	Depreciation expense 20X5	1,375
	1,375		1,375
		Balance b/f	1,375

Depreciation expense

	$		$
Accumulated depreciation (cash register)	375		
Accumulated depreciation delivery van)	1,375	Income statement	1,750
	1,750		1,750

Statement of financial position extract at 31 August 20X5

	Cost	Accumulated depreciation	NBV
	$	$	$
Cash register	5,000	(375)	4,625
Delivery van	22,000	(1,375)	20,625
Total	27,000	(1,750)	25,250

Test your understanding 4

Coco acquired two fixed assets for cash on 1 August 20X5 for use in her party organising business:

- a 25-year lease on a shop for $200,000
- a chocolate fountain for $4,000.

The fountain is to be depreciated at 25% pa using the reducing balance method.

A full year of depreciation is charged in the year of acquisition and none in the year of disposal.

Show the ledger account entries for these assets for the years ending 31 October 20X5, 20X6 and 20X7.

8 Consistency and subjectivity when accounting for depreciation

The following are all based on estimates made by the management of a business:

- depreciation method
- residual value
- useful life.

Different estimates would result in varying levels of depreciation and, consequently, profits.

It can be argued that these subjective areas could therefore result in manipulation of the accounts by management.

In order to reduce the scope for such manipulation and increase consistency of treatment, **IAS 16 Property, Plant and Equipment** requires the following:

- Depreciation method should be reviewed at each year end and changed if the method used no longer reflects the pattern of use of the asset.
- Residual value and useful life should be reviewed at each year end and changed if expectations differ from previous estimates.

Illustration 3 – Changes to estimates

Alfie purchased a non-current asset for $100,000 on 1 January 20X2 and started depreciating it over five years. Residual value was taken as $10,000.

At 1 January 20X3 a review of asset lives was undertaken and the remaining useful life was estimated at eight years. Residual value was estimated as nil.

Calculate the depreciation charge for the year ended 31 December 20X3 and subsequent years.

Expandable text

Solution

Initial depreciation charge pa	= ($100,000 2 $10,000) / 5 years
	= $18,000
NBV at date of change	= $100,000 – ($18,000 x 1 year)
	= $82,000
New depreciation charge	= ($82,000 - nil) / 8 years
	= $10,250

Test your understanding 5

Alberto bought a wood-burning oven for his pizza restaurant for $30,000 on 1 January 20X0. At that time he believed that the oven's useful life would be 20 years after which it would have no value.

On 1 January 20X3, Alberto revises his estimations: he now believes that he will use the oven in the business for another 12 years after which he will be able to sell it second-hand for $1,500.

What is the depreciation charge for the year ended 31 December 20X3?

A $2,000

B $2,125

C $1,875

D $2,375

9 Disposal of non-current assets

Profit/Loss on disposal

Proceeds (cash or part disposal allowance) > NBV at disposal date	Profit
Proceeds (cash or part disposal allowance) < NBV at disposal date	Loss
Proceeds (cash or part disposal allowance) = NBV at disposal date	Neither profit nor loss

A disposals T account is required when recording the disposal of a non-current asset. This is an income statement account which reflects any profit or loss on disposal.

Disposal for cash consideration

This is a three-step process:

(1) Remove the original cost of the non-current asset from the 'non-current asset' account.

Dr Disposals original cost

Cr NC assets original cost

(2) Remove accumulated depreciation on the non-current asset from the 'accumulated depreciation' account.

Dr Acc'd dep'n acc'd dep'n

Cr Disposals acc'd dep'n

(3) Record the cash proceeds.

Dr Cash proceeds

Cr Disposals proceeds

The balance on the disposals T account is the profit or loss on disposal:

Disposal

Original cost	X	Accumulated depreciation	X
		Proceeds	X
Profit on disposal	ß	Loss on disposal	ß
	—		—
	X		X
	—		—

The profit or loss on disposal can also be calculated as proceeds less NBV of asset at disposal.

Test your understanding 6

Percy Throwerp runs a landscape gardening business. On 1 February 20X2, he purchased a sit-on lawnmower costing $3,000. He depreciates it at 10% straight line on a monthly basis. A few years later he decides to replace it with one which has an enclosed cabin for when it rains. He sells the lawnmower to an old friend, Alan Titchmuck, for $2,000 on 31 July 20X5.

How much is charged to Percy's income statement in respect of the asset for the year ended 31 December 20X5?

Disposal through a part exchange agreement

A part exchange agreement arises where an old asset is provided in part payment for a new one, the balance of the new asset being paid in cash.

The procedure to record the transaction is very similar to the three-step process seen for a cash disposal. The first two steps are identical, however steps 3 and 4 are as follows:

(3) Record the part exchange allowance (PEA) as proceeds.

Dr NC assets (= part of cost of new asset) PEA

Cr Disposals (= sale proceeds of old asset) PEA

(4) Record the cash paid for the new asset.

Dr NC assets cash

Cr Cash cash

Again, the balance on the disposals T account is the profit or loss on disposal:

Disposal

Original cost	X	Accumulated depreciation	X
		Proceeds	X
Profit on disposal	ß	Loss on disposal	ß
	X		X

Expandable text

There are two debits to the non-current asset account in respect of the new asset:

- PEA
- cash balance.

Together these are the cost of the new asset. If preferred you can show the total as one debit (however do not forget to record both credits).

Test your understanding 7

Bindi Bobbin runs a business altering and repairing clothes. When she started business on 1 January 20X2, she bought a Soopastitch II sewing machine for $2,500. She depreciates sewing machines using the straight-line method at a rate of 20% pa, and she charges a full year of depreciation in the year of acquisition and none in the year of disposal.

The business has now grown such that she needs a faster machine, and she will upgrade to the Soopastitch V during December 20X5. The Soopastitch salesman has offered her a part exchange deal as follows:

Part exchange allowance for Soopastitch II $750

Balance to be paid in cash for Soopastitch V $4,850

Show the ledger entries for the year ended 31 December 20X5 to reflect this transaction.

10 Revaluation of non-current assets

- Some non-current assets, such as land and buildings may rise in value over time. Businesses may choose to reflect the current value of the asset in their statement of financial position. This is known as revaluing the asset.

- The difference between the NBV of the asset and the revalued amount (normally a gain) is recorded in a revaluation reserve in the capital section of the statement of financial position.

- This gain is not recorded in the income statement because it is unrealised, i.e. it is not realised in the form of cash.

- IAS 1 requires that a revaluation gain is disclosed in "other comprehensive income" on the statement of comprehensive income. (this is later covered within chapter 17)

Expandable text

If the fair value of a non-current asset can be measured reliably, it can be carried at its fair value at the date of revaluation, less any subsequent depreciation and impairment losses. The revaluation should be repeated regularly to ensure that the fair value of the asset does not differ materially from the carrying amount.

An upward revaluation should be credited to revaluation surplus, unless it reverses a previous downward revaluation which was charged as an expense.

A downward revaluation should be charged as an expense, unless it reverses a previous upward revaluation, when it may be charged against the revaluation surplus for that same asset.

If one asset in a class is revalued, all assets of that class must be revalued. This is to prevent selective revaluation of only those assets that have increased in value.

Illustration 4 – Revaluation of non-current assets

Vittorio owns land which originally cost $250,000. No depreciation has been charged on the land in accordance with IAS 16. Vittorio wishes to revalue the land to reflect its current market value, which he has been advised is $600,000.

What is the double entry to record this revaluation?

Expandable text

Solution

The land is currently held at cost of $250,000. This needs to be increased by $350,000 to reflect the new valuation of $600,000. Therefore the double entry required is:

Dr Land cost $350,000

Cr Revaluation reserve $350,000

Illustration 5– Revaluation of non-current assets

Hamish runs a kilt-making business in Scotland. He has run the business for many years from a building which originally cost $300,000 and on which $100,000 total depreciation has been charged to date. Hamish wishes to revalue the building to $750,000.

What is the double entry required to record the revaluation?

Expandable text

Solution

The current balances in the accounts are:

Building cost $300,000

Accumulated depreciation $100,000

- The building cost account needs to be raised by $450,000 to $750,000.

- On revaluation, the accumulated depreciation account is cleared out.

Therefore the double entry required is:

Dr Building cost $450,000

Dr Accumulated depreciation $100,000

Cr Revaluation reserve $550,000

The gain of $550,000 reflects the difference between the NBV pre-revaluation of $200,000 and the revalued amount of $750,000.

Cost (building)

	$		$
Balance b/f	300,000		
Revaluation reserve	450,000	Balance c/f	750,000
	750,000		750,000
Balance b/f	750,000		

Accumulated depreciation (building)

	$		$
Revaluation reserve	100,000	Balance b/f	100,000
	100,000		100,000

Revaluation reserve

	$		$
		Cost (building)	450,000
Balance c/f	550,000	Accumulated depreciation (building)	100,000
	550,000		550,000
		Balance b/f	550,000

Extract from the Statement of comprehensive income: (covered in more detail within chapter 17)

Other comprehensive income:

Gain on property revaluation $450,000

In summary:

Revaluation surplus = Revalued amount – NBV

For a non-depreciated asset:

Dr Non-current asset – cost   revaluation surplus

Cr Revaluation reserve   revaluation surplus

For a depreciated asset:

Dr Accumulated depreciation   depreciation to date

Dr Non-current asset – cost   ß

Cr Revaluation reserve   revaluation surplus

The revaluation gain is disclosed on the face of the statement of comprehensive income under "other comprehensive income" and in the statement of changes in equity (SOCIE).

Test your understanding 8

Max owns a fish-finger factory. The premises were purchased on 1 January 20X1 for $450,000 and depreciation charged at 2% pa straight line.

Max now wishes to revalue the factory premises to $800,000 on 1 January 20X7 to reflect the market value.

What is the balance on the revaluation reserve after this transaction?

A $350,000

B $395,000

C $404,000

D $413,000

11 Depreciation and disposal of a revalued asset

Depreciation of a revalued asset

- When a non-current asset has been revalued, the charge for depreciation should be based on the revalued amount and the remaining useful life of the asset.

- this charge will be higher than depreciation prior to the revaluation.

- the excess of the new depreciation charge over the old depreciation charge should be transferred from the revaluation reserve to accumulated profits (within the capital section of the statement of financial position):

    Dr Revaluation reserve X

    Cr Accumulated profits X

Illustration 6 – Depreciation of a revalued asset

Eddie owns a retail unit in central Springfield. He bought it 25 years ago for $100,000, depreciating it over 50 years. At the start of 20X6 he decides to revalue the unit to $800,000. The unit has a remaining useful life of 25 years.

What accounting entries should be made in 20X6?

Expandable text

Solution

On revaluation at start of 20X6

    Dr Retail unit cost $700,000

    Dr Accumulated depreciation $50,000

    Cr Revaluation reserve $750,000

Depreciation for 20X6

    Dr Depreciation expense($800,000/25 yrs) $32,000

    Cr Accumulated depreciation $32,000

Reserves transfer for 20X6

    Dr Revaluation reserve ($32,000 – $2,000) $30,000

    Cr Accumulated profits $30,000

Disposal of a revalued asset

- The disposal of a revalued asset is recorded as already seen.

Test your understanding 9

Spartacus United football club's statement of financial position at 31 December 20X7 includes the following information:

	$
Stadium cost	1,500,000
Depreciation	450,000
	1,050,000

Depreciation has been provided at 2% on the straight-line basis.

The stadium is revalued on 30 June 20X8 to $1,380,000. There is no change in its remaining estimated future useful life.

What is the depreciation charge for the year ended 31 December 20X8?

Test your understanding 10

Tiger Trees owns and runs a golf club. Some years ago Tiger purchased land next to the existing course with the intention of creating a smaller nine-hole course. The cost of the land was $260,000. Tiger hasn't yet built the additional course but has revalued this land to $600,000. He has now decided that building the new course is uneconomical and has found a buyer who is willing to pay $695,000 for the land.

What are the ledger entries on disposal?

12 Disclosure of non-current asset balances in company financial statements

Statement of financial position

Aggregate NBV of non-current assets disclosed on the face of the statement of financial position.

Income statement

Depreciation charge included within relevant expense categories.

Notes to the accounts
- Disclosure of depreciation methods and rates used.
- Non-current assets disclosure.
- Details of revaluations.

Expandable text

IAS 16 Property Plant and Equipment contains a number of disclosure requirements relating to non-current assets. Here are the main ones:

(1) The measurement bases used for arriving at the carrying amount of the asset (e.g. cost or valuation). If more than one basis has been used, the amounts for each basis must be disclosed.

(2) Depreciation methods used, with details of useful lives or the depreciation rates used.

(3) The gross amount of each asset heading and its related accumulated depreciation (aggregated with accumulated impairment losses) at the beginning and end of the period.

(4) A reconciliation of the carrying amount at the beginning and end of the period, showing:

- additions

- assets classified as held for sale

- disposals

- revaluations

- depreciation.

(5) Any commitments for future acquisition of property, plant and equipment.

KAPLAN PUBLISHING

(6) If assets are stated at revalued amounts, the following should be disclosed:

- the effective date of the revaluation

- whether an independent valuer was involved

- the methods and assumptions applied in estimating the items' fair value

- the carrying amount that would have been recognised had the assets been carried at cost

- the revaluation surplus, indicating the change for the period.

13 Intangible non-current assets

Non-current assets are assets used within the business on an ongoing basis in order to generate revenue.

They can be split into two distinct types:

Tangible non-current assets

Normally have physical substance, e.g land and buildings.

Normally involve expenditure being incurred.

Cost of the tangible non-current asset is capitalised.

Depreciation is a reflection of the wearing out of the asset.

Intangible non-current assets

Do not normally have physical substance, e.g. copyright.

Can be purchased or may be created within a business without any expenditure being incurred, i.e. internally generated, e.g. brands.

Purchased intangible non-current assets are capitalised. Generally, internally generated assets may not be capitalised.

Amortisation is a reflection of the wearingout of the (capitalised) asset.

Examples:
- Development costs
- Goodwill
- Trade marks
- Licences
- Patents
- Copyrights
- Franchises

Chapter summary

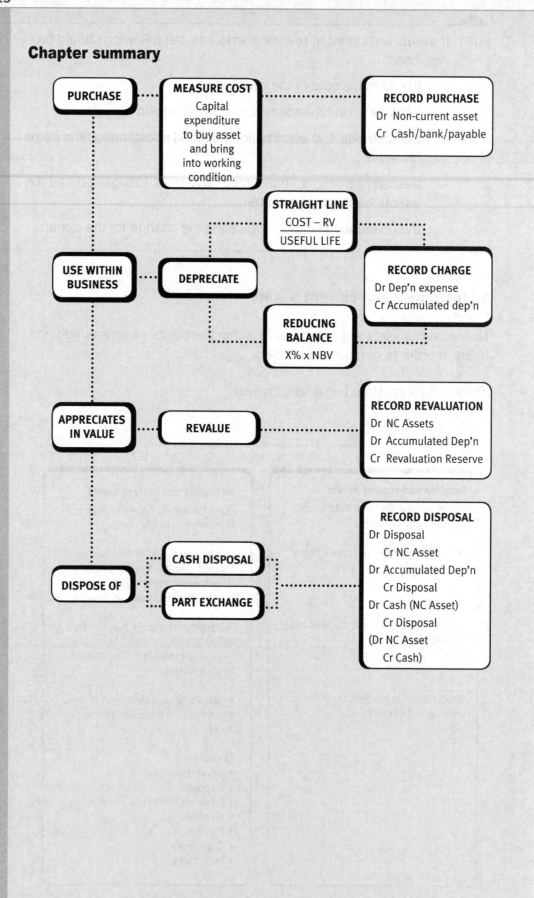

Test your understanding answers

Test your understanding 1

The correct answer is A

Land and buildings

Office premises: $250,000

Legal fees: $10,000

Total: $260,000

- The cost of the purple paint does not form part of the cost of the office and so should not be capitalised. Instead it should be taken to the income statement as a revenue expense.

Motor vehicles

3 Mercedes E series $116,000

Number plates $210

Delivery charges $180

Total $116,390

- The number plates are one-off charges which form part of the purchase price of any car.
- The road licence fee, drivers' wages and receipts are ongoing expenses, incurred every year. They cannot be capitalised, but should be taken to the income statement as expenses.

Test your understanding 2

The correct answer is D

	20X6
Oven	$
£2,000 x 10%	200
Minibus	
20X4 : 25% x $18,000 = $4,500	
20X5: 25% x $(18,000 – 4,500) = $3,375	
20X6: 25% x $(18,000 – 7,875) = $2,531	2,531
	———
Total depreciation charge	2,731

Test your understanding 3

The correct answer is B

Machine 1 $ $

    20X5: 20% x $12,000 x 5/12 = 1,000

    20X6: 20% x $12,000 = 2,400

Machine 2

    20X6: 10% x $8,000 x 3/12 = 200

Total depreciation charge

    20X5: 1,000

    20X6: $2,400 + $200 2,600

KAPLAN PUBLISHING

Test your understanding 4

Leases (cost)

	$		$
1.8.X5 Cash	200,000	Balance c/f	200,000
	200,000		200,000
Balance b/f	200,000		

Fixtures and fittings (cost)

	$		$
1.8.X5 Cash	4,000	Balance c/f	4,000
	4,000		4,000
Balance b/f	4,000		

Depreciation charge

	$		$
X5 accumulated depreciation	9,000	Income statement	9,000
X6 accumulated depreciation	8,750	Income statement	8,750
X7 accumulated depreciation	8,563	Income statement	8,563

Depreciation charge

	$		$
		X5 depreciation charge	8,000
Balance c/f	8,000		
	8,000		8,000
		Balance b/f	8,000
		X6 depreciation charge	8,000
Balance c/f	16,000		
	16,000		16,000
		Balance b/f	16,000
		X7 depreciation charge	8,000
Balance c/f	24,000		
	24,000		24,000
		Balance b/f	24,000

Accumulated depreciation (fixtures and fittings)

	$		$
		X5 depreciation charge	1,000
Balance c/f	1,000		
	1,000		1,000
		Balance b/f	1,000
		X6 depreciation charge	750
Balance c/f	1,750		
	1,750		1,750
		Balance b/f	1,750
		X7 depreciation charge	563
Balance c/f	2,313		
	2,313		2,313
		Balance b/f	2,313

Annual depreciation workings:

Note, details of the depreciation method and rate for the lease are not given in the question. We are however told that the lease term is 25 years. This suggests that it would be appropriate to use the straight-line method with a useful life of 25 years.

20X5
Lease: $200,000/25 years = 8,000
Fountain: $4,000 x 25% = 1,000

Total: 9,000

20X6
Lease: $200,000/25 years = 8,000
Fountain: $3,000 x 25% = 750

Total: 8,750

20X7
Lease: $200,000/25 years = 8,000
Fountain: $2,250 x 25% = 563

Total: 8,563

Test your understanding 5

The correct answer is A

Initial depreciation charge = $30,000 /20 years = $1,500

NBV at date of change = $30,000 – ($1,500 x 3yrs)

   = $25,500

New depreciation charge = $25,500 – $1,50 / 12 years0

   = $2,000 pa

Test your understanding 6

(1) Dr Disposals $3,000

Cr Fixtures and fittings cost $3,000

(2) Dr Accumulated depreciation $1,050

Cr Disposals $1,050

Depreciation working:

X2 10% x 3,000 x 11/12 = 275

X3 10% x 3,000 = 300

X4 10% x 3,000 = 300

X5 10% x 3,000 x 7/12 = 175

Total: 1050

(3) Dr Cash $2,000

Cr Disposals $2,000

Disposals:

	$		$
31.7.X5 fixtures and fittings cost	3,000	Accumulated depreciation	1,050
Profit on disposal (ß)	50	Cash proceeds	2,000
	3,050		3,050

The charge to the income statement for the year ended 31 December 20X5 is: $

Depreciation charge for the year 175

profit/loss on disposa(50)

Note: As depreciation is charged monthly, it is necessary to charge an amount to the income statement for the period 1 January 20X5 to the disposal date 31 July 20X5.

Test your understanding 7

Sewing machine

	$		$
Balance b/f	2,500	Disposal	2,500
New asset			
PEA	750		
Cash	4,850	Balance c/f	5,600
	_____		_____
	8,100		8,100
	_____		_____
Balance b/f	5,600		

Accumulated depreciation (Sewing machine)

	$		$
Disposal	1,500	Balance b/f	1,500
		Depreciation	
Balance c/f	1,120	charge X5	1,120
	_____		_____
	2,620		2,620
	_____		_____
		Balance b/f	1,120

Depreciation b/f working:

$2,500 x 20% x 3 years = $1,500

Disposals

	$		$
Sewing machine cost	2,500	Sewing machine accumulated depreciation	1,500
		PEA	750
		Loss on disposal (ß)	250
	_____		_____
	2,500		2,500
	_____		_____

KAPLAN PUBLISHING

Depreciation charge

	$		$
Sewing machine accumulated depreciation	1,120	Income statement	1,120

Depreciation charge working:

$5,600 x 20% = $1,120

Test your understanding 8

The correct answer is C

Factory cost

	$		$
Balance b/f	450,000		
Revaluation	350,000	Balance c/f	800,000
	800,000		800,000
	800,000		

Accumulated depreciation (factory)

	$		$
Revaluation	54,000	Balance b/f	54,000
(2% x $450,000		Balance c/f	800,000
x 6 years)	350,000		
	54,000		54,000

Revaluation reserve			
	$		$
		Factory cost	350,000
		Accumulated	
Balance c/f	404,000	depreciation	54,000
	————		————
	404,000		404,000
	————		————
		Balance b/f	404,000

Test your understanding 9

Depreciation must continue to be charged on the original cost until the date of revaluation. Thereafter it is charged on the revalued amount:

1 January to 30 June 20X8

2% x $1,500,000 x 6/12

15,000

Note that this is part of the depreciation cleared out on revaluation and so is not part of the accumulated depreciation balance at the year end.

1 July to 31 December 20X8

(1,380,000/34.5 years)x (6/12)

20,000

This amount will form the accumulated depreciation at the year end.

Total depreciation charge

Test your understanding 10

Land (valuation)

	$		$
Balance b/f	600,000	Disposal	600,000

Disposal

	$		$
Land valuation	600,000	Proceeds	695,000
Profit on disposal	95,000		

From trial balance to financial statements

Chapter learning objectives

Upon completion of this chapter you will be able to:

- illustrate the process of adjusting the financial statements for accruals and prepayments, depreciation, irrecoverable debts and the allowance for receivables.

1 Trial balance

In this chapter we will bring together the material from the previous chapters and produce a set of financial statements from a trial balance.

This will involve adjusting for the following items:

- closing inventory
- depreciation
- accruals and prepayments
- irrecoverable debts and the allowance for receivables.

Once these adjustments have been made, the income statement and statement of financial position can be prepared.

When making the adjustments it is important to ensure that each transaction contains the correct double entry.

Expandable Text

Purpose of the trial balance

The purpose of the trial balance is

- to check that for every debit entry made, an equal credit entry has been made
- as a first step in preparing the financial statements.

> **Limitations of the trial balance**
>
> Although the trial balance is useful in ensuring that double entry has been maintained, it will not:
>
> - identify errors such as mispostings to the wrong account or a double entry for the wrong amount
> - identify where errors have been made, or what those errors are.

2 Adjustments

Here is a reminder of the accounting entries for the adjustments required when preparing the financial statements:

Closing inventory

    Dr Inventory (SFP)

    Cr Cost of sales (IS)

With the closing inventory at the end of the period.

Depreciation

    Dr Depreciation expense (IS)

    Cr Accumulated depreciation (SFP)

With depreciation charge for the year for each class of asset.

Accruals

    Dr Expenses (IS)

    Cr Accrual (Liability) (SFP)

With each accrued expense.

Prepayments

    Dr Prepayment (Receivables) (SFP)

    Cr Expenses (IS)

With each prepaid expense.

Irrecoverable debts

> Dr Irrecoverable debt expense (IS)

> Cr Receivables (SFP)

With the total of receivables written off.

Allowance for receivables

> Dr Irrecoverable debt expense (IS)

> Cr Allowance for receivables (SFP)

With the increase or decrease in the allowance for the period.

Illustration 1– Preparation of financial statements

In this example, we will account for the period-end adjustments and prepare a set of financial statements from a TB.

The trial balance of Tyndall at 31 May 20X6 is as follows:

Trial balance of Tyndall at 31 May 20X6

	$	$
Capital account		15,258
Drawings by proprietor	5,970	
Purchases	73,010	
Returns inwards	1,076	
Returns outwards		3,720
Discounts	1,870	965
Credit sales		96,520
Cash sales		30,296
Customs duty	11,760	
Carriage inwards	2,930	
Carriage outwards	1,762	
Salesman's commission	711	
Salesman's salary	3,970	
Office salaries	7,207	
Bank charges	980	
Loan interest	450	
Light and heat	2,653	
Sundry expenses	2,100	

	$	$
Rent	3,315	
Insurance	4,000	
Printing and postage	2,103	
Advertising	1,044	
Irrecoverable debts	1,791	
Allowance for receivables		437
Inventory	7,650	
Receivables	10,760	
Payables		7,411
Cash at bank	2,634	
Cash in hand	75	
New delivery van (less trade-in)	2,200	
Motor expenses	986	
Furniture and equipment:		
Cost	8,000	
Depreciation at 1 June 20X5		2,400
Old delivery van:		
Cost	2,000	
Depreciation at 1 June 20X5		1,000
Loan account at 9% (repayable in five years)		5,000
	163,007	163,007

The following information is relevant:

(1) Closing inventory has been valued for accounts purposes at $8,490.

(2) The motor van was sold on 31 August 20X5 and traded in against the cost of a new van. The trade-in price was $1,400 and the cost of the new van was $3,600. No entries have yet been made for this transaction apart from debiting the $2,200 cash paid to the New delivery van account.

(3) Straight-line depreciation is to be provided on a monthly basis at the following annual rates:

Motor vans 25%

Furniture and equipment 10%

(4) Past experience indicates that an allowance for receivables should be made equivalent to 5% of the closing receivables.

(5) An accrual of $372 is required in respect of light and heat.

(6) A quarter's rent to 30 June 20X6 amounting to $900 was paid on 2 April 20X6. Insurance for the year to 31 March 20X7 amounting to $1,680 was paid on 16 April.

Prepare an income statement and a statement of financial position for the year ended 31 May 20X6.

Expandable text

Solution

Step 1 Inventory

The closing inventory figure of $8,490 must be included in the financial statements. The accounting journal is:

Dr Inventory (SFP) $8,490

Cr Inventory (Cost of sales in IS) $8,490

Step 2 Non-current assets and depreciation

As well as calculating the depreciation for the year, we must also deal with the part-exchange of the van during the year.

Depreciation of van from 1 June 20X5 to 31 August 20X5:

Cost $2,000 x 25% x 3/12 = $125

Disposal of van:

The van has been part-exchanged against the cost of a new van. The trade-in value of $1,400 is equivalent to the disposal proceeds of the van. The new van has a total cost of $3,600 consisting of $1,400 trade-in allowance and $2,200 cash.

The double entry to record the disposal is:

Dr Delivery van accumulated

depreciation account ($1,000 + 125) $1,125

Dr New delivery van cost account $1,400

Cr Delivery van cost account $2,000

Cr Profit on sale of asset $525

KAPLAN PUBLISHING

This can be shown in the disposal account as follows:

Old delivery van-disposal

	$		$
Old delivery van – cost	2,000	Old delivery van – accumulated depreciation	1,125
Profit on disposal	525		
		New delivery van	1,400
	2,525		2,525

Don't forget to add on the depreciation for the first three months of the year when you are calculating the profit on disposal.

Note that this question specifically requires monthly depreciation. Some questions may state that there is no depreciation in the year of acquisition or year of disposal of an asset. Make sure you read the question carefully.

Depreciation of van from 1 September 20X5 to 31 May 20X6:

Cost $3,600 x 25% x 9/12 = $675.

The total depreciation for the year for delivery vans is $800 (675 + 125).

Depreciation on furniture and equipment:

Cost $8,000 x 10% = $800.

Step 3 Irrecoverable debts

- The TB shows us that:
- $1,791 has been written off in the year for irrecoverable debts; and
- the balance on the allowance for receivables is $437.

The closing allowance should be 5% of closing receivables.

$10,760 x 5% = $538.

The charge to the income statement is the movement between the opening and closing allowance.

$538 – $437 = $101 increase in the allowance which is debited to the income statement.

The double entry to record this transactions is:

Dr Irrecoverable debts expense $101

Cr Allowance for receivables $101

The charge in the income statement for irrecoverable debts will amount to $1,892 including the debt already written off ($1,791 + $101).

Step 4 Light and heat

$372 needs to be accrued for light and heat expenses. The double entry is:

Dr Light and heat expense $372

Cr Current liabilities $372

This journal entry ensures that the business has recorded all of its expenses in the period.

Step 5 Rent

The rent has been paid in advance and part of the payment relates to the next accounting period. This must be taken out of expenses for the current period and shown in the statement of financial position as a prepayment.

Rent prepaid (1/3 x $900) = $300

Step 6 Insurance

Insurance has also been paid in advance and must be adjusted.

Insurance prepaid 10/12 x $1,680 = $1,400

Step 7 Prepare the income statement and statement of financial position

	$	$
Sales revenue:		
Credit sales		96,520
Cash sales		30,296
		126,816
Less: Sales returns		(1,076)
		125,740
Opening inventory	7,650	
Purchases	73,010	
Less: Purchase returns	(3,720)	
Carriage inwards	2,930	
Customs duty	11,760	
Closing inventory	(8,490)	
Cost of sales		(83,140)
Gross profit		42,600
Discount received		965
Profit on sale of van		525
		44,090
Less: Expenses:		
Depreciation:		
Van (Step 2)	800	
Equipment (Step 2)	800	
Irrecoverable debts (Step 3)	1,892	
Light and heat ($2,653 + 372)(Step 4)	3,025	
Rent ($3,315 – 300)(Step 5)	3,015	
Insurance ($4,000 – 1,400) (Step 6)	2,600	
Discount allowed	1,870	
Carriage outwards	1,762	
Salesman's commission	711	
Salesman's salary	3,970	

	$	$
Office salary	7,207	
Bank charges	980	
Loan interest	450	
Sundry expenses	2,100	
Printing and postage	2,103	
Advertising	1,044	
Motor expenses	986	
		(35,315)
Net profit		8,775

Statement of financial position at 31 May 20X6

	Cost $	Acc $	NBV $
Non-current assets			
Motor van (step 2)	3,600	675	2,925
Furniture and equipment	8,000	3,200	4,800
	11,600	3,875	7,725
Current assets:			
Inventory		8,490	
Receivables	10,760		
Less: Allowance for receivables (Step 3)	(538)		
		10,222	
Prepayments (rent and insurance)		1,700	
Cash at bank		2,634	
Cash in hand		75	
			23,121
			30,846
Capital account:			
Balance at 1 June 20X5		15,258	
Net profit		8,775	
			24,033
Less: Drawings by proprietor		(5,970)	18,063
Non-current liabilities:			
Loan			5,000

	NBV $	Cost $	Acc $
Current liabilities			
Payables		7,411	
Accrued expenses		372	
			7,783
			30,846

Test your understanding 1

Kevin Suri carries on business as a retail trader. The trial balance of his business as at 31 December 20X5 was as follows:

	Dr $	Cr $
Capital		225,600
Sales and purchases	266,800	365,200
Inventory at 1 January 20X5	23,340	
Returns	1,200	1,600
Wages	46,160	
Rent	13,000	
Motor expenses	3,720	
Insurance	760	
Irrecoverable debts	120	
Allowance for receivables		
1 January 20X5		588
Discounts	864	1,622
Light and heat	3,074	
Bank overdraft interest	74	
Motor vehicles at cost	24,000	
– aggregate depreciation		
1 Jan 20X5		12,240
Fixtures and fittings at cost	28,000	
– aggregate depreciation		
1 Jan 20X5		16,800
Land	100,000	
Receivables and payables	17,330	23,004

	Dr	Cr
	$	$
Bank	3,412	
Buildings at cost	100,000	
– aggregate depreciation		
1 Jan 20X5		6,000
Drawings	20,800	
	652,654	652,654

You are given the following additional information:

(1) Inventory at 31 December 20X5 was $25,680.

(2) Rent was prepaid by $1,000 and light and heat owed was $460 at 31 December 20X5.

(3) Land is to be revalued to $250,000 at 31 December 20X5.

(4) Following a final review of the receivables at 31 December 20X5, Kevin decides to write off another debt of $130. He also wishes to maintain the allowance for receivables at 3% of the year end balance.

(5) Depreciation is to be provided as follows:

(a) building – 2% annually, straight-line

(b) fixtures & fittings – straight line method, assuming a useful economic life of five years with no residual value

(c) motor vehicles – 30% annually on a reducing balance basis.

A full year's depreciation is charged in the year of acquisition and none in the year of disposal.

Prepare an income statement for the year ended 31 December 20X5 and a statement of financial position as at that date for Kevin Suri.

Chapter summary

```
┌─────────────────────────────┐
│      TRIAL BALANCE          │
│                             │
│  •  Lists out all the       │
│     balances on the         │
│     ledger accounts         │
└─────────────────────────────┘
                │
┌─────────────────────────────┐
│       Adjustment            │
│  •  Closing inventory       │
│  •  Depreciation            │
│  •  Accruals and            │
│     prepayments             │
│  •  Irrecoverable debts     │
│     and allowance for       │
│     receivables.            │
└─────────────────────────────┘
        │                 │
┌──────────────────┐  ┌──────────────────────┐
│ Income statement │  │ Statement of financial│
│                  │  │      position         │
│ •  Shows the     │  │  •  Shows the financial│
│    financial     │  │     position of the    │
│    performance   │  │     business.          │
│    of the        │  │                        │
│    business.     │  │                        │
└──────────────────┘  └──────────────────────┘
```

Test your understanding answers

Test your understanding 1

Kevin Suri Income statement for the year ended 31 December 20X5

	$	$
Sales		365,200
Returns in		(1,200)
		_____
		364,000
Cost of sales		
Opening Inventory	23,340	
Purchases	266,800	
Returns out	(1,600)	
	_____	
	288,540	
Closing inventory	(25,680)	
	_____	
		(262,860)
		_____
Gross profit		101,140
Sundry income		
Discount received		1,622
Decrease in allowance for receivables		72
		_____
		102,834
Expenses		
Wages	46,160	
Rent ($13,000 – 1,000)	12,000	
Motor expenses	3,720	
Insurance	760	
Irrecoverable debts ($120 + 130)	250	
Discounts allowed	864	
Light and heat ($3,074 + 460)	3,534	
Bank interest	74	

KAPLAN PUBLISHING

	$	$
Depreciation		
Buildings (W1)	2,000	
Fixtures and fittings (W1)	5,600	
Motor vehicles (W2)	3,528	
		(78,490)
Net profit		24,344
Other Comprehensive Income		
Revaluation Gain		150,000
Total Comprehensive Income		174,344

Statement of financial position as at 31 December 20X5

	Cost $	Acc dep'n $	NBV $
Non-current assets			
Land	250,000	–	250,000
Buildings	100,000	8,000	92,000
Fixtures and fittings	28,000	22,400	5,600
Motor vehicles	24,000	15,768	8,232
	402,000	46,168	355,832
Current assets			
Inventory		25,680	
Receivables ($17,330 – 130)	17,200		
Allowance for receivables ($17,200 X 3%)	(516)		
			16,684

Prepaid expenses (rent)	1,000	
Bank	3,412	
	46,776	
	402,608	

Capital		225,600
Profit		24,344
Revaluation reserve/surplus		
($250,000 – 100,000)		150,000
Drawings		(20,800)
		379,144
Current liabilities		
Payables	23,004	
Accrued expenses		
(light and heat)	460	
		23,464
		402,608

Working

	Motor vehicles
Cost	$24,000
Accumulated depreciation	($12,240)
NBV	$11,760
Depreciation rate	x 30%
Annual depreciation charge	$3,528

Books of prime entry and control accounts

Chapter learning objectives

Upon completion of this chapter you will be able to:

- identify the main data sources and records in an accounting system

- describe the contents and purpose of different types of business documentation

- outline the form of accounting records in a typical manual system

- record credit sale and purchase transactions (with and without sales tax) using day books

- post day book totals to the ledger accounts

- explain the division of the ledger into sections

- explain the nature and purpose of control accounts for the accounts receivable and accounts payable ledgers

- account for contras between trade receivables and payables

- record cash transactions using the cash book

- explain the need for a record of petty cash transactions

- illustrate the typical format of the petty cash book

- explain the importance of using the imprest system to control petty cash

- list the necessary controls and security over petty cash that would normally be found in a business

- explain the uses of the journal

- illustrate the use of the journal and the posting of journal entries into ledger accounts.

1 Business documentation

The table below summarises the main types of business documentation and sources of data for an accounting system, together with their content and purpose.

	Contents	**Purpose**
Quotation	Quantity/ description/details of goods required.	To establish price from various suppliers and cross refer to purchase requisition.
Purchase order	Details of supplier, e.g. name, address. Quantity/ description/details of goods required and price. Terms and conditions of delivery, payment, etc.	Sent to supplier as request for supply. To check to the quotation and delivery note.
Sales order	Quantity/ description/details of goods required and price.	Cross checked with the order placed by customer. Sent to the stores/warehouse department for processing of the order.
Delivery note (goods delivery note – GDN)	Details of supplier, e.g. name and address. Quantity and description of goods	Provided by supplier. Checked with goods received and purchase order.
Goods received note (GRN)	Quantity and description of goods.	Produced by company receiving the goods as proof of receipt. Matched with delivery note and purchase order.

	Contents	**Purpose**
Purchase invoice	Details of supplier, e.g. name and address. Contains details of goods, e.g. quantity, price, value, sales tax, terms of credit, etc.	Issued by supplier as request for payment. Cross checked with delivery note, and purchase order. Statement
Statement	Details of supplier, e.g. name and address. Has details of date, invoice numbers and values, payments made, refunds, amount owing.	Issued by the supplier. Checked with other documents to ensure that the amount owing is correct.
Credit note	Details of supplier, e.g.name and address. Contains details of goods returned, e.g. quantity, price, value,sales tax, terms of credit, etc.	Issued by the supplier. Checked with documents regarding goods returned.
Debit note	Details of the supplier.Contains details of goods returned, e.g. quantity, price, value, sales tax, terms of credit, etc.	Issued by the company receiving the goods. Cross referred to the credit note issued by the supplier.
Remittance advice	Method of payment,invoice number, account number, date, etc.	Sent to supplier with, or as notification of, payment.
Receipt	Details of payment received.	Issued by the selling company indicating the payment received.

2 Accounting records

Books of prime entry

- If ledgers were updated each time a transaction occurred, the ledger accounts would quickly become cluttered and errors might be made.

- To avoid this, all transactions are initially recorded in a book of prime entry.

- Several books of prime entry exist, each recording a different type of transaction:

Book of prime entry	Transaction type
Sales day book	Credit sales
Purchases day book	Credit purchases
Sales returns day book	Returns of goods sold on credit
Purchases returns day book	Returns of goods bought on credit
Cash book	All bank transactions
Petty cash book	All small cash transactions
The journal	All transactions not recorded elsewhere

- Entry of a transaction to a book of prime entry does not record the double entry required for that transaction.

- The book of prime entry is, however, the source for double entries to the ledger accounts.

- The double entry arising from the book of prime entry will be recorded periodically (daily, weekly, monthly) depending on the volume of transactions.

3 Ledger accounts and the division of the ledger

In a manual system, ledgers can be thought of as books containing the individual accounts:

- The **general ledger** contains all accounts or a summary of all accounts necessary to produce the trial balance and financial statements.

- The **accounts receivable ledger** contains an account for each credit customer to show how much each one owes.

   An account to summarise this information, the **receivables control account**, is normally contained within the general ledger.

- The **accounts payable ledger** contains an account for each credit supplier to show how much they are owed.

   An account to summarise this information, the **payables control account**, is normally contained within the general ledger.

Where there are individual accounts in a receivables or payables ledger AND a control account in the general ledger, only one can form part of the double entry system. The other exists for memorandum purposes. It is normally the case that the control accounts form part of the double entry.

Expandable text

Not all businesses maintain a receivables ledger control account and purchases ledger control account, however where they do it is usually these control accounts that form part of the double entry system.

Where control accounts are maintained, they are effective in reducing the time it takes to ascertain the total amount owed by receivables and owed to payables. The scope for making errors when realising these numbers through totalling several individual accounts is also reduced.

Even where control accounts are maintained, a business must still keep a record of how much each customer owes them and how much they owe each supplier, therefore the accounts payable ledger and accounts receivable ledger are always part of the accounting system.

4 Sales and purchases day books

Sales day book

Date	Invoice	Customer	Ledger Ref	$
4.1.X6	1	Jake	RL3	4,500
4.1.X6	2	Bella	RL18	3,000
4.1.X6	3	Fizz	RL6	2,200
4.1.X6	4	Milo	RL1	10,000
4.1.X6	5	Max	RL12	500
Total for 4.1.X6				20,200

The format of the double entry resulting from the sales day book will depend upon whether the individual accounts in the accounts receivable ledger OR the receivables control account in the general ledger is part of the double entry system:

Individual Accounts part of double entry:		Receivables ledger control account part of double entry:	
Dr Jake (RL3)	$4,500	Dr SLCA	$20,200
Dr Bella (RL18)	$3,000	Cr Sales	$20,200
Dr Fizz (RL6)	$2,200	Care must then be taken to update the individual memorandum accounts with the new amounts that Jake, Bella, Fizz, Milo and Max owe.	
Dr Milo (RL1)	$10,000		
Dr Max (RL12)	$500		
Cr Sales	$20,200		
The total receivables of $20,200 should then be posted to the memorandum control account (assuming one is maintained).			

KAPLAN PUBLISHING

Purchases day book, sales returns day book and purchases returns day book

The format of the remaining day books is similar to that of the sales day book. The double entries arising are:

	Individual accounts part of double entry	Control accounts part of double entry
Purchases day book	Dr Purchases. Cr Individual accounts in accounts payable ledger.	Dr Purchases. Cr Payables ledger control account.Each entry also posted to individual memorandum accounts in accounts payable ledger.
Sales returns day book	Dr Sales returns. Cr Individual accounts in accounts receivable ledger.	Dr Sales Returns. Cr Receivables ledger control account. Each entry also posted to individual memorandum accounts in accounts Receivables ledger.
Purchases returns day book	Dr Individual accounts in accounts payable ledger. Cr Purchases returns.	Dr Payables ledger control account. Cr Purchases returns. Each entry also posted to individual memorandum accounts in accounts payable ledger.

Expandable text

Format of the purchases day book

Date	Invoice	Customer	Ledger Ref	$
4.1.X6	34	JHarry	RL3	2,700
4.1.X6	11	Ron	RL18	145
4.1.X6	5609	Hermione	RL6	4,675
4.1.X6	2	Neville	RL1	750
4.1.X6	577	Draco	RL12	345
				_____
Total for 4.1.X6				8,615

Dr Purchases $8,615

Cr Payables ledger control account $8,615

Individual purchases posted as credits to individual suppliers accounts in accounts payable ledger.

Format of the sales returns day book

Date	Invoice	Customer	Ledger Ref	$
4.1.X6	1	Max	RL12	50
4.1.X6	2	Ernie	RL2	450
4.1.X6	3	Pat	RL20	390
4.1.X6	4	Sam	RL27	670
4.1.X6	5	Milo	RL1	2,300
Total for 4.1.X6				3,860

Dr Sales returns $3,860

Cr Receivables ledger control account $3,860

Individual returns posted as credits to individual customers' accounts in accounts receivable ledger.

Format of the purchases returns day book

Date	Invoice	Customer	Ledger Ref	$
4.1.X6	112	Harry	PL3	600
4.1.X6	56	Cho	PL16	75
4.1.X6	7	Fleur	PL2	800
4.1.X6	890	Neville	PL1	50
4.1.X6	12	Draco	PL12	100
Total for 4.1.X6				1,625

Dr Payables ledger control account $1,625

Cr Purchases returns $1,625

Individual returns posted as debits to individual suppliers accounts in accounts payable ledger.

Illustration

Mr Kipper-Ling runs a business providing equipment for bakeries. He always makes a note of sales and purchases on credit and associated returns, but he is not sure how they should be recorded for the purposes of his accounts.

Write up the following credit transactions arising in the first two weeks of August 20X6 into day books and advise Mr Kipper-Ling of the correct double entries assuming that control accounts are maintained as part of the double entry system.

1 August Mrs Bakewell buys $500 worth of cake tins.

1 August Mr Kipper-Ling purchases $2,000 worth of equipment from wholesalers TinPot Ltd.

2 August Mr Kipper-Ling returns goods costing $150 to another supplier, I Cook.

3 August Jack Flap buys $1,200 worth of equipment.

3 August Mrs Bakewell returns $100 worth of the goods supplied to her.

4 August Victoria Sand-Witch buys a new oven for $4,000.

5 August Mr Kipper-Ling purchases $600 worth of baking trays from regular supplier TinTin Ltd.

8 August Mr Kipper-Ling purchases ovens costing $10,000 from Hot Stuff Ltd.

8 August Mr Kipper-Ling returns equipment costing $300 to TinPot Ltd.

9 August Pavel Ova purchases goods costing $2,200.

11 August Mrs Bakewell buys some oven-proof dishes costing $600.

Expandable text

Solution

Sales day book			Sales returns day book		
Aug	Customer	$	Aug	Customer	$
1	Mrs Bakewell	500			
3	Jack Flap	1,200	3	Mrs Bakewell	100
4	Victoria Sand-Witch	4,000			___
					100
9	Pavel Ova	2,200			
11	Mrs Bakewell	600			
		___			
		8,500			
Dr Receivables ledger control account		$8,500	Dr Sales returns		$100
Cr Sales		$8,500	Cr Receivables ledger control account		$100
And update the memorandum accounts:			And update the memorandum accounts:		
Dr Mrs Bakewell		$1,100	Cr Mrs Bakewell		$100
Dr Jack Flap		$1,200			
Dr Victoria Sand-Witch		$4,000			
Dr Pavel Ova		$2,200			

KAPLAN PUBLISHING

Purchases day book					
Aug	Supplier	$			
1	TinPot Ltd	2,000			
5	TinTin Ltd	600			
8	Hot Stuff	10,000			
		12,600			
Dr Purchases		$12,600			
Cr Payables ledger control account		$12,600			
And update the memorandum accounts:					
Cr TinPot Ltd	$2,000				
Cr TinTin Ltd	$600				
Cr Hot Stuff	$10,000				

Purchases returns day book		
Aug	Supplier	$
2	I Cook	150
8	TinPot Ltd	300
		450
Dr Payables ledger control account		$450
Cr Purchases returns		$450
And update the memorandum accounts:		
Dr I Cook		$150
Dr TinPot Ltd		$300

5 Sales tax in day books

If a business is registered for sales tax, the sales and purchases day books must include entries to record the tax.

Illustration 1– Sales tax in day books

Sales day book

Date	Invoice	Customer	Ledger Ref	Gross	Sales tax	Net
				$	$	$
8.7.X6	1	Spencer	J1	587.50	87.50	500.00
10.7.X6	2	Archie	S5	705.00	105.00	600.00
				1,292.50	192.50	1,100.00

Purchases day book

Date	Customer	Ledger Ref	Gross	Sales tax	Net
			$	$	$
8.7.X6	Peggy	Y1	1,762.50	262.50	1,500
10.7.X6	Zena	Z8	352.50	52.50	300
			2,115.00	315.00	1,800

Expandable text

The double entry for the above transaction will be:

Dr Sales tax $315

Dr Purchases $1,800

Cr Payables ledger control account $2,115

The double entry for the above transaction will be:

Dr Receivables ledger control account $1,292.50

Cr Sales tax $192.50

Cr Sales $1,100.00

Test your understanding 1

The following sales invoices have been issued by Quincy. in July:

Date	Customer	Inv No	Ledger ref.	Sales tax
8 July	Simpson	1100	A8	$ 411.25 (including sales tax)
10 July	Burns	1101	B5	$ 1,300 (excluding sales tax)

Quincy is registered for sales tax, applied at a rate of 17.5%

KAPLAN PUBLISHING

What double entry arises from the day book?

		Dr		Cr
A	Receivables ledger control account	$1,711.25	Sales	$2,010.72
	Sales tax	$299.47		
B	Receivables ledger control account	$2,010.72	Sales	$1,711.25
			Sales tax	$299.47
C	Receivables ledger control account	$1,650.00	Sales	$1,938.75
	Sales tax	$288.75		
D	Receivables ledger control account	$1,938.75	Sales	$1,650.00
			Sales tax	$288.75

Control accounts

Control accounts are ledger accounts that summarise a large number of transactions.

Control accounts do form part of the double entry system.

The receivables ledger control account may include any of the following entries:

Receivables ledger control account

Balance b/f	X	Balance b/f	X
Credit sales (SDB)	X	Sales returns (SRDB)	X
		Bank (CB)	X
Bank (CB) dishonoured cheques	X	Irrecoverable debts (journal)	X
Bank (CB) refunds of credit balances	X	Discounts allowed	X
		Contra	X
Balance c/f	X	Balance c/f	X
	X		X
Balance b/f	X	Balance b/f	X

The payables ledger control account may include any of the following entries:

Payables ledger control account

Balance b/f	X	Balance b/f	X
Bank (CB)	X	Credit purchases (PDB)	X
Purchases returns (PRDB)	X	Bank (CB) refunds of debit balances	X
Discounts received	X		
Contra	X		
Balance c/f	X	Balance c/f	X
	___		___
	X		X
	___		___
Balance b/f	X	Balance b/f	X

SDB Sales day book

PDB Purchases day book

SRDB Sales returns day book

PRDB Purchases returns day book

CB Cash book

Note that any entries to the control accounts must also be reflected in the individual accounts within the accounts receivable and payable ledgers.

KAPLAN PUBLISHING

Expandable Text

Contra entries

The situation may arise where a customer is also a supplier. Instead of both owing each other money, it may be agreed that the balances are contra'd, i.e. cancelled.

The double entry for this type of contra is:

> Dr Payables ledger control account

> Cr Receivables ledger control account

The individual receivable and payable accounts must also be updated to reflect this.

Expandable Text

Credit balances on the receivables ledger control account

Sometimes the receivables ledger control account may show a credit balance, i.e. we owe the customer money. These amounts are usually small and arise when:

- The customer has overpaid.
- Credit notes have been issued for fully-paid-for goods.
- Payment is received in advance of raising invoices.

The payables ledger control account may show a debit balance for similar reasons.

Test your understanding 2

Jones prepares monthly Receivables and Payables ledger control accounts. At 1 November 2005 the following balances existed in the company's records.

	Dr $	Cr $
Receivables ledger control account	54,000	1,000
Payables ledger control account	200	43,000

The following information is extracted in November 2005 from the company's records:

	$
Credit sales	251,000
Cash sales	34,000
Credit purchases	77,000
Cash purchases	29,000
Credit sales returns	11,000
Credit purchases returns	3,000
Amounts received from credit customers	242,000
Dishonoured cheques	500
Amounts paid to credit suppliers	74,000
Cash discounts allowed	3,000
Cash discounts received	2,000
Irrecoverable debts written off	1,000
Increase in allowances for receivables	1,200
Interest charged to customers	1,400
Contra settlements	800

At 30 November 2005 the balances in the Receivables and Payables ledgers, as extracted, totalled:

	Dr $	Cr $
Receivables ledger balances	To be calculated	2,000
Payables ledger balances	200	To be calculated

Prepare the receivables ledger control account and the payables ledger control account for the month of November 2005 to determine the closing debit and closing credit balances on the receivables ledger control account and payables ledger control account respectively.

6 The cash book

- All transactions involving cash at bank are recorded in the cash book.

- Many businesses have two distinct cash books – a **cash payments book** and a **cash receipts book.**

- A note of cash discounts given and received is also recorded in the cash book. This is to facilitate the recording of discounts in both the general and accounts payable/receivable ledgers.

- It is common for businesses to use a columnar format cash book in order to analyse types of cash payment and receipt.

Illustration 2– The cash book

The cash payments book

The following is the cash payments book of a small print business.

Date	Detail	Bank	Discount ledger	Payables	Rent
		$	$	$	$
18.7.X6	Mr A	1,400	100	1,400	
18.7.X6	Office	3,000			3,000
18.7.X6	Mr B	210		210	
18.7.X6	Mr C	1,600	80	1,600	
18.7.X6	Shop	400			400
		———	———	———	———
		6,610	180	3,210	3,400

What are the accounting entries arising from the totals in the cash book at the end of the day, assuming control accounts are kept?

Expandable text

Solution

The cash transactions are recorded in total as follows:

Dr Payables ledger control account $3,210

Dr Rent expense $3,400

Cr Bank $6,610

The discount is recorded as follows:

Dr Payables ledger control account $180

Cr Discounts received $180

Entries must also be made to Mr A, Mr B and Mr C's individual accounts in the accounts payable ledger in order to reflect the payments made and discounts received.

Test your understanding 3

The following is the cash receipts book of the SM Art Gallery.

Date	Detail	Bank received	Discount ledger	Receivables	Rent
		$	$	$	$
18.7.X6	C Monet	10,000	500	10,000	
18.7.X6	Interest Acc # 1	20			20
18.7.X6	VV Gogh	25,000		25,000	
18.7.X6	Interest Acc # 2	100			100
18.7.X6	P Picasso	13,700	300	13,700	
		48,820	800	48,700	120

What are the accounting entries arising from the totals in the cash book at the end of the day, assuming control accounts are kept?

7 The petty cash book

- All transactions involving small amounts of cash are recorded in the petty cash book.

- The petty cash system is usually designed to deal with sundry small payments in cash made by a business, e.g. paying the milkman, purchasing biscuits, buying stationery or reimbursing travel expenses.

- The cash receipts will be recorded together with the payments which will be analysed in the same way as a cash book.

KAPLAN PUBLISHING

The imprest system

The best way of dealing with petty cash is by means of an imprest system, which works as follows.

Step 1

The business decides on the amount of cash to be held as a float.

Dr Petty cash   X

Cr Bank   X

This round sum amount will be referred to as the 'petty cash float'.

Step 2

As the petty cashier makes payments he records these in the petty cash book, which is not part of the double entry system. All expenditure must be evidenced by an expense receipt and the petty cashier will attach an expense voucher to each expense.

Step 3

When the petty cash runs low, a cheque is drawn to return the petty cash to the exact amount of the original float. At this stage the expense vouchers should be produced by the petty cashier to the cheque signatory which will exactly equal the cheque required.

This aspect of control is the essential feature of the petty cash system. At any stage :

Float = Cash in petty cash box + sum total of expense vouchers since last reimbursement

Expandable Text

Controls over petty cash

The following controls and security over petty cash should be found in a business:

- Petty cash must be kept in a petty cash box.
- Petty cash box must be secured in a safe.
- Person responsible for petty cash must be reliable and know what he/she is doing.
- All petty cash must be supported by invoices.
- Petty cash vouchers must be signed by the claimant and the person responsible for running the petty cash.
- Regular spot checks must be carried out to ensure that the petty cash is accurate.

Illustration 3 – The petty cash book

On 1 March 20X9 a petty cash float of $100 is introduced by Dialex. During March the following payments are made out of petty cash:

		$
2 March	Biscuits	10
8 March	Stationery	20
11 March	Bus fare	3
16 March	Train fare	5
25 March	Stationery	40

On 31 March the cash is reimbursed. Write up the petty cash book for the month and show the resulting entries to the general ledger.

Expandable text

Solution

Received	Date	Details	Voucher	Total	Stationery expenses	Sundry expenses	Travelling
			$	$	$	$	$
100	1 Mar	Cash book					
	2 Mar	Gateway biscuits	1	10		10	
	8 Mar	Basildon Bond	2	20	20		
	11 Mar	Bus fares	3	3			3
	16 Mar	Rail fares	4	5			5
	25 Mar	Office International	5	40	40		
				——	——	——	——
				78	60	10	8
				——	——	——	——
78	31 Mar	Cash Balance c/f					
				100			
				——			
				178			
				——			
	1 Apr	Balance b/f					

No double entry bookkeeping entries are made from the receipts side of the petty cash book – in a good system the only receipt should be the reimbursement of the float, the double entry of which is dealt with in the posting of the cash book.

As regards the payments, the double entry in the general ledger is performed as follows:

Stationery

20X9	$	20X9	$
Mar Petty cash book	60		

Sundry expenses

20X9	$	20X9	$
Mar Petty cash book	10		

Travelling expenses

20X9	$	20X9	$
Mar Petty cash book	8		

8 The journal

The journal is a book of prime entry which records transactions which are not routine (and not recorded in any other book of prime entry), for example:

- year-end adjustments
    - depreciation charge for the year
    - irrecoverable debt write-off
    - record movement in allowance for receivables
    - accruals and prepayments
    - closing inventory
- acquisitions and disposals of non-current assets
- opening balances for statement of financial position items
- correction of errors.

The journal is a clear and comprehensible way of setting out a bookkeeping double entry that is to be made.

Presentation of a journal

A journal should be laid out in the following way:

    Dr Non-current asset   X

    Cr Cash   X

to record the purchase of a new non-current asset.

A brief narrative should be given to explain the entry.

Test your understanding 4

Igor Romanov runs a Russian restaurant. He is a very good chef but not quite so good at accounting and needs help to record the following transactions:

(1) Closing inventory of 250 bottles of vodka at a cost of $2,750 has not been recorded.

(2) Igor needs to charge depreciation on his restaurant. He holds a 25-year lease which cost him $150,000 ten years ago.

(3) A regular customer, V Shady, keeps a tab behind the bar. He currently owes $350 but was last seen buying a one-way ticket to Moscow. Igor has given up hope of payment and intends to write the debt off.

(4) On the last day of the year Igor bought two new sofas for cash for the bar area of the restaurant. They cost $600 each but the purchase has not been reflected in the accounts.

What journals should Igor post?

Chapter summary

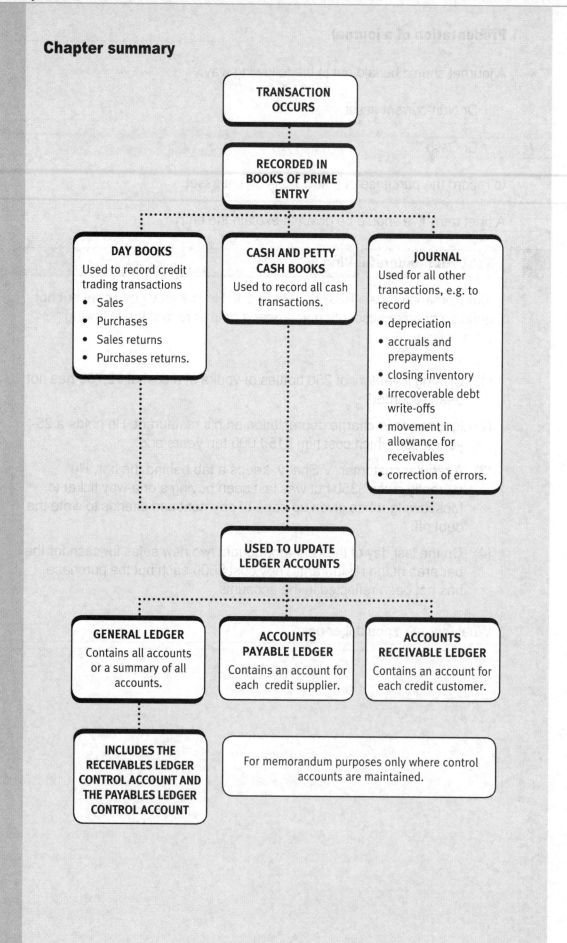

TRANSACTION OCCURS

RECORDED IN BOOKS OF PRIME ENTRY

DAY BOOKS
Used to record credit trading transactions
- Sales
- Purchases
- Sales returns
- Purchases returns.

CASH AND PETTY CASH BOOKS
Used to record all cash transactions.

JOURNAL
Used for all other transactions, e.g. to record
- depreciation
- accruals and prepayments
- closing inventory
- irrecoverable debt write-offs
- movement in allowance for receivables
- correction of errors.

USED TO UPDATE LEDGER ACCOUNTS

GENERAL LEDGER
Contains all accounts or a summary of all accounts.

ACCOUNTS PAYABLE LEDGER
Contains an account for each credit supplier.

ACCOUNTS RECEIVABLE LEDGER
Contains an account for each credit customer.

INCLUDES THE RECEIVABLES LEDGER CONTROL ACCOUNT AND THE PAYABLES LEDGER CONTROL ACCOUNT

For memorandum purposes only where control accounts are maintained.

Test your understanding answers

The correct answer is D

Sales day book

Date	Customer	Invoice	Ledger ref.	Gross	Sales tax	Net
				$	$	$
8 July	Simpson	1100	A8	411.25	61.25	350.00
10 July	Burns	1101	B5	1,527.50	227.50	1,300.00
				1,938.75	288.75	1,650.00

The double entry for the above transaction will be:

Dr	Receivables ledger control account	$1,938.75
Cr	Sales tax	$288.75
Cr	Sales	$1,650.00

Test your understanding 2

Receivables ledger control account

	$		$
Balance b/f	54,000	Balance b/f	1,000
Credit sales	251,000	Sales returns	11,000
Dishonoured cheques	500	Cash received	242,000
Interest charged	1,400	Discounts allowed	3,000
		Irrecoverable debts	1,000
		Contra	800
Balance c/f	2,000	Balance c/f	50,100
	308,900		308,900
Balance b/f	50,100	Balance b/f	2,000

Payables ledger control account

	$		$
Balance b/f	200	Balance b/f	43,000
Purchases returns	3,000	Credit purchases	77,000
Cash paid	74,000		
Discounts received	2,000		
Contra	800		
Balance c/f	40,200	Balance c/f	200
	120,200		120,200
Balance b/f	200	Balance b/f	40,200

Test your understanding 3

The cash transactions are recorded in total as follows:

Dr Bank $48,820

Cr Receivables ledger control account $48,700

Cr Interest income $120

The discount is recorded as follows:

Dr Discounts allowed $800

Cr Receivables ledger control account $800

Entries must also be made to Monet, Gogh and Picasso's individual accounts in the accounts receivable ledger in order to reflect the payments received and discounts allowed.

Test your understanding 4

(1) Dr Closing inventory (statement of financial position) $2,750

   Cr Closing inventory (cost of sales) $2,750

To record the closing inventory of vodka.

(2) Dr Depreciation expense $6,000 ($150,000/25 yrs)

   Cr Accumulated depreciation $6,000

To record depreciation on the restaurant lease.

(3) Dr Irrecoverable debt expense $350

   Cr Receivables ledger control account $350

To record the write-off of a debt outstanding from V Shady.

NB Igor must also remember to update V Shady's individual account in the accounts receivable ledger.

(4) Dr Fixtures and Fittings cost $1,200

   Cr Cash $1,200

To record the purchase of two sofas for the bar.

Control account reconciliations

Chapter learning objectives

Upon completion of this chapter you will be able to:

- prepare, reconcile and understand the purpose of supplier statements

- identify errors which would be highlighted by performing a control account reconciliation

- perform basic control account reconciliations for receivables and payables, identifying and correcting errors in control accounts and ledgers.

1 Control accounts

- Control accounts are a means of proving the accuracy of the ledger accounts, such as receivables and payables.

- The diagram above shows the information that is included in the **accounts receivables ledger**.

- If we wanted to check the accuracy of the accounts receivables ledger, one way we can do this is by getting the information from different sources:

  - The sales can be taken from the sales day book.

  - The cash received and discounts allowed are recorded in the cash book.

  - The opening balances can be taken from the prior month's closing balances.

- An alternative way to check the accuracy of the accounts receivables ledger is to compare the sum total of the individual receivables accounts with the balance on the receivables ledger control account.

- Remember, the control account is normally part of the double entry system, whereas the ledger contains memorandum accounts which are not part of the double entry system. Nevertheless, both are updated using the same sources and therefore should agree.

2 Supplier statements

These statements are issued to a business by suppliers to summarise the transactions that have taken place during a given period, and also to show the balance outstanding at the end of the period.

- Their purpose is to ensure that the amount outstanding is accurate and agrees with underlying documentation.

- The payables ledger control account and individual list of payables balances should agree with the total of the supplier statements.

- As such, these are a further way to prove the accuracy of accounting records.

3 Control account reconciliations

The reconciliation is a working to ensure that the entries in the ledger accounts agree with the entries in the control account. The two should have the same closing balance as ideally they have had exactly the same entries in both accounts.

- A **receivables ledger reconciliation** compares the total of the accounts in the receivables ledger with the balance on the receivables ledger control account.

- A **payables ledger reconciliation** compares the total of the accounts in the payables ledger with the balance on the payables ledger control account.

If there are differences between the control account and the ledger accounts, they must be identified and reconciled. Differences may arise due to:

- errors in the receivables or payables ledger

- errors in the receivables or payables ledger control accounts

- errors in both the control account and ledger account.

It is also possible to reconcile a supplier statement to the control account.

The purpose for doing this is as follows:

- before any payments are made to suppliers it is important to ensure that the suppliers statement is correct – else we could make over or under payments.

- each invoice and credit note listed on the statement should be checked to the original documentation for accuracy.

- once accuracy has been established, it is then possible to decide which invoices need paying ans when by.

Below is an example extract of a statement from a supplier:

STATEMENT					
Date	Transaction	Total	Current	30+	60+
		$	$	$	$
10 May 20X9	Invoice 100	94.50			94.50
1 June 20X9	CN 2008	(24.56)			(24.56)
4 July 20X9	Invoice 110	101.99		101.99	
15 July 20X9	Invoice 156	106.72	106.72		
	TOTALS	278.65	106.72	101.99	69.94

May I remind you that our credit terms are 30 days.

Here is the payables ledger which corresponds with this supplier:

Nino Ltd

		$			$
1 June 20X9 CN		24.56	10 May 20X9	Invoice 100	94.50
			4 July 20X9	Invoice 110	110.99
			15 July 20X9	Invoice 156	106.72

You can see that the invoice dated 4 July 20X9 in the ledger is of a total $110.99, however in the statement it appears as $101.99.

The purchase invoice itself should be reviewed to check which is the correct amount. If the suppliers statement is incorrect, then a polite telephone call to the supplier should be made or a letter sent explaining the problem.

If it is the ledger that is incorrect then it should be updated.

Test your understanding 1

Suggest reasons why there might be a difference between the balance on the receivables ledger control account and the total of the list of accounts receivable ledger balances.

4 Preparing a control account reconciliation

The format of a control account reconciliation, in this case for sales is as follows:

Receivables ledger control account

	$		$
Balance given by the examiner	X	Adjustments for errors	X
Adjustments for errors	X	Revised balance c/f	X
	___		___
	X		X

Reconciliation of individual receivables balances with control account balance

	$
Balance as extracted from list of receivables	X
Adjustments for errors	X/(X)
	___
Revised total agreeing with balance c/f on control account	X

- The examiner will provide details of the error(s).

- You must decide for each whether correction is required in the control account, the list of individual balances or both.

- When all errors have been corrected, the revised balance on the control account should agree to the revised total of the list of individual balances.

- Due to the nature of the F3 exam, you will not be asked to produce a full control account reconciliation, however you may be asked for the revised balance on the control account / list of individual balances after one or two errors have been corrected.

---

e.g

Illustration 1 – Preparing a control account reconciliation

Alston's payables ledger control account is an integral part of the double entry system. Individual ledger account balances are listed and totalled on a monthly basis, and reconciled to the control account balance. Information for the month of March is as follows:

(1) Individual ledger account balances at 31 March have been listed out and totalled $19,766.

(2) The payables ledger control account balance at 31 March is $21,832.

(3) On further examination the following errors are discovered:

- The total of discount received for the month, amounting to $1,715, has not been entered in the control account but has been entered in the individual ledger accounts.

- On listing-out, an individual credit balance of $205 has been incorrectly treated as a debit.

- A petty cash payment to a supplier amounting to $63 has been correctly treated in the control account, but no entry has been made in the supplier's individual ledger account.

- The purchases day book total for March has been undercast (understated) by $2,000.

- Contras (set-offs) with the receivables ledger, amounting in total to $2,004, have been correctly treated in the individual ledger accounts but no entry has been made in the control account.

(i) Prepare the part of the payables ledger control account reflecting the above information.

(ii) Prepare a statement reconciling the original total of the individual balances with the corrected balance on the control account.

Expandable text

Solution:

The best way to approach the question is to consider each of the points above in turn and ask to what extent they affect (i) the payables ledger control account and (ii) the listing of payables ledger balances.

Step 1

The total of discount received in the cash book should have been debited to the payables ledger control account and credited to discount received. Thus, if the posting has not been entered in either double entry account it clearly should be. As this has already been entered into the individual ledger accounts, no adjustment is required to the list of balances.

Step 2

Individual credit balances are extracted from the payables ledger. Here, this error affects the ledger accounts balance. No adjustment is required to the control account, only to the list of balances.

Step 3

The question clearly states that the error has been made in the individual ledger accounts. Amendments should be made to the list of balances. Again, no amendment is required to the control accounts.

Step 4

The total of the purchases day book is posted by debiting purchases and crediting payables ledger control account. If the total is understated, the following bookkeeping entry must be made, posting the $2,000 understatement:

Dr Purchases

Cr Payables ledger control account

As the individual ledger accounts in the payables ledger are posted individually from the purchases day book, the total of the day book being understated will not affect the listing of the balances in the payables ledger.

Step 5

Here it is clear that the error affects the control account, not the payables ledger. Correction should be made by the bookkeeping entry:

Dr Payables ledger control account

Cr Receivables ledger control account

Payables ledger control account

20X9	$	20X9	$
Discount received	1,715	31 Mar	
Sales receivable ledger control	2,004	Balance	21,832
Balance c/f	20,113	Purchase	2,000
	23,832		23,832

Reconciliation of individual balances with control account balance

	Cr $
Balances as extracted	19,766
Credit balance incorrectly treated 2 x $205	410
Petty cash payment	(63)
Net total agreeing with control account	20,113

Test your understanding 2

Rayneydaze is a business selling umbrellas branded with corporate logos. The umbrellas are sold in bulk lots on credit. The accountant is carrying out a reconciliation of the receivables ledger control account balance, which is $172,120 to the total of the balances on the individual accounts in the receivables ledger, which is $176,134.

The following has been found:

(1) A contra item of $1,500 has not been entered in the receivables ledger control account.

(2) A cheque for $555 from a customer has been dishonoured. The correct double entry has been posted but the individual accounts have not been updated.

(3) A payment of $322 from a customer has incorrectly been entered in the accounts receivable ledger as $233.

(4) Discounts allowed totalling $120 have not been entered in the control account.

(5) Cash received of $800 has been debited to the individual customer's account in the accounts receivable ledger.

(6) Total credit sales of $4,500 to a large accountancy firm, Close & Counter have been posted correctly to the ledger account but not recorded in the control account.

Correct the receivables ledger control account and reconcile this to the sum total of the individual accounts in the accounts receivable ledger.

KAPLAN PUBLISHING

Test your understanding 3

Tonga received a statement from a supplier, Cook, showing a balance of $14,810. Tonga's Payables ledger shows a balance due to Cook of $10,000. Investigation reveals the following:

(1) Cash paid to Cook of $4,080 has not been allowed for by Cook.

(2) Tonga's recorded the fact that a $40 cash discount was not allowed by Cook, but forgot to record this in the payables ledger.

What discrepancy remains between Tonga and Cook's records after allowing for these items?

A $9,930

B $9,850

C $770

D $690

Chapter summary

CONTROL ACCOUNTS

- Control accounts include a summary of transactions that have occurred in the period.
- They are a means of checking that the information in the ledger accounts is correct.
- They are part of the double entry system.

LEDGER ACCOUNTS

- Ledger accounts include a separate account for each credit customer/ credit supplier.
- They are memorandum accounts and not part of the double entry system.

CONTROL ACCOUNT RECONCILIATIONS

- These are a means of checking that the balance on the control account agrees with the balance on the ledger account.
- There may be errors in the ledger account, the control account or both.

PREPARING A CONTROL ACCOUNT RECONCILIATION

- Compare the balance on the ledger account with the control account.
- Review the list of errors to see which account needs amending.
- Set up a T account for the control accounts.
- Prepare a reconciliation for the ledger account.

Test your understanding answers

Test your understanding 1

The following are reasons why the accounts receivable control account may not agree with the ledger account:

- The sales day book, sales returns day book or cash receipts book have been incorrectly totalled.

- A total from a book of prime entry has been transferred to the control account as a different figure.

- An individual entry from a book of prime entry has been transferred to the individual customer's account as a different figure.

- An entry in the control account or the individual customer's account has been omitted or posted to the wrong side of the account.

- The double entry for a day book total has been incorrectly made.

- An individual customer's account has been incorrectly balanced.

- The list of accounts receivable ledger balances has been incorrectly totalled.

- An entry has been made in either the control account or the individual customer's account but not in both.

- An individual customer's balance has been omitted from the list of balances.

Test your understanding 2

Receivables ledger control account

	$		$
Balance b/f	172,120	Contra (1)	1,500
Credit sales (6)	4,500	Discounts (4)	120
		Balance c/f	175,000
	176,620		176,620
Balance b/f	175,000		

Receivables ledger reconciliation

Balance per accounts receivable ledger	176,134
Dishonoured cheque (2)	555
Misposting (3)	(89)
Cash received (5)	(1,600)
Revised balance	175,000

Test your understanding 3

The correct answer is D.

	Cook $	Tonga $	
Difference			
Balance per question	14,810	10,000	
Adjustment	(4,080)	40	
Revised balance	10,730	10,040	690

KAPLAN PUBLISHING

Bank reconciliations

Chapter learning objectives

Upon completion of this chapter you will be able to:

- describe the purpose of bank reconciliations
- identify the main differences between the cash book and the bank statement
- identify the bank balance to be reported in the final accounts
- correct cash book errors or omissions
- prepare bank reconciliation statements
- derive bank statement and cash book balances from given information.

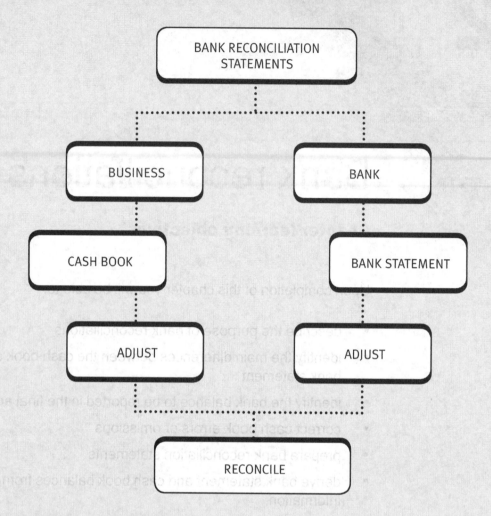

1 The bank reconciliation

The objective of a bank reconciliation is to reconcile the difference between:

- the cash book balance, i.e. the business' record of their bank account, and

- the bank statement balance, i.e. the bank's records of the bank account.

Note that debits and credits are reversed in bank statements because the bank will be recording the transaction from its point of view, in accordance with the business entity concept.

Expandable text

Nature and purpose of a bank reconciliation statement.

The cash book records all transactions with the bank. The bank statement records all the bank's transactions with the business.

The contents of the cash book should be exactly the same as the record provided by the bank in the form of a bank statement, and therefore our records should correspond with the bank statement.

This is in fact so, but with three important provisos:

(1) The ledger account maintained by the bank is the opposite way round to the cash book. This is because the bank records the balance in favour of an individual as a credit balance, i.e. a liability of the bank to the individual. From the individual's point of view it is, of course, an asset, i.e. a debit balance in his cash book.

(2) Timing differences must inevitably occur. A cheque payment is recorded in the cash book when the cheque is despatched. The bank only records such a cheque when it is paid by the bank, which may be several days later.

(3) Items such as interest may appear on the bank statement but are not recorded in the cash book as the cashier is unaware that they have arisen.

The existence of the bank statement provides an important check on the most vulnerable of a company's assets – cash. However, the differences referred to above make it essential to reconcile the balance on the ledger account with that of the bank statement.

The reconciliation is carried out frequently, usually at monthly intervals.

2 Differences between the bank statement and the cash book

When attempting to reconcile the cash book with the bank statement, there are three differences between the cash book and bank statement:

- unrecorded items
- timing differences
- errors

Expandable Text

Unrecorded items

These are items which arise in the bank statements before they are recorded in the cash book. Such 'unrecorded items' may include:

- interest
- bank charges
- dishonoured cheques.

They are not recorded in the cash book simply because the business does not know that these items have arisen until they see the bank statement.

The cash book must be adjusted to reflect these items.

Test your understanding 1

On which side of the cash book should the following unrecorded items be posted?

- bank charges
- direct debits/standing orders
- direct credits
- dishonoured cheques
- bank interest.

Expandable Text

Timing differences

These items have been recorded in the cash book, but due to the bank clearing process have not yet been recorded in the bank statement:

- Outstanding/unpresented cheques (cheques sent to suppliers but not yet cleared by the bank).
- Outstanding/uncleared lodgements (cheques received by the business but not yet cleared by the bank).

KAPLAN PUBLISHING

The bank statement balance needs to be adjusted for these items:

	$
Balance per bank statement	X
Less: Outstanding/unpresented cheques	(X)
Add: Outstanding/uncleared lodgements	X
Balance per cash book (revised)	X

Errors in the cash book

The business may make a mistake in their cash book. The cash book balance will need to be adjusted for these items.

Errors in the bank statement

The bank may make a mistake, e.g. record a transaction relating to a different person within our business' bank statement. The bank statement balance will need to be adjusted for these items.

Expandable text

Outstanding or unpresented cheques

Suppose a cheque relating to a payment to a supplier of Poorboy is written, signed and posted on 29 March. It is also entered in the cash book on the same day. By the time the supplier has received the cheque and paid it into his bank account, and by the time his bank has gone through the clearing system, the cheque does not appear on Poorboy's statement until, say, 6 April. Poorboy would regard the payment as being made on 29 March and its cash book balance as reflecting the true position at that date.

Outstanding deposits

In a similar way, a trader may receive cheques by post on 31 March, enter them in the cash book and pay them into the bank on the same day. Nevertheless, the cheques may not appear on the bank statement until 2 April. Again the cash book would be regarded as showing the true position. Outstanding deposits are also known as outstanding lodgements.

3 Proforma bank reconciliation

Cash book

Bal b/f	X	Bal b/f	X
Adjustments	X	Adjustments	X
Revised bal c/f	X	Revised bal c/f	X
	───		───
	X		X
	───		───
Revised bal b/f	X	Revised bal b/	X

Bank reconciliation statement as at .....

	$
Balance per bank statement	X
Outstanding cheques	(X)
Outstanding lodgements	X
Other adjustments to the bank statement	X/(X)
	───
Balance per cash book (revised)	X

- Beware of overdrawn balances on the bank statement.

- Beware of debits/credits to bank statements.

- Beware of aggregation of deposits in a bank statement.

- **Note that the bank balance on the statement of financial position is always the balance per the revised cash book.**

Test your understanding 2

In preparing a company's bank reconciliation statement, the accountant finds that the following items are causing a difference between the cash book balance and bank statement balance:

(1) Direct debit $530.

(2) Lodgements not credited $1,200.

(3) Cheque paid in by the company and dishonoured $234.

(4) Outstanding cheques $677.

(5) Bank charges $100.

(6) Error by bank $2,399 (cheque incorrectly credited to the account.

Which of these items will require an entry in the cash book?

A   3, 4 and 6

B   1, 3 and 5

C   1, 2 and 4

D   2, 5 and 6

Test your understanding 3

The following information has been extracted from the records of N Patel:

Bank account

		$			Chq no	$
1Dec	Balance b/f	16,491	1 Dec	Alexander	782	857
2 Dec	Able	962	6 Dec	Burgess	783	221
	Baker	1,103	14 Dec	Barry	784	511
10 Dec	Charlie	2,312	17 Dec	Cook	785	97
14 Dec	Delta	419	24 Dec	Hay	786	343
21 Dec	Echo	327	29 Dec	Rent	787	260
23 Dec	Cash sales	529				
30 Dec	Fred	119	31 Dec	Balance c/f		19,973
		22,262				22,262

High Street Bank

Bank Statement – N. Patel

Date	Details	With-drawals $	Deposits $	Balance $
1 December	Balance b/f			17,478
2 December	780	426		
2 December	781	737		16,315
2 December	Deposit		176	16,491
5 December	782	857		
5 December	Bank charges	47		15,587
6 December	Deposit		2,065	17,652
10 December	Standing order (rates)	137		17,515
11 December	783	212		17,303
13 December	Deposit		2,312	19,615
17 December	784	511		19,104
17 December	Deposit		419	19,523
23 December	Deposit		327	19,850
24 December	Deposit		528	20,378
28 December	786	343		20,035
30 December	310923	297		19,738
31 December	Balance c/f			19,738

(a) Prepare a bank reconciliation statement at 1 December.

(b) Update the cash book for December.

(c) Prepare a bank reconciliation statement at 31 December.

Test your understanding 4

The following is a summary of Ami's cash book as presented to you for the month of December 20X6:

	$		$
Receipts	1,469	Balance b/f	761
Balance c/f	554	Payments	1,262
	2,023		2,023

All receipts are banked and payments made by cheque.

On investigation you discover:

(1) Bank charges of $136 entered on the bank statement had not been entered in the cash book.

(2) Cheques drawn amounting to $267 had not been presented to the bank for payment.

(3) A cheque for $22 had been entered as a receipt in the cash book instead of as a payment;

(4) A cheque drawn for $6 had been incorrectly entered in the cash book as $66.

What balance is shown on the bank statement at 31 December 20X6?

A $913

B $941 overdraft

C $941

D $407 overdraft

Chapter summary

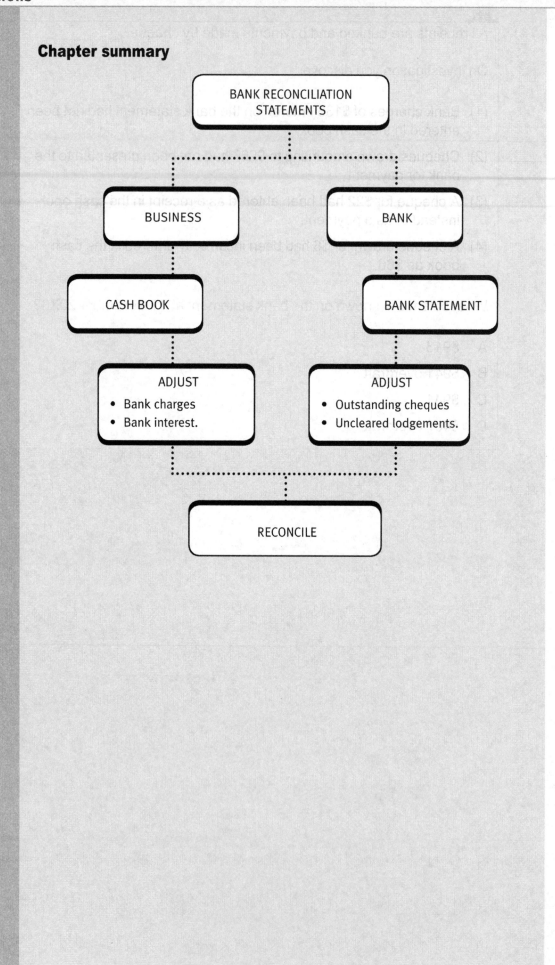

Test your understanding answers

Test your understanding 1

Cash book

	$		$
Bank interest	X	Bank charges	X
Direct credits	X	Direct debits/ standing orders	X
		Dishonoured cheques	X

Test your understanding 2

The correct answer is B

Test your understanding 3

Bank reconciliation statement as at 1December	$
Balance per bank statement	17,478
Less: Outstanding cheques ($426 + 737)	(1,163)
Add: Outstanding lodgements	176
Balance per cash book	
	16,491

Bank

	$		$
Balance b/f	19,973	Deposit difference ($529 – 528)	1
Error – cheque 783 ($221–212)	9	Bank charges	47
		Rates – s/order	137
		Revised balance c/f	19,797
	19,982		19,982
Revised balance b/f	19,797		

Bank reconciliation statement as at 31 December	$
Balance per bank statement	19,738
Less: Outstanding cheques ($97 + 260)	(357)
Add: Outstanding lodgements (Fred)	119
Bank error (Cheque 310923)	297
Balance per cash book	
	19,797

KAPLAN PUBLISHING

Test your understanding 4

The correct answer is D

Cash book

	$		$
Adjustment re cheque (4)	60	Balance b/f	554
Balance c/f	674	Bank charges (1)	136
		Adjustment re paid cheque entered as receipt (3)	44
	734		734
		Balance b/f	674

Bank reconciliation statement as at 31 December 20X6

	$
Balance per bank statement at 31 December 20X6 (derived)	(407) O/D
Less:Cheques issued but not yet presented (2)	(267)
Balance per cash book at 31 Dec 20X6	
	(674) O/D

Correction of errors and suspense accounts

Chapter learning objectives

Upon completion of this chapter you will be able to:

- identify the types of error which may occur in bookkeeping systems
- identify errors which would not be highlighted by the extraction of a trial balance
- identify errors leading to the creation of a suspense account.
- describe the purpose of a suspense account
- prepare journal entries to correct errors and clear out a suspense account
- prepare statements correcting profit for errors discovered.

1 Type of error

Errors where the trial balance still balances

- **Error of omission:** A transaction has been completely omitted from the accounting records, e.g. a cash sale of $100 was not recorded.

- **Error of commission**: A transaction has been recorded in the wrong account, e.g. rates expense of $500 has been debited to the rent account in error.

- **Error of principle:** A transaction has conceptually been recorded incorrectly, e.g. a non-current asset purchase of $1,000 has been debited to the repair expense account rather than an asset account.

- **Compensating error:** Two different errors have been made which cancel each other out, e.g. a rent bill of $1,200 has been debited to the rent account as $1,400 and a casting error on the sales account has resulted in sales being overstated by $200.

- **Error of original entry:** The correct double entry has been made but with the wrong amount, e.g. a cash sale of $76 has been recorded as $67.

- **Reversal of entries:** The correct amount has been posted to the correct accounts but on the wrong side, e.g. a cash sale of $200 has been debited to sales and credited to bank.

When correcting these errors, a good approach is to consider:

(1) What was the double entry? ('did do').

(2) What should the double entry have been? ('should do').

(3) Therefore what correction is required? ('to correct').

Always assume that if one side of the double entry is not mentioned, it has been recorded correctly.

Test your understanding 1

Provide the journal to correct each of the following errors:

(1) A cash sale of $100 was not recorded.

(2) Rates expense of $500, paid in cash has been debited to the rent account in error.

(3) a non-current asset purchase of $1,000 on credit has been debited to the repairs expense account rather than an asset account.

(4) A rent bill of $1,200 paid in cash has been debited to the rent account as $1,400 and a casting error on the sales account has resulted in sales being overstated by $200.

(5) A cash sale of $76 has been recorded as $67.

(6) A cash sale of $200 has been debited to sales and credited to cash.

Errors where the trial balance does not balance

- Single sided entry – a debit entry has been made but no corresponding credit entry or vice versa.

- Debit and credit entries have been made but at different values.

- Two entries have been made on the same side.

- An incorrect addition in any individual account, i.e. miscasting.

- Opening balance has not been brought down.

- Extraction error – the balance in the trial balance is different from the balance in the relevant account.

If there is a difference on the trial balance, then a suspense account is used to make the total debits equal the total credits:

	$	$
Non-current assets	5,000	
Receivables	550	
Inventory	1,000	
Cash	200	
Payables		600
Loan		2,000
Capital		4,000
Suspense account		150
	6,750	6,750

The balance on the suspense account must be cleared before final accounts can be prepared.

Corrections to any of the six errors mentioned above will affect the suspense account.

Approach to questions:

- Take the approach as before.

- Use the suspense account to make the 'did do' Dr = the 'did do' Cr and then part of the correction journal will be to reverse this suspense account entry.

E.g. The purchase of a non-current asset costing $100 has been recorded by debiting $10 to the non-current assets account and crediting $100 to cash.

What was the double entry? ('Did do')	What should the double entry have been? ('Should do')	Correcting journal	
Dr Non-current assets	$10 Dr Non-current assets	$100 Dr Non-current assets	$90
(Dr suspense	$90) Cr Cash	$100 Cr Suspense	$90
Cr Cash	$100		

- Where an opening balance has not been brought down, journal it in and send the opposite entry to suspense.

- The correction journal must always include an equal debit and credit.

Suspense accounts

A suspense account is an account in which debits or credits are held temporarily until sufficient information is available for them to be posted to the correct accounts.

Suspense accounts are often encountered and must be dealt with according to the usual rules of double entry bookkeeping.

There are two main reasons why suspense accounts may be created:

- On the extraction of a trial balance the debits are not equal to the credits and the difference is put to a suspense account.

- When a bookkeeper performing double entry is not sure where to post one side of an entry he may debit or credit a suspense account and leave the entry there until its ultimate destination is clarified.

Test your understanding 2

The debit side of a company's TB totals $1,200 more than the credit side. Which of the following errors would fully account for the difference?

A   The petty cash balance of $1,200 has been omitted from the TB.

B   A receipt of $1,200 for commission receivable has been omitted from the records.

C $600 paid for plant maintenance has been correctly entered into the cash book and credited to the plant cost account.

D   Discount received of $600 has been debited to the discount allowed account.

Test your understanding 3

Bond's TB failed to agree and a suspense account was opened for the difference. Bond does not maintain control accounts for sales and purchases. The following errors were found in Bond's accounting records:

(1) In recording the sale of a non-current asset, cash received of $33,000 was credited to the disposals account as $30,000.

(2) An opening accrual of $340 had been omitted.

(3) Cash of $8,900 paid for plant repairs was correctly accounted for in the cash book but was credited to the plant cost account.

(4) A cheque for $12,000 paid for the purchase of a machine was debited to the machinery account as $21,000.

Which of the errors will require an entry to the suspense account to correct them?

A   1, 3 and 4 only.

B   All.

C   1 and 4 only.

D   2 and 3 only.

Suspense accounts

On extracting a trial balance, the accountant of ETT discovered a suspense account with a debit balance of $1,075 included therein; she also found that the debits exceeded the credits by $957. She posted this difference to the suspense account and then investigated the situation. She discovered:

(1) A debit balance of $75 on the postage account had been incorrectly extracted on the list of balances as $750 debit.

(2) A payment of $500 to a credit supplier, X, had been correctly entered in the cash book, but no entry had been made in the supplier's account.

(3) When a motor vehicle had been purchased during the year the bookkeeper did not know what to do with the debit entry so he made the entry Dr Suspense, Cr Bank $1,575.

(4) A credit balance of $81 in the sundry income account had been incorrectly extracted on the list of balances as a debit balance.

(5) A receipt of $5 from a credit customer, Y, had been correctly posted to his account but had been entered in the cash book as $625.

(6) The bookkeeper was not able to deal with the receipt of $500 from the owner's own bank account, and he made the entry Dr Bank and Cr Suspense.

(7) No entry has been made for a cheque of $120 received from a credit customer M.

(8) A receipt of $50 from a credit customer, N, had been entered into his account as $5 and into the cash book as $5.

What journals are required to correct the errors and eliminate the suspense account?

Expandable Text

Solution:

Process of clearing a suspense account

The starting position we have is as follows (once we have posted our $957):

Suspense account

	$		$
Balance b/f	1,075	Trial balance difference	957

We now need to work our way through the information given in numbered points 1 to 8 to try and clear this suspense account.

You need to ask yourself the following questions for each point:

a) what was the double entry that has been made?

b) what should the double entry have been?

c) what is the journal we need to correct this?

1. a) They have posted Dr postage 750, Cr bank 75, so the other Dr of 675 will auitomatically go to the suspense a/c.

b) It should have been : Dr postage 75, Cr bank 75

c) correction = Dr suspense a/c 675, Cr postage 675

2. a) They have posted Dr suspense a/c 500, Cr cash 500.

b) It should have been: Dr payables (X) 500, Cr cash 500

c) correction = Dr payables (X) 500, Cr suspense a/c 500

3. a) They have posted: Dr suspense a/c 1575, Cr cash 1575.

b) It should have been Dr Motor vehicles cost 1575, Cr bank 1575

c) correction = Dr motor vehicles 1575, Cr suspense a/c 1575

4. a) They have posted Dr sundry income 81, Dr bank 81 Cr suspense a/c 162

b) should have been: Dr bank/cash 81. Cr sundry income 81

c) Correction = Dr suspense a/c 162, Cr sundry income 162

5. a) They have posted Dr cash 625, Cr receivables 5, so Cr suspense a/c 620

b) Should have been Dr cash 5, Cr receivables 5

c) Correction = Dr suspense a/c 620, Cr cash 620

6. a) They have posted Dr bank 500, Cr suspense a/c 500

b) Should have been: Dr bank 500, Cr capital 500

c) correction = Dr suspense a/c 500, Cr capital 500

7. a) They have posted nothing

b) They should have posted Dr bank 120, Cr receivables (M) 120

c) Correction = Dr bank 120, Cr receivables (M) 120

8.a) They have posted Dr cash 5, Cr receivables 5

b) Should have been Dr cash 50, Cr receivables 50

c) Correction = Dr cash 45, Cr receivables 45

Now you can post all of the journals that you have listed under the c) corrections which affect the suspense a/c.

Then you can balance off your suspense a/c and it should balance on both the debit and credit sides. Hence, this will clear your suspense a/c and leave it with a nil balance.

Once you have done so, you should get the following result:

Suspense Account

	$		$
Balance b/f	1,075	Trial balance difference	957
Postage (1)	675	Payable X (2)	500
Sundry income (4)	162	Motor vehicle cost (3)	1,575
Cash (5)	620		
Capital (6)	500		
	3,032		3,032

2 Adjustments to profit

The correction journal may result in a change in profit, depending on whether the journal debits or credits the income statement:

Dr Statement of financial position account Cr Statement of financial position account	No impact on profit
Dr Income statement account Cr Income statement account	No impact on profit
Dr Income statement account Cr Statement of financial position account	Profit decreases
Dr Statement of financial position account Cr Income statement account	Profit increases

For this purpose the suspense account is defined as a statement of financial position account.

Test your understanding 4

The following correction journals have been posted by Boris Brokovitch, a self-employed plumber:

(1) Dr Suspense $4,000

   Cr Rent $4,000

(2) Dr Payables $2,500

   Cr Suspense $2,500

(3) Dr Loan interest $1,000

      Cr Loan $1,000

(4) Dr Suspense $650

      Cr Sundry income $650

(5) Dr Suspense $6,000

      Cr Cash $6,000

Boris' draft profit figure prior to the posting of these journals is $355,000.

What is the revised profit figure?

A $354,000
B $358,650
C $356,150
D $358,000

What affect will these correction journals have on the Statement of financial position?

3 Statement of comprehensive income

Your correction journals may also affect the Statement of comprehensive income. (this is covered in detail in chapter 17).

The only correction journals which would affect this would be revaluation journals.

Chapter summary

```
                          ┌─────────────────┐
                          │     ERRORS      │
                          └─────────────────┘
```

Errors where the trial balance still balances

- Error of omission
- Error of commission
- Error of principle
- Compensating error
- Error of original entry
- Reversal of entries.

Errors where the trial balance does not balance

- Single-sided entry
- Debit ≠ credit
- Same side entries
- Casting error in one account
- Opening balance not brought down
- Extraction error.

SUSPENSE ACCOUNT USED TO MAKE THE TB BALANCE

CORRECTION JOURNALS
CORRECT THE ERRORS AND REMOVE ANY SUSPENSE ACCOUNT

Impact of correction journals on profit:

Dr Income statement	
Cr Income statement	No impact on profit
Dr Statement of financial position	
Cr Statement of financial position	No impact on profit
Dr Income statement	
Cr Statement of financial position	Profit decreases
Dr Statement of financial position	
Cr Income statement	Profit increases

(the suspense account is a balance sheet account).

Test your understanding answers

Test your understanding 1

	What was the double entry?	What should the double entry have been?	Correcting journal
1)		Dr cash $100 Cr sales $100	Dr cash $100 Cr sales $100 to record both sides of the sale correctly
2)	Dr rent $500 Cr cash $500	Dr rates $500 Cr cash $500	Dr rates $500 to record the rates expense correctly Cr rent $500 to reverse the incorrect debit to the rent account
3)	Dr repairs $1,000 Cr payables $1,000	Dr NC asset $1,000 Cr payables $1,000	DR NC asset $1,000 to record the asset correctly Cr repairs $1,000 to reverse the incorrect debit to the repairs account
4)	Dr rent $1,400 Cr cash $1,200	Dr rent $1,200 Cr cash $1,200	Cr rent $200 to reverse the extra £200 debited to the rent account Dr sales $200 to correct the casting error
5)	Dr cash $67 Cr sales $67	Dr cash $76 Cr sales $76	Dr cash $9 Cr sales $9 to record the extra $9 sales not previously recorded
6)	Dr sales $200 Cr cash $200	Dr cash $200 Cr sales $200	Dr cash $400 Cr sales $400 to firstly reverse the error of $200 and then record the sale of $200 correctly in noth accounts

Test your understanding 2

The correct answer is D

A and C would result in the credit side of the TB being $1,200 higher than the debit side.

B would have no effect on the TB since neither the debit nor the credit side of the transaction has been accounted for.

Test your understanding 3

The correct answer is B

An entry to the suspense account is required wherever an account is missing from the trial balance or the initial incorrect entry did not include an equal debit and credit.

Test your understanding 4

Income statement profits

The correct answer is B.

	Increase $	Decrease $	$
Draft profit			355,000
1 Rent	4,000		
2 No impact			
3 Loan interest		1,000	
4 Sundry income	650	——	
	——		
5 No impact			
			3,650
			——
Revised profit			358,650

Statement of financial position

Journal 1.

The Dr entry would go towards clearing any suspense a/c balance.

Journal 2.

The Dr payables would decrease the current liabilities. The Cr suspense a/c would go towards clearing the account balance.

Journal 3.

The Cr loan would increase the loan liability balance. It does not state whether it is current or non-current.

Journal 4.

The Dr suspense a/c would work towards clearing any balance left.

Journal 5.

Dr suspense a/c would completely clear the balance in this account. The Cr cash would decrease the cash balance held, which is a current asset.

Applications of information technology

Chapter learning objectives

Upon completion of this chapter you will be able to:

- outline the form of accounting records in a typical computerised system

- compare manual and computerised accounting systems

- identify the advantages and disadvantages of computerised systems

- explain the use of integrated accounting packages

- explain the nature and use of microcomputers

- describe the main elements of a computerised accounting system

- describe typical data processing work

- explain other business uses of computers

- explain the nature and purpose of spreadsheets

- explain the nature and purpose of database systems.

1 Manual accounting systems

A typical **manual system** consists of the following:

- separate **books of original entry**, which are the original accounting records of a business and are not part of the double entry

- **general ledger**, a book within which there is a page for each ledger account in the double entry system

- further ledgers, the main ones being the **accounts receivable ledger**, the **accounts payable ledger** and the **cash book.**

Expandable text

Often these records are in the form of books but they are equally likely to be in some other form. For example, an accounts receivable ledger may be a collection of individual cards with one or more cards for each customer. The advantage of cards lies in the ability to insert additional cards for customers with many transactions or cards for new customers, and still retain the alphabetical order of customers.

KAPLAN PUBLISHING

Often the subsidiary ledgers may not be laid out as ledger accounts but as running totals of amounts owing. For example:

Sales ledger
Customer: J Bloggs

Date	Dr $	Cr $	Balance $
1 Mar Brought forward			3,978.45
19 Mar Invoice 2354	1,549.00		5,527.45
23 Mar Cash receipt book		3,978.45	1,549.00

Whatever the format, the reasons for the types of records and the double entry principles remain the same no matter how the system is displayed.

2 Computerised accounting systems

Computerised accounting systems can vary in the form they take. They may be:

- completely computerised
- partially computerised.

Expandable text

A fully computerised system will operate under the same principles as a manual system except that all the records will be stored in one place, i.e. the hard disk of the computer. This does not necessarily mean that all accounting personnel have access to all records. The system will be broken down into sections in the same way as the manual system.

Another difference in a computerised system may be that when the data is printed out, the form of that information may look very different from a manual system, particularly with regard to the general ledger.

Whereas in a manual system the general ledger is a collection of 'T' accounts, the general ledger on a computer system will probably appear as an arithmetical listing of debits and credits. This does not mean, however, that the system is not performing double entry; it is.

3 Manual versus computerised accounting systems

Advantages of computers in a modern business environment include:

- speed
- stored program
- decision making
- file storage and processing
- accuracy and reliability.

Expandable text

The advantages of computerisation include:

(1) Speed. The computer is very fast – much faster than a clerk or any office machine. This speed can be of value to the business in two ways:

- High volumes of work can be handled by a computer.
- Rapid turnaround and response can be achieved.

Thus, one company might value a computer primarily for its ability to cope with large numbers of orders; another might be more interested in speeding up its order processing.

(2) Stored program. Once the programs have been written and tested, the computer can perform vast amounts of work with minimum labour costs. Only small teams of operators are needed for the largest machines. This is possible because the computer runs under the control of its stored program, and operator activity is limited to loading and unloading peripherals and indicating what work is to be done.

(3) Decision making. The computer can be programmed to undertake complicated decision-making processes. It can handle work to a much higher degree of complexity than other office machines – and the manager.

(4) File storage and processing. Large files of data can be stored on magnetic media which require very little space. More importantly, files thus stored can be reviewed and updated at high speeds, and information can be retrieved from them very quickly.

(5) Accuracy and reliability. The computer is very accurate (provided that its programs are free from faults) and generally reliable.

KAPLAN PUBLISHING

Disadvantages of computers in a modern business environment include:

- lack of intelligence
- quantifiable decisions
- initial costs
- inflexibility
- vulnerability.

Expandable text

Disadvantages of computers

(1) Lack of intelligence. The computer is a machine. It cannot recognise errors made in its program, or notice that data is incomplete or incorrect. Errors that would be detected by clerks in a manual system may go unnoticed in a computer-based system. It is therefore necessary to devote the utmost care to the development of computer-based systems, to foresee every contingency and to test every instruction. Thus, system development is often both prolonged and costly.

(2) Quantifiable decisions. The program can only take decisions that can be quantified, e.g. that can be expressed as two numbers or amounts that can be compared with each other. It cannot make value judgements of the type involved in, for example, selecting personnel, or deciding whether to take legal action if debts are overdue. The solution indicated by the program may have to be modified because of intangible factors known to the manager but incapable of being expressed in the program.

(3) Initial costs. Initial costs, e.g. hardware, software, site preparation and training, tend to be high. Note that nowadays software costs often exceed hardware costs.

(4) Inflexibility. Because of the care and attention to detail needed in systems and program development and maintenance, computer systems tend to be inflexible. They take longer and cost more to alter than manual systems.

(5) Vulnerability. The more work an organisation transfers to a computer, the greater is its dependence on a single resource. If the machine breaks down or is damaged, or if computer staff take industrial action, many systems may be brought to a halt.

4 Integrated accounting packages

The usual pattern for financial accounting has been for computerisation on a piecemeal basis, tackling the aspects involving most work first, e.g.:

- accounts receivable ledger
- accounts payable ledger
- payroll.

A number of integrated accounting packages exist which handle all parts of the process and ultimately produce the financial statements. Each package varies, but the broad groups are:

- cash book systems
- basic bookkeeping systems, and
- bookkeeping and accounting systems.

Expandable text

Cash book systems

This system emulates a manual cash book. Such a system might be suitable for a small business which does not sell on credit and which either (i) provides a service or (ii) buys its inventory for cash or on credit from a small number of suppliers.

Basic bookkeeping systems

These might be suitable for the smaller business selling mainly on a cash basis, requiring basic bookkeeping. Such a system will normally offer basic facilities for maintaining an accounts receivable ledger, an accounts payable ledger and a general ledger. There should be facilities for automatically producing a full printout of transactions and perhaps bank reconciliation statements. The package will also generate trial balances, income statements and statement of financial position.

Bookkeeping and accountancy systems

In addition to offering the basic facilities described above, these packages can cope with a greater number of customer and supplier accounts and offer more sophisticated credit control facilities. They can generate invoices, print out customers' statements and produce ageing schedules of receivables. They may be able to produce standard letters automatically to send to customers whose accounts are overdue or who have exceeded their agreed credit limit.

Within this group the more advanced packages may incorporate inventory control facilities. Separate records are maintained for each inventory item recording units purchased and sold and the balance of inventory in hand.

5 Microcomputer packages

Most microcomputer accounting packages are used by people who are not computer programmers or systems analysts.

The users of such systems are normally accountants and their accounting staff.

To run an accounting package, the user will normally have the program on a hard disk. Data may be on separate disks or discs. The program will probably operate on a 'menu system', i.e. the user will select the required options from a list of choices (the menu).

A typical initial menu would include the following options:

(1) create new accounts

(2) edit account data

(3) post transactions

(4) create report layouts

(5) print reports

(6) quit.

Expandable text

To select an option, the user will key in the appropriate number. For example, to create new accounts, number one would be keyed in.

Each of these options would involve another sub-menu.

The initial setup of a computerised accounting system is similar to a manual system, i.e. accounts receivable and payable ledgers and general ledger are set up and account codes allocated for each individual account.

In the majority of cases, the bank account is contained within the general ledger.

- sales invoices
- credit notes (re sales)
- purchase invoices

- credit notes (re purchases)
- receipts
- payments
- journals.

To post to the ledger, the user would batch up the appropriate source documents – for example, sales invoices, and compute the batch total.

The user would then select the 'Post to ledger' option from the appropriate sub-menu and key in the following data for each sales invoice:

- customer account code
- date
- invoice number
- description
- total value of goods sold.

Provided valid code numbers are used and the totals agree, the posting will be accepted; similarly, the batch total will need to be verified before the program will actually post the transactions to the ledgers. An additional security measure is that of passwords, e.g. the user would have to know the appropriate password to load the system in the first place and possibly different passwords for each ledger.

Expandable text

Entering the text

Text is typed into the word processor using a keyboard, with the text visible on a VDU. Each 'document' is assigned a reference so that it can be stored and subsequently retrieved. As the text is typed in, it appears on the VDU to enable the 'typist' to check visually that there are no typing errors. Any errors can be corrected by moving the cursor to the error and overtyping.

The way the text appears on the screen is not necessarily how the final document will appear.

Storing the text

After the text has been typed in, it is stored on disk (or disc) under its unique reference number. Once the text has been stored, a hard copy of the text can be printed to be reviewed by the author for errors or subsequent amendments.

Retrieving the text

If for any reason amendments need to be made to any stored text, it is retrieved from store into the main memory of the word processor and displayed on the VDU. Retrieval is by means of the unique reference assigned to the text when it was first entered.

Editing the text

This is the stage where the text is made ready for printing. There are two aspects. First, any errors are corrected and any amendments made. Amendments may include changing the order of paragraphs, adding and deleting whole, or parts of, paragraphs. This is known as editing.

The second aspect is text formatting. This means arranging the text exactly as the author wishes it to appear. What size of paper (e.g. A4, A5) or special form (like a polling card) is to be used? How wide should the margins be, what line spacing, etc.?

All the instructions for editing and formatting are keyed in using the VDU. All word processors enable 'on screen' editing – i.e. you can see the results of the amendments on the VDU; many enable 'on screen' formatting (WYSIWYG – 'what you see is what you get').

Printing the text

After all amendments have been made, the text is put back into store in its final form. A copy is printed to enable the author to ensure that his instructions have been carried out. Provided that the author is satisfied with the finished product it can then be sent to its intended recipient.

6 Database systems

A **database** is a collection of information that can be used for many different purposes, and by a number of business applications.

For example supplier database contains the data relating to suppliers, and may use headings (fields) such as:

- supplier name
- supplier code
- supplier address.

The advantages of a database over a manual card index system would include:

- The amount of information held in each record/field can be much larger than a card index.
- Calculations can be performed automatically, e.g. return on capital employed.
- Records may be sorted, or those matching a certain criterion selected, automatically, and in a variety of orders.
- Reports based on the information may be prepared and printed.

Expandable text

Database design

There are various ways of designing database systems so as to link the data together:

- A flat file database is a single file database. All records in this type of database are of a standard format. Data can be stored, accessed, sorted and updated.
- A relational database is one where files can be linked together and data can be accessed from any file.

A programmable database is one with its own programming language which enables the database to be tailored to individual needs.

Database systems will continue to be a major area of expansion of computer applications in the future.

Database management system

The software that runs the database is known as the database management system. The database management system organises the data input into the database and allows various application programs to use the database.

Chapter summary

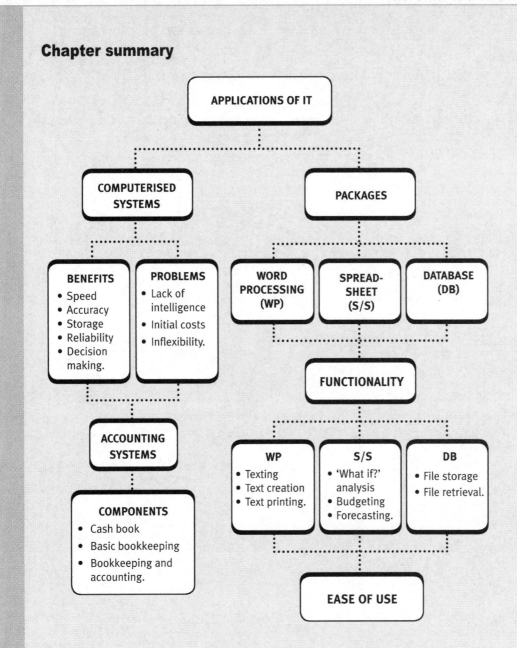

15

Incomplete records

Chapter learning objectives

Upon completion of this chapter you will be able to:

- explain and illustrate the calculation of profit or loss as the difference between opening and closing net assets

- explain techniques used in incomplete record situations:
  - calculation of opening capital
  - use of ledger total accounts to calculate missing figures.
  - use of cash and/or bank summaries
  - use of given gross profit percentage to calculate missing figures.

1 Incomplete records

When you are preparing a set of accounts, it is likely that you may not have all of the information available to you to complete a set of financial statements.

It is likely that you may have an incomplete ledger or control accounts system.

If this is the case, you will have to use the best information that it available to you and 'guestimate' any missing figures.

There are a number of different ways which we can use to calculate missing figures and balances, such as:

- Accounting equation method

- Opening capital calculations

- Balancing figure approach

- Ratios - mark up and margin

- Lost inventory methods

2 Identification of profit figure using the accounting equation

If a business has recorded very little information of its transactions it may only be possible to calculate net profit for the year. This can be done using the accounting equation as follows:

Net assets = Capital + Profit – Drawings

Therefore:

Change in net assets = Capital introduced + Profit for the period – Drawings for the period.

NB: Net assets = Assets – Liabilities

Test your understanding 1

Andy Carp's statement of financial position at 31 December 2004 shows that his fishing business has net assets of $5,000. The statement of financial position as at 31 December 20X5 shows that the business has net assets of $8,000. Andy's drawings for the year amounted to $2,500 and he didn't introduce any further capital in that year.

What profit is made by Andy Carp in the year ended 31 December 2005?

(a) $5,500

(b) $500

(c) $10,500

(d) $7,500

NB: Net assets = Assets – Liabilities

3 Identification of individual account balances within financial statements

- In most cases a business will keep limited accounting records from which it is possible to prepare a full set of financial statements. You may be asked to calculate any of the balances within these financial statements.

- In these types of questions the opening asset and liability balances will be given together with details of transactions during the year.

- Opening capital can be calculated as:

Opening assets – Opening liabilities

- Two further methods may be used to identify other missing figures:

    (1) Use of ledger accounts to find a balancing figure

    (2) Use of ratios.

4 The balancing figure approach

The balancing figure approach, using ledger accounts, is commonly used in the following way:

Ledger account	Missing figure
Receivables	Credit sales, Money received from receivables
Payables	Credit purchases, Money paid to payables
Cash at bank	Drawings, Money stolen
Cash in hand	Cash sales, Cash stolen

Cash at bank

	$		$
Cash received from customers	X	Cash paid to suppliers	X
Bankings from cash in hand	X	Expenses	X
Sundry income	X	Drawings	X
		Money stolen	X
	—	Balance c/f	X
	X		—
Balance b/f	—		X

Cash in hand

	$		$
Cash sales	X	Cash purchases	X
Sundry income	X	Sundry Expenses	X
	—	Bankings	X
	X	Money stolen	X
		Balance c/f	X
			—
Balance b/f			X

In the case of receivables and payables, you may need to use total receivables and total payables accounts where information given cannot be split between cash and credit sales and purchases:

Total receivables

	$		$
Balance b/f	X	Total cash received	X
Total sales	X	in respect of sales	
(cash and credit)	—	(from cash and credit customers)	
		Balance c/f	X
	—		—
Balance b/f	X		X

Total payables

	$		$
		Balance b/f	
Total cash paid in	X	Total purchases	X
respect of purchases		(cash and credit)	
(cash purchases and payments to credit suppliers)	—		—
Balance c/f	X		X
	—		—
		Balance b/f	

Test your understanding 2

Suppose that opening receivables for B Rubble's business are $30,000. There have been total receipts from customers of $55,000 of which $15,000 relates to cash sales and $40,000 relates to receipts from receivables. Discounts allowed in the year totalled $3,000 and closing receivables were $37,000.

What are total sales for the year?

(a) $65,000

(b) $50,000

(c) $47,000

(d) $62,000

Test your understanding 3

The opening payables of Dick Dastard-Lee's business are $15,000. Total payments made to suppliers during the year were $14,000. Discounts received were $500 and closing payables were $13,000.

What are total purchases for the year?

(a) $16,500

(b) $16,000

(c) $12,000

(d) $12,500

Questions may require you to calculate 'missing' income statement figures, for example rent and rates values, from a list of information including payments and opening/closing accruals and prepayments.

To calculate the missing value for each expense use either:

- T-accounts, or
- Equations

Test your understanding 4

The following information relates to Ivor Big-Head's business:

On 1 January	Electricity accrued	$250
	Rent prepaid	$300
Cash paid in the year	Electricity	$1,000
	Rent	$2,000
On 31 December	Electricity accrued	$300
	Rent prepaid	$400

What are the income statement charges for electricity and rent for the year?

> Electricity Rent
>
> $ $

(a) 1,050 2,100

(b) 1,050 1,900

(c) 950   1,900

(d) 950   2,100

Test your understanding 5

On 1 January Elma Fudd's bank account is overdrawn by $1,367. Payments in the year totalled $8,536 and on 31 December the closing balance is $2,227 (positive).

What are total receipts for the year?

(a) $4,942

(b) $7,676

(c) $9,396

(d) $12,130

Test your understanding 6

On 1 January, Daisee Chain's business had a cash float of $900. During the year cash of $10,000 was banked, $1,000 was paid out as drawings and wages of $2,000 were paid. On 31 December the float was $1,000.

How much cash was received from customers for the year?

(a) $12,900

(b) $14,900

(c) $13,100

(d) $6,900

5 Ratios – mark up and margin

Gross profit can be expressed as a percentage of either sales or cost of sales:

GROSS PROFIT MARGIN

$$= \frac{\text{Gross profit}}{\text{Sales}} \times 100$$

Therefore

Gross profit = margin x sales

MARK-UP

$$= \frac{\text{Gross profit}}{\text{Cost of sales}} \times 100$$

Therefore

Gross profit = mark-up x sales

E.g.

Sales $5,000

Cost of sales ($4,000)

Gross profit $1,000

- Gross profit margin = (1,000/5,000) x 100 = 20%
- Mark up = (1,000/4,000) x 100 = 25%

Test your understanding 7

Padraig O'Flaherty has sales of $1,000. He makes a margin of 25%.

What is the cost of sales figure?

(a) $200

(b) $800

(c) $750

(d) $250

KAPLAN PUBLISHING

Test your understanding 8

Ratios

Lorna McDuff has cost of sales of $600 and a 25% mark up.

What is her sales figure?

(a) $750

(b) $800

(c) $250

(d) $200

Using margin and mark up

An exam question will often provide you with margin and cost of sales or mark up and sales. You will then be required to calculate the remaining figures in the income statement. This can be done using the following 'relationship' columns:

Margin 25%			Mark up 25%		
Sales	2	100%	Sales 3	3	Logic!
Cost of sales	3	Logic!	Cost of sales	2	100%
Gross profit	1	Ratio	Gross profit	1	Ratio

Therefore, if we know the mark up or margin percentage and one of the figures in the income statement, we can calculate the remaining figures in the income statement.

Test your understanding 9

Jethro Longhorn can tell you the following with regard to his business:

Margin 5%

Opening inventory $800

Closing inventory $600

Purchases $2,840

Complete Jethro's income statement with the above figures.

6 Cost of lost inventory

- In incomplete record questions, inventory may have been lost – probably due to a fire or flood.

- Closing inventory that has not been lost is subtracted from cost of sales because by definition, the inventory has not been sold in the year.

- Lost inventory has not been sold in the year and therefore also needs subtracting within cost of sales.

- Therefore, to work out the cost of lost inventory, complete the trading account from the information given and then lost inventory can be calculated as a balancing figure.

Test your understanding 10

Jack Spratt provides the following information about his business:

Margin	20%
Sales	$100,000
Opening inventory	$10,000
Purchases	$82,000
Closing inventory after fire	$3,000

What is the cost of inventory lost in the fire?

(a) $12,000

(b) $9,000

(c) $69,000

(d) $5,667

Double entries for inventory and lost inventory

Actual closing inventory is posted by:

Dr Inventory (SFP)   X

Cr Income statement X

Lost inventory will still be credited to the income statement so that it is removed from cost of sales. However, the debit side of the entry will depend on whether or not the lost inventory has been insured:

If insured: Dr Insurance company (Current asset)

                 Cr Income statement   (Cost of sales)

If not insured: Dr Income statement   (Expense)

                 Cr Income statement   (Cost of sales)

Test your understanding 11

Fred lost his entire inventory in a fire. His unsigned insurance policy is still in the pocket of his good suit. Fred has supplied you with the following information:

Mark up 25%

Sales $10,000

Opening inventory $2,000

Purchases $7,500

Prepare Fred's income statement and show the journal to record closing inventory.

7 Reconstruction of full financial statements

Although you will not face an exam question of this length, the following illustration will help you to see how a full set of financial statements can be reconstructed using the methods within this chapter.

Illustration 1-Reconstruction of full financial statements

Malcolm is a retailer, selling stationery. He does not keep a full set of records. The following records have been extracted from his books.

	30 September 2004	30 September 2005
	$	$
Fixtures and fittings: Cost	20,000	To be determined
Accumulated depreciation	8,000	To be determined
Motor vehicles: Cost	22,000	To be determined
Accumulated depreciation	4,180	To be determined
Inventory	18,000	33,900
Receivables	10,000	12,000
Allowances for receivables	500	To be determined
Prepayments – Rates	400	450
Bank	2,000	(15,500)
Cash	600	600
Payables	4,000	4,600
Accruals – Light and heat	250	300

He also has the following cash and bank transactions for the year ended 30 September 2005.

	Cash $	Bank $
Balance b/f	600	2,000
Receipts:		
Cash sales	15,000	
From receivables		140,000
Loan received (long-term)		30,000
Sale proceeds of a motor vehicle sold during the year		8,200
Cash banked		15,000
	15,600	195,200
Payments:		
Payables		110,000
Rates		9,000
Light and heat		2,000
Telephone		1,500
Loan interest		1,500
Insurance		1,000
Rent		20,000
Wages and salaries		25,000
Withdrawals		15,000
Purchase of fixtures		5,000
Purchase of new motor vehicle		20,000
Sundry expenses		700
Cash paid into bank	15,000	
Balance c/f	600	(15,500)

The following further information is available:

(1) The loan was received at the beginning of the year and is entitled to 5% interest pa.

(2) The motor vehicle disposed of during the year had cost $10,000 and the accumulated depreciation on it as at 30 September 2004 was $1,900.

(3) Discount received during the year amounted to $500.

(4) Goods amounting to $1,000 at cost were withdrawn by Malcolm during the year.

(5) The depreciation policy is as follows:

    (a) Fixtures and fittings, 20% pa on a straight-line basis.

    (b) Motor vehicles, 10% pa on a reducing-balance basis.

(6) The allowance for receivables is to be provided at 5% pa on the closing receivables.

    (a) Prepare Malcolm's income statement for the year ended 30 September 2005.

    (b) Prepare Malcolm's statement of financial position as at 30 September 2005.

KAPLAN PUBLISHING

Expandable text

Solution

(a) Malcolm's income statement for the year ended 30 September 2005

	$	$
Sales: Cash		15,000
– Credit (W1)		142,000
		———
		157,000
Less: Cost of sales		
Opening Inventory	18,000	
Purchases (W2)	111,100	
Goods withdrawn	(1,000)	
	———	
	128,100	
Less: Closing inventory	(33,900)	
	———	
		(94,200)
		———
Gross profit		62,800
Add: Discount received	500	
Profit on sale of motor vehicle (W3)	100	
	——	
		600
		———
		63,400
Less: Increase in allowances for receivables (W4)	(100)	
Rates (9,000 + 400 – 450)	(8,950)	
Light and heat (2,000 + 300 – 250)	(2,050)	
Telephone	(1,500)	
Loan interest	(1,500)	
Insurance	(1,000)	
Rent	(20,000)	
Wages and salaries	(25,000)	

	$	$
Depreciation:		
Motor vehicles (W6)	(2,972)	
Fixtures and fittings (W5)	(5,000)	
Sundry expenses	(700)	
		(68,772)
Net loss		(5,372)

(b) Malcolm's statement of financial position as at 30 September 2005

	Cost	Accumulated depreciation	Net book value (NBV)
	$	$	$
Non-current assets: Fixtures and fittings(W5)	25,000	(13,000)	12,000
Motor vehicles (W6)	32,000	(5,252)	26,748
	57,000	18,252)	38,748
Current assets			
Inventory		33,900	
Receivables	12,000		
Less: Allowances for receivables	(600)		
		11,400	
Rates prepaid		450	
Cash		600	
			46,350
			85,098
Capital (W7)			56,070
Less: Net loss			(5,372)
			50,698
Less: Drawings (W8)			(16,000)
			34,698

Non-current liabilities		
Loan		30,000
Current liabilities		
Payables	4,600	
Lighting and heating accrued	300	
Bank overdraft	15,500	
		20,400
		85,098

(W1)

Receivables

	$		$
Balance b/f	10,000	Bank	140,000
Credit sales (derived)	142,000	Balance c/f	12,000
	152,000		152,000

(W2)

Payables

	$		$
Discount received	500	Balance b/f	4,000
Bank	110,000	Credit purchases (derived)	111,100
Balance c/f	4,600		
	115,100		115,100

(W3)

	$	$
Disposal proceeds		8,200
Less: Net book value:		
Cost	10,000	
Accumulated depreciation	(1,900)	
	————	
		8,100
Profit on disposal		————
		100
		————

(W4) Allowances for receivables

	$
– Required (5% x $12,000)	600
– B/f	(500)
Increase in allowance	100
	————

(W5) Fixtures and fittings

	Cost	Accumulated depreciation	NBV
	$	$	$
Balance b/f	20,000	(8,000)	12,000
Additions	5,000	–	5,000
	————	————	————
	25,000	(8,000)	17,000
Charge for the year:			
20% x $25,000		(5,000)	(5,000)
		————	————
		(13,000)	12,000
	25,000		
	————		

KAPLAN PUBLISHING

(W6) Motor vehicles

	Cost	Accumulated depreciation	NBV
	$	$	$
Balance b/f	22,000	(4,180)	17,820
Disposals	(10,000)	1,900	(8,100)
	12,000	(2,280)	9,720
Additions	20,000		20,000
	32,000	(2,280)	29,720
Charge for the year:			
10% x $29,720		(2,972)	(2,972)
Balance c/f	32,000	(5,252)	26,748

(W7) Capital as at 30 September 2004

	$	$
Fixtures and fittings ($20,000 – 8,000)		12,000
Motor vehicles ($22,000 – 4,180)		17,820
Motor vehicles ($22,000 – 4,180)		17,820
Inventory		18,000
Receivables ($10,000 – 500)		9,500
Rates prepaid		400
Bank		2,000
Cash		600
		60,320
Payables	4,000	
Light and heat accrued	250	
		(4,250)
		56,070

(W8) Drawings

	$
Bank	15,000

Chapter summary

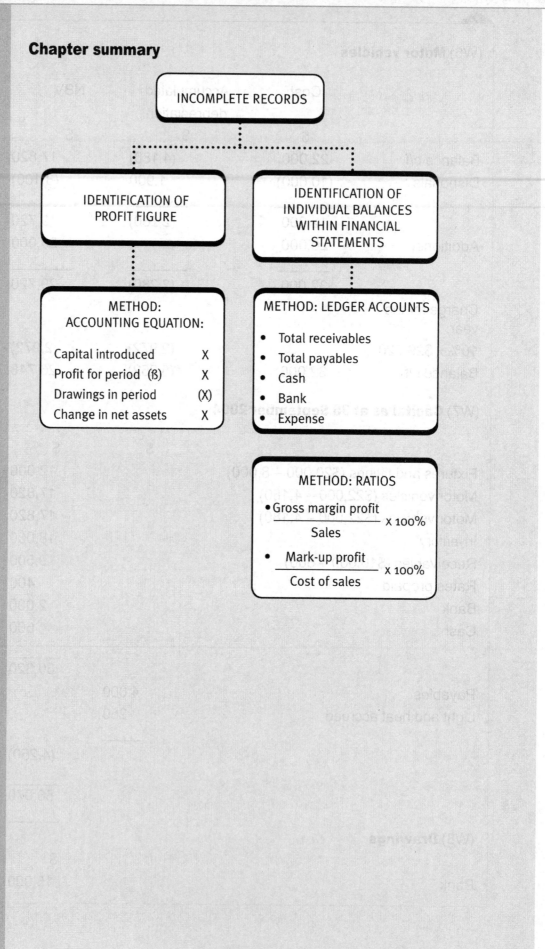

Test your understanding answers

Test your understanding 1

The correct answer is A

Change in net assets = Capital introduced + Profit for the year-
Drawings for the year

$8,000 – $5,000 = 0 + Profit for the year – $2,500

Profit = $3,000 + $ 2,500

= $5,500

Test your understanding 2

The correct answer is A

Receivables

	$		$
Balance b/f	30,000	Bank	40,000
Credit sales (ß)	50,000	Discount allowed	3,000
		Balance c/f	37,000
	80,000		80,000
Balance b/f	37,000		

Receivables

Total sales = $50,000 + $15,000 = $65,000

OR

Total receivables

	$		$
Balance b/f	30,000	Bank (total cash rec'd)	55,000
Total sales (ß)	65,000	Discount allowed	3,000
		Balance c/f	37,000
	95,000		95,000

Test your understanding 3

The correct answer is D

Total payables

	$		$
Bank	14,000	Balance b/f	15,000
Discount received	500	Purchases (ß)	12,500
Balance c/f	13,000		
	27,500		27,500
		Balance b/f	13,000

Test your understanding 4

The correct answer is B

Income statement (extracts):

Expenses

Electricity(-250 + 1,000 + 300)   = $1,050

Rent (300 + 2,000 – 400)   = $1,900

Test your understanding 5

The correct answer is D

Bank

	$		$
Receipts (ß)	12,130	Balance b/f	1,367
		Payments	8,536
		Balance c/f	2,227
	12,130		12,130
Balance b/f	2,227		

Test your understanding 6

The correct answer is C

Cash in till

	$		$
Balance b/f	900	Bank	10,000
Receipts	13,100	Drawings	1,000
		Wages	2,000
		Balance c/f	1,000
	14,000		14,000
Balance c/f	1,000		

Test your understanding 7

The correct answer is C

Gross profit: $1,000 x 25% = $250
Cost of sales:

	$
Sales	1,000
Cost of sales (ß)	(750)
Gross profit	250

Test your understanding 8

The correct answer is A

Gross profit: $ 600 x 25% = $150

Sales:

	$
Sales (ß)	750
Cost of sales	(600)
Gross profit	150

Test your understanding 9

	$	$	%
Sales:		3,200	100
Cost of sales:	800		
Opening inventory	2,840		
Purchases	(600)		
		(3,040)	(95)
Gross profit:		160	5

Test your understanding 10

The correct answer is B

	$	$	%
Sales:		100,000	100
Cost of sales:			
Opening inventory	10,000		
Purchases	82,000		
Closing inventory	(3,000)		
Inventory lost (ß)	(9,000)		
		(80,000)	(80)
Gross profit:		20,000	20

Test your understanding 11

	$	$	%
Sales:		10,000	125
Cost of sales:			
Opening inventory	2,000		
Purchases	7,500		
Inventory lost (ß)	(1,500)		
		(8,000)	(100)
Gross profit:		2,000	25
Dr Income statement (expense):		1,500	
Cr Income statement (cost of sales):		1,500	

Being the recording of uninsured inventory destroyed by the fire.

Partnerships

Chapter learning objectives

Upon completion of this chapter you will be able to:

- define the circumstances creating a partnership

- explain the advantages and disadvantages of operating as a partnership compared with operating as a sole trader or limited liability company

- explain the typical contents of a partnership agreement, including profit-sharing terms

- explain the accounting differences between partnerships and sole traders:
  - capital accounts
  - current accounts
  - division of profits

- explain and illustrate how to record partners' shares of profits/losses and their drawings in the accounting records and financial statements

- explain and illustrate how to account for guaranteed minimum profit share

- explain how to account for loans from partners

- define goodwill in relation to partnership accounts

- identify the factors leading to the creation of goodwill in relation to partnership accounts

- calculate the value of goodwill from information given

- account for the effect of the admission of a new partner.

1 Definition of a partnership

- A partnership is 'the relationship which subsists amongst persons carrying on a business in common with a view of making profit'.

- Therefore a partnership is a business which has two or more joint owners.

- As in the case of a sole trader, the profits of the business are owed to the owners.

- It is therefore necessary to share the profits of the business amongst the partners.

Expandable text

A partnership is a natural progression from a sole trader, the sole proprietor taking in one or more partners (co-proprietors) in common with a view to profit. In many countries a partnership is not a corporate entity, but a collection of individuals jointly carrying on business.

2 Advantages and disadvantages of partnerships

SOLE TRADER   VERSUS   PARTNERSHIP   VERSUS   LIMITED LIABILITY COMPANY

Advantages of a partnership over a sole trader

- A partnership shares business risks between more than one person.

- Each partner can develop special skills upon which the other partners can rely, whereas a sole trader has responsibility for everything.

- Greater resources will be available since more individuals will be contributing to the business.

Disadvantages of a partnership

- There may be disputes in the running of the business.

- Partners are jointly and severally liable for their partners. Thus if one partner is being sued in relation to the business, all partners share the responsibility and potential liability.

Advantages of a partnership over a limited liability company

- The arrangement is less formal than setting up a company, which requires the issue of shares and the appointment of directors.

- If the partners wish to dissolve the business, this is easier to achieve by a partnership than by a company.

Disadvantage of a partnership

- The partners are not protected from the creditors of the business. Unless the partnership is set up as a limited liability partnership, partners have unlimited liability.

3 The partnership agreement

A partnership will usually have a partnership agreement which will state how the profits are to be shared ('appropriated') amongst the partners.

The division of profit stated in the agreement may be quite complex in order to reflect the expected differing efforts and contributions of the partners.

Salaries	May be awarded to partners who take on extra responsibility within the business.
Interest on capital	May be provided at a set percentage to reflect the differing amounts of capital invested.
Interest on drawings	To penalise those partners who take out more drawings from the business, the partnership may charge interest on drawings. Interest may be charged on all drawings or only those above a certain level This results in a reduction in the amount of profit that the partner is allocated
Profit share ratio (PSR)	This is the ratio in which any remaining profits should be shared amongst the partners after they have been allocated salaries, interest on capital and interest on drawings.

It is important to appreciate that the above suggestions are means of dividing the profits of the partnership and are not expenses of the business. **A partnership salary is merely a device for calculating the division of profit; it is not a salary in the normal meaning of the term.**

Expandable text

A partnership agreement, which need not necessarily be in written form, will govern the relationship amongst the partners. Important matters to be covered include:

- name of firm, the type of business, and duration

- capital to be introduced by partners

- distribution of profits amongst partners

- drawings by partners

- arrangements for dissolution, or on the death or retirement of partners

- settling of disputes

- preparation and audit of accounts.

In the absence of a partnership agreement in the UK, the Partnership Act 1890 states that profits should be shared as follows:

- No partner should receive a salary.

- No interest on capital should be allowed.

- Profits should be shared equally between the partners.

- Where a partner advances funds in excess of the agreed capital amount (possibly as a loan), they are entitled to interest on the excess at 5 % pa.

Other countries will have their own rules in place.

4 Financial statements for a partnership

- The **income statement** for a partnership is exactly the same as that for a sole trader.

- An extra statement is required in which the profit from the income statement is shared between the partners. This is referred to as a **statement of division of profit** or **appropriation account**:

	Partner A	Partner B	Total
Salaries	$	$	$
Interest on capital	X		X
Interest on drawings	X	X	X
Profit share ratio 3:2		(X)	(X)
	X	X	ß
	___	___	___
Total profit share	X	X	
Net profit from income statement			X

- The profit from a partnership does not belong to just one individual (like a soletrader), so must be appropriated (as shown above) at the end of the financial year.

- The profits allocated to each partner are credited to the partners' **current account**. Drawings are also recorded in this account.

Current account

	Ptnr A	Ptnr B		Ptnr A	Ptnr B
			Balance b/f	X	X
Drawings	X	X	Profit share (from profit appropriation account)	X	X
Balance c/f	X	X		——	——
	X	X		X	X

The partners' **capital account** records the initial capital invested in the business by each partner. Transactions in this account are rare, being the injection of further capital or withdrawal of capital by a partner:

Capital account

	Ptnr A	Ptnr B		Ptnr A	Ptnr B
			Balance b/f	X	X
Withdrawals of long-term capital	X	X	Injection of long-term capital	X	X
Balance c/f	X	X			
	X	X		X	X
				——	——
			Balance b/f	X	X

- The closing balances on the partners' **current** and **capital accounts** form the capital section of the statement of financial position:

		$	$
Capital accounts	Partner A		
	Partner B	X	
		X	
		———	
			X
Current accounts	Partner A	X	
	Partner B	X	
		———	
			X
			X

- The remainder of the statement of financial position(assets and liabilities) is as for a sole trader.

Expandable text

Capital accounts

At the commencement of the partnership, an agreement will have to be reached as to the amount of capital to be introduced. This could be in the form of cash or other assets. Whatever the form of assets introduced and debited to asset accounts, it is normal to make the credit entry to fixed capital accounts. These are so called because they are not then used to record drawings or shares of profits but only major changes in the relations between partners. In particular, fixed capital accounts are used to deal with:

- capital introduced or withdrawn by new or retiring partners
- revaluation adjustments.

The balances on fixed capital accounts do not necessarily bear any relation to the division of profits. However, to compensate partners who provide a larger share of the capital, it is common for interest to be paid on capital accounts.

This is dealt with in the calculations for the profit shares transferred from the income statement.

Current accounts

Current accounts are used to deal with the regular transactions between the partners and the firm, i.e. matters other than those sufficiently fundamental to be dealt with through the capital accounts. Most commonly these are:

- share of profits, interest on capital and partners' salaries, usually computed annually

- monthly drawings against the annual share of profit.

Both accounts are presented in a columnar format. This is convenient for examination purposes and is quite common in a partnership set of books as each partner will have similar transactions during the year. A columnar format allows two (or more) separate accounts to be shown using the same narrative. It is important to remember that each partner's account is separate from that (those) of the other partner(s).

Statement of financial position presentation

One of the main differences between the capital section of the statement of financial position of a sole trader and a partnership is that the partnership statement of financial position will often give only the closing balances whereas the sole trader's movements in capital are shown. The main reason for the difference is simply one of space.

Movements in the capital and current accounts for a few partners cannot be easily accommodated on the face of the statement of financial position.

Illustration 1– Profit allocation

Parvati and Lavender run a business selling home-made potions and lotions. They have been very successful in their first year of trading and have made a profit of $48,000.

Their partnership agreement makes the following provisions:

- Parvati is to be allocated a salary of $11,000 to reflect her extensive potion knowledge.

- Interest on capital is to be provided at 7% per annum.

- The balance of profits is to be split equally.

When they set the business up, Parvati injected capital of $8,000 and Lavender $12,000.

How much profit is allocated to Lavender?

A $18,360

B $24,140

C $18,640

D $29,360

Expandable Text

The correct answer is C

	Parvati	Lavender	Total
	$	$	$
Salaries	11,000		11,000
Interest on capital	560	840	1,400
Profit share ratio 1:1	17,800	17,800	35,600 (ß)
Total profit share	29,360	18,640	
Net profit from income statement			48,000

Test your understanding 1

Britney, Justin and Cameron are in partnership selling CDs and DVDs via their website Bigstars.com. They haven't been very successful in the past year and in the year ended 30 June 20X6, recorded a loss of $120,000 Their partnership agreement states the following:

- interest on capital to be provided at 4% per annum
- Cameron to be allocated a salary of $25,000, and Justin $14,000
- no interest to be charged on drawings
- balance of profits to be shared in the ratio 4:3:1.

Capital balances at the start of the year stood as follows:

Britney $35,000

Justin $26,000

Cameron $40,000

How much profit or loss is allocated to Cameron?

A $6,220

B $36,220

C   ($34,540)

D $54,920)

Test your understanding 2

Hamish and Campbell started a business making and distributing haggis on 1 January 20X6. This was largely prompted by Hamish winning $40,000 at bingo just before Christmas. Hamish invested half his winnings in the business and Campbell borrowed $14,000 from his Uncle Hoolie to invest.

In the first year of trade, the business made $25,000 profit, with which both partners were rather pleased.

They have set up a partnership agreement, but even so are not sure how much profit they are each allocated. The agreement says the following:

- Neither partner receives a salary.

- Interest on capital is to be provided at 4%.

- Interest on drawings is to be charged at 2%.

- The balance of profit is to be split in the ratio 3:2.

Both Hamish and Campbell drew $5,000 from the business in the year, to pay for their annual fishing holiday in Spain.

Show how this information appears in the partners' capital and current accounts and in the statement of financial position.

5 Guaranteed minimum profit share

A partner may be guaranteed a minimum share of the profits.

If the partner has not received this guaranteed amount after allocating profits in the usual way, the shortfall should be given to the partner.

This amount is funded by the other partners in accordance with the profit share ratio.

KAPLAN PUBLISHING

Illustration 2– Profit allocations

A partnership, organising European holidays, has four partners – Pierre, Wolfgang, Edwin and Carmen. In the year to 30 June 20X5 the partnership made profits of $106,250.

Pierre invested $100,000 in the partnership. He withdrew $30,000 from the business on 1 July 20X4.

Wolfgang invested $20,000 in the partnership. He withdrew $30,000 on 30 June 20X5.

Edwin invested $50,000 into the business. He withdrew $25,000 on 1 July 2004 and a further $25,000 on 1 January 2005.

Carmen also invested $50,000 and withdrew $30,000 on 1 July 20X4.

Allocate the profits of the business in accordance with the following partnership agreement:

interest on capital at 5% pa

- Wolfgang to receive $5,000 salary
- interest on drawings at 10% pa
- profit share ratio 2:1:3:4
- guaranteed minimum profit share of $42,500 for Carmen.

Expandable Text

	P	W	E	C	Total
	$	$	$	$	$
Salaries		5,000			5,000
Interest on capital	5,000	1,000	2,500	2,500	11,000
Interest on drawings	(3,000)	–	(3,750)	(3,000)	(9,750)
Profit share	20,000	10,000	30,000	40,000	100,000
					(ß)
ratio 2:1:3:4					
	22,000	16,000	28,750	39,500	
Adjustment					3,000
Pierre 2/6 x $3,000	(1,000)				
Wolfgang 1/6 x $3,000		(500)			
Edwin 3/6 x $3,000			(1,500)		
	21,000	15,500	27,250	42,500	106,250

Working – interest on drawings

Pierre	$30,000 x 10%	$3,000
Wolfgang	No interest as drawings at year end	
Edwin	$25,000 x 10%	$2,500
	$25,000 x 10% x 6/12	$1,250
		$3,750
Carmen	$30,000 x 10%	$3,000

6 Loans from partners

- A partner may loan the business some money and may then receive interest on this loan.

- The double entry when the loan is made is:

Dr Cash   X

Cr Loan (liability) X

- The interest arising is treated as a business expense which is charged to profits before the profits are shared.

- The double entry for the loan interest is:

 Dr Loan interest expense X

 Cr Bank (if paid) or   X

 Current account (if outstanding)

7 Full partnership accounts

The following illustrates the process of drawing up a full set of financial statements for a partnership. Although you will not face a question as long as this in your examination, it is useful to understand how full partnership accounts are produced from the trial balance and other information.

Illustration 3– Full partnership accounts

Ken and Barbie are in partnership making and selling gourmet pies. The TB of their business at 30 June 20X6 was:

	Dr $	Cr $
Irrecoverable debts	2,350	
Rent and rates	35,000	
Motor expenses (including depreciation)	17,400	
Allowance for receivables		5,450
Motor vehicles – cost	32,750	
Motor vehicles – accumulated depreciation		15,578
Cash at bank	467	
Drawings – Ken	13,500	
Drawings – Barbie	15,000	
Inventory	3,000	
Fixtures and fittings – cost	27,000	
Fixtures and fittings – accumulated depreciation		13,500
Sundry expenses	14,780	
Sales		157,000
Payables		9,800
Receivables	16,000	
Purchases	96,000	
Current account – Ken		7,655
Current account – Barbie		9,264
Capital account – Ken		35,000
Capital account – Barbie		20,000
	273,247	273,247

They provide the following further information which is not reflected in the TB:

- Inventory held at the year end cost $4,500.

- Fixtures and fittings have not yet been depreciated – the applicable rate is 10% straight line.

- Prepayments at the year end were $2,500 in respect of rates.

- On the last day of the year, Ken paid $13,000 to the business bank account as a loan.

- Barbie is awarded a salary of $7,500.
- Interest on capital is provided at 8% per annum.
- The balance of profits is split equally.

You are required to prepare an income statement, statement of division of profits, partners' current accounts and a statement of financial position at 30 June 20X6

Expandable text

Income statement for Ken and Barbie Gourmet Pies for the year ended 30 June 20X6

	$	$
Revenue		157,000
Cost of sales:		
Opening inventory	3,000	
Purchases	96,000	
Closing inventory	(4,500)	
		(94,500)
Gross profit		62,500
Irrecoverable debts	2,350	
Rent and Rates (35,000 - 2,500)	32,500	
Motor expenses	17,400	
Sundry expenses	14,780	
Depreciation expense		
(fixtures and fittings: 10% x 27,000)	2,700	
		(69,730)
Net loss		(7,230)

Statement of financial position for Barbie and Ken Gourmet Pies at 30 June 20X6

	Cost $	Acc'd Dep'n $	NBV $
Non-current assets			
Motor vehicles	32,750	15,578	17,172
Fixtures and fittings (13,500 + 2,700)	27,000	16,200	10,800
			27,972
Current assets:			
Inventory		4,500	
Receivables (16,000 - 5,450)		10,550	
Prepayments		2,500	
Cash at bank (467 + 13,000)		13,467	
			31,017
			58,989

	Ken $	Barbie $	
Partners' accounts			
Capital accounts	35,000	20,000	55,000
Current accounts	(12,610)	(6,201)	(18,811)
Current liabilities			
Payables			9,800
Loan			13,000
			58,989

Current accounts

	Ken $	Barbie $		Ken $	Barbie $
Share of loss	6,765	465	Balance b/f	7,655	9,264
Drawings	13,500	15,000	Balance c/f	12,610	6,201
	20,265	15,465		20,265	15,465
Balance b/f	12,610	6,201			

Statement of division of profit

	Ken $	Barbie $	Total $
Salary		7,500	7,500
Interest on capital	2,800	1,600	4,400
Profit share ratio (1:1)	(9,565)	(9,565)	(19,130) (ß)
	———	———	———
	(6,765)	(465)	(7,230)

8 Partnership accounts and goodwill

Goodwill is the difference between the value of the partnership business as a whole and the aggregate of the fair values of the net assets:

Value of the business	X
Fair value of net assets	(X)
	——
Goodwill	X

A number of factors will lead to the creation of goodwill in a partnership business:

- good reputation
- location
- technical know-how
- excellent profits over the past years
- good prospects in the future.

Goodwill 'belongs' to the partners in the same ratio as their profit share agreement, although attributing goodwill is only necessary when:

(1) The partners elect to change their profit share ratio.

(2) A partner retires or dies.

(3) A new partner joins the partnership.

Expandable text

8.1 The calculation of goodwill

Partnership goodwill can be calculated in a number of ways:

(1) the difference between the fair value of purchase consideration and the fair value of the separable net assets

(2) a multiple of the previous year's profit or any other mathematical formulae

(3) a share/percentage paid by an incoming partner for goodwill can be used to determine the total goodwill

(4) any other basis given in the question.

Expandable text

Calculate the goodwill in each of these cases.

(1) The fair value of purchase consideration and fair value of the net assets are given as $750,000 and $500,000 respectively.

(2) Goodwill is to be valued at 4 times the profit of last year. Last year's profit is given as $25,000.

(3) The incoming partner introduces $6,000 in payment for his share of a quarter of the goodwill.

Solution:

(1) $250,000 ($750,000 - $500,000)

(2) $100,000 (4 x $25,000)

(3) $24,000 (4 x $6,000)

9 Adjustments to partnership accounts

If any of the following situations occur:

- the profit share ratio is changed

- a partner retires or dies

- a new parter joins the business

KAPLAN PUBLISHING

then the profit-sharing ratio will change and so ownership of the goodwill also changes. Adjustments to the capital accounts of the partners are required before such a change takes place in order that partners retain their share of goodwill generated to date. This can be done with or without a goodwill account.

Use of a goodwill account

Calculate the goodwill in the business and then:

Dr Goodwill account   X

Cr Capital accounts in old ratio   X

Adjustment without a goodwill account

Calculate the goodwill in the business and then:

Dr Capital accounts of partners in **new** ratio   X

Cr Capital accounts of partners in **old** ratio   X

In order that partners now taking a smaller share of the profits are 'compensated' for the goodwill 'lost', this 'compensation' is funded by the partners now taking a larger share of the profits.

Note that the death of a partner is not examinable.

Illustration 4– Goodwill on change of PSR (profit share ratio)

John, Lewis and Fraser have been partners in a delicatessen for 10 years. They share their profits in the ratio 3:4:2. As Lewis wishes to step back from the operational side of the business in order to spend more time with his family, it has been agreed that the profit share ratio will be changed to 3:1:2. The value of the goodwill in the business is $54,000.

What journals are required to account for this

(a) If a goodwill account is used

(b) without a goodwill account?

Expandable text

(a) **using a goodwill account**

Dr Goodwill	$54,000	
Cr Capital (John)	$18,000	(3/9 x $54,000)
Cr Capital (Lewis)	$24,000	(4/9 x $54,000)
Cr Capital (Fraser)	$12,000	(2/9 x $54,000)

(b) **without a goodwill account**

Dr Capital (John)	$27,000	(3/6 x $54,000)
Dr Capital (Lewis)	$9,000	(1/6 x $54,000)
Dr Capital (Fraser)	$18,000	(2/6 x $54,000)
Cr Capital (John)	$18,000	(3/9 x $54,000)
Cr Capital (Lewis)	$24,000	(4/9 x $54,000)
Cr Capital (Fraser)	$12,000	(2/9 x $54,000)

Test your understanding 3

Harvey, Nichol and Selfridge have been in partnership for a number of years with a profit share ratio of 1:1:4. They have agreed to change this ratio to 1:1:2. The value of goodwill in the business is $24,000.

How should this be accounted for?

10 Revaluation of assets on a change in partnership structure

- When there is a change in the structure of the partnership due to an admission, retirement or death of a partner, then the assets will generally be revalued.

- Any revaluation profits or losses are awarded to the partners in the old profit share ratio.

- This reflects the fact that the old partners have built up the business and they are therefore entitled to the gain or must bear the loss.

Illustration 5– Revaluation of assets

Proper and Quibble are partners sharing profits and losses in the ratio of 4:1. On 1 January 20X6, when Proper and Quibble's capital balances stand at $27,000 and $12,000 respectively, a new partner Right joins the business, and the following take place:

- Right introduces capital of $10,000.
- Land and buildings are revalued upwards by $80,000.
- Goodwill is valued at $40,000.
- The profit share is revised to 2:2:1 (P:Q:R).

Write up the capital accounts of the partners to record the above, assuming that a goodwill account is used.

Expandable text

Solution

Capital accounts

	Proper $	Quibble $	Right $		Proper $	Quibble $	Right $
				Balance b/f	27,000	12,000	
				Revaluation Old ratio (4:1)			
				- Land and buildings	64,000	16,000	
				Goodwill	32,000	8,000	
				Bank			10,000
Balance c/f	123,000	36,000	10,000				
	123,000	36,000	10,000		123,000	36,000	10,000
				Bal b/f	123,000	36,000	10,000

Test your understanding 4

Miranda and Charlotte are partners sharing profits and losses equally. Capital account balances at 1 January 20X6 are $50,000 and $50,000 respectively. On this date, a new partner, Carrie, joins the business, introducing capital of $30,000. Land and buildings are revalued by $100,000 and goodwill is valued at $20,000. After the admission of Carrie, the profit share is revised to 2:2:1 and goodwill is to be eliminated from the books.

What is the balance on Charlotte's capital account after this transaction has been accounted for?

A $60,000

B $102,000

C $110,000

D $52,000

Chapter summary

PARTNERSHIP
A business with two or more joint owners.

INCOME STATEMENT
As for a sole trader

PARTNERSHIP AGREEMENT

PROFIT SHARED BETWEEN PARTNERS
in statement of division of profit (appropriation account)
- Salaries
- Interest on capital
- Interest on drawings
- Profit-share ratio
- Minimum guaranteed profit share.

CURRENT ACCOUNTS

Drawings	Balance b/f
	Profit share
	Interest on
	Loan
Balance c/f	

LOANS FROM PARTNERS
- Included in statement of financial position as if a third party loan.
- Interest expensed and accrued to current account.

STATEMENT OF FINANCIAL POSITION
Capital section includes balances on partners' capital and current accounts.

CAPITAL ACCOUNTS
- Show long-term capital invested in business
- Movements are rare.

Test your understanding answers

The correct answer is A

	Britney $	Justin $	Cameron $	Total $
Salaries		14,000	25,000	39,000
Interest on capital	1,400	1,040	1,600	4,040
Profit share ratio	(81,520)	(61,140)	(20,380)	(163,040) (ß)
Total profit share	(80,120)	(46,100)	6,220	
Net profit from income statement				(120,000)

Test your understanding 2

Statement of division of profit

	Hamish $	Campbell $	Total $
Interest on capital	800	560	1,360
Interest on drawings (w)	(50)	(50)	(100)
Profit share ratio 3:2	14,244	9,496	23,740 (ß)
Total profit share	14,994	10,006	
Net profit from income statement			25,000

Working – interest on drawings

$5,000 x 2% x 6/12 = 50

Capital account

	Hamish $	Campbell $		Hamish $	Campbell $
Balance c/f	20,000	14,000	1.1.X6 injection	20,000	14,000
	20,000	14,000		20,000	14,000
			Balance b/f	20,000	14,000

Current account

	Hamish $	Campbell $		Hamish $	Campbell $
Drawings	5,000	5,000	Profit share	14,994	10,006
Balance c/f	9,994	5,006			
	14,994	10,006		14,994	10,006
			Balance b/f	9,994	5,006

Statement of financial position presentation

		$	$
Capital accounts	Hamish	20,000	
	Campbell	14,000	
			34,000
Current accounts	Hamish	9,994	
	Campbell	5,006	
			15,000
			49,000

Test your understanding 3

With goodwill account:

Dr Goodwil	24,000
Cr Capital (Harvey) 1/6 x $24,000	4,000
Cr Capital (Nichol) 1/6 x $24,000	4,000
Cr Capital (Selfridge) 4/6 x $24,000	16,000

Without goodwill account:

	Capital							
	Harvey	**Nichol**	**Selfridge**			**Harvey**	**Nichol**	**Selfridge**
	$	$	$			$	$	$
				Balance b/f		X	X	X
				Goodwill adjustment		4,000	4,000	16,000
Goodwill adjustment	6,000	6,000	12,000					
Balance c/f	X	X	X					
	X	X	X			X	X	X
				Balance b/f		X	X	X

Therefore the overall effect is to:

Dr Capital (Harvey) 2,000

Dr Capital (Nichol) 2,000

Cr Capital (Selfridge) 4,000

Thus Harvey and Nichol, who have a greater share of goodwill under the new profit-share ratio, are compensating Selfridge, who is entitled to a lesser share under the new profit-share ratio.

Test your understanding 4

The correct answer is B

Without goodwill account

	Miranda $	Charlotte $	Carrie $		Miranda $	Charlotte $	Carrie $
				Balance b/f	50,000	50,000	
				Revaluation Old ratio (1:1)	50,000	50,000	
Goodwill adjustment 2:2:1	8,000	8,000	4,000	Goodwill adjustment	10,000	10,000	
				Bank			30,000
Balance c/f	102,000	102,000	26,000		110,000	110,000	30,000
	110,000	110,000	30,000	Balance c/f	102,000	102,000	26,000

Company accounts

Chapter learning objectives

Upon completion of this chapter you will be able to:

*   explain the difference between a sole trader and a limited liability company

*   illustrate the IAS1 required presentation of financial statements

*   identify items requiring separate disclosure on the face of the income statement

*   explain the capital structure of a limited liability company

*   explain and illustrate the share premium account

*   define a rights issue and its advantages and disadvantages

*   record a rights issue in ledger accounts and show the effect in the statement of financial position

*   define a bonus (capitalisation) issue and its advantages and disadvantages

*   record a bonus issue in ledger accounts and show the effect in the statement of financial position

*   explain and illustrate other reserves which may appear in a company statement of financial position

*   explain why the heading, retained earnings, appears in a company statement of financial position

*   explain how finance is raised by borrowing rather than by the issue of shares

*   calculate and record finance costs in the ledger accounts and the financial accounts

- explain the requirements of IAS as regards current assets and liabilities
- explain the impact of tax on company profits and illustrate the ledger account required to record it
- record tax in the income statement and statement of financial position of a company
- explain and illustrate the recording of dividends.

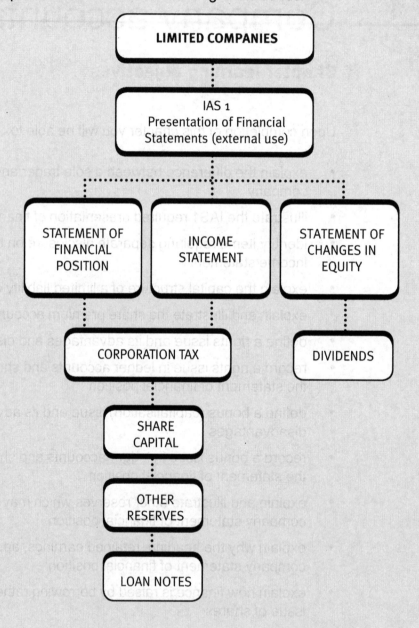

1 Characteristics of limited companies

	Limited liability company	Sole trader
Separate legal entity	A limited company is a separate legal entity, i.e. in the eyes of the law it is a person in its own right and is distinct from its owners.	A sole trader is legally not separate from his business even though he is treated as such for accounting purpose
Liability	A company is fully liable for its own debts. This means that if the company goes into liquidation, the owners (shareholders) of the company are liable only for amounts that they have not yet paid for their shares. Thus the shareholders are said to have limited liability.	If a sole trader goes into liquidation then he is personally liable for any outstanding debts of his business.
Ownership and management	A company is owned by shareholders. The managers of the company are called directors and are appointed by the shareholders. The directors may or may not be shareholders in the company. Thus most shareholders do not play a part in the day-to-day running of the company.	A sole trader is generally both the owner and manager of his or her business.
Formalities	Formalities involved vary from country to country, but frequently require public availability of financial statements and an annual audit by qualified auditors.	No such formalities exist for sole traders.

Expandable text

The advantages of operation as a limited company rather than as a sole trader can be as follows:

- The liability of the shareholders is limited to the capital already introduced by them.

- There is a formal separation of the business from the owners of the business, which may be helpful to the running of the business. For example, if several members of a family are the shareholders in a company, but only two of the family are directors, it is clear to all concerned who is running the company.

- Ownership of the business can be shared between people more easily than in other forms of business organisation, e.g. a partnership.

- Shares in the business can be transferred relatively easily.

- There may be tax advantages.

The disadvantages of operation as a limited company rather than as a sole trader can be as follows:

- The costs of formation of the company.

- Costs of complying with companies' legislation, including the audit requirement, if any.

- Directors of a company are subject to greater legislative duties than others running an unincorporated business.

- It is difficult/expensive to return capital surplus to the business's requirements back to the shareholders.

- There may be tax disadvantages.

2 IAS 1 presentation of financial statements

IAS 1 incorporates the recommended formats for company published accounts. The following financial summaries are required:

- statement of financial position

- income statement

- statement of comprehensive income (only examinable where a revaluation of non-current assets has occurred)

- statement of changes in equity

- notes to the accounts (the F3 syllabus does not require knowledge of these).

- a statement of cash flows and supporting notes

3 Statement of financial position

There are many similarities to the statement of financial position of a sole trader, although some items will require further explanation.

Note that IAS 1 requires an asset or liability to be classified as current if:

- it will be settled within 12 months of the statement of financial position date, or

- it is part of the enterprise's normal operating cycle.

Statement of financial position for XYZ at 31 December XXXX

	$m	$m
Assets		
Intangible		
Non-current assets		
Property, plant and equipment	X	
Investments	X	
	___	
		X
Current assets		
Inventories	X	
Trade and other receivables	X	
Prepayments	X	
Cash	X	
	___	
		X
Total assets		X
		___
Equity and liabilities		
Capital and reserves		
Ordinary share capital	X	
Preference share capital	X	
Share premium account	X	
Reserves	X	
Accumulated profits	X	
	___	
		X
Non-current liabilities		
Loan notes		X
Current liabilities		
Trade and other payables	X	
Overdrafts	X	
Tax payable	X	
	___	
		X
		___
Total equity and liabilities		X
		___

Expandable text

The suggested statement of financial position format makes a distinction between current and non-current assets and liabilities. IAS 1 sets down the rules to be applied in making this distinction.

Current assets

An asset should be classified as a current asset if it is:

*   part of the enterprise's operating cycle

*   held primarily for trading purposes

*   expected to be realised within 12 months of the statement of financial position date; or

*   cash or a cash equivalent.

All other assets should be classified as non-current assets.

Note that this definition allows inventory or receivables to qualify as current assets under (a) above, even if they may not be realised into cash within twelve months.

Current liabilities

The rules for current liabilities are similar to those for current assets.

A liability should be classified as a current liability if:

*   it is expected to be settled in the normal course of the enterprise's operating cycle

*   it is held primarily for the purpose of being traded

*   it is due to be settled within 12 months of the statement of financial position date or

*   the company does not have an unconditional right to defer settlement for at least 12 months after the statement of financial position date.

All other liabilities should be classified as non-current liabilities.

KAPLAN PUBLISHING

4 Income statement

Income statement

A recommended format for the Income statement is as follows:

XYZ Group
Income statement for the year ended 31 December 20X2

	$
Revenue	X
Cost of sales	(X)
	—
Gross profit	X
Distribution costs	(X)
Administrative expenses	(X)
	—
Profit from operations	X
Finance costs	(X)
	—
Profit before tax	X
tax expense	(X)
	—
Net profit for the period	X

5 Statement of comprehensive income

The suggested format is as follows.

Note that all expenses are classified under one of three headings:

- **Cost of sales**

  This is calculated as for a sole trader. However the calculation should be shown in a note to the accounts rather than on the face of the income statement.

- **Distribution costs**

  These are all expenses relating to selling or delivering products or services.

- **Administrative expenses**

  This includes all expenses not classified within cost of sales or distribution costs.

Some expenses such as depreciation will be split across all three expense categories.

Statement of comprehensive income for XYZ for the year ended 31 December XXXX

	$m
Revenue	X
Cost of sales	(X)
Gross profit	X
Other operating income	X
Distribution costs	(X)
Administrative expenses	(X)
Profit from operations	X
Net interest cost (interest paid less interest received)	X
Profit before tax	X
Tax expense	(X)
Net profit for the period	X

Other comprehensive income:

Gain on property revaluation	X
Total comprehensive income for the year	X

There are certain circumstances where large one-off items require separate disclosure on the face of the Statement of comprehensive income, these are:

- restructuring or the reorganisation of the entity
- disposal of items of property, plant and equipment
- disposal of investment
- write downs of inventory or property, plant and equipment

These will be clearly shown in the question and should be shown on a separate line on the Statement of comprehensive income.

Relationship between the income statement and statement of financial position

The link between the statement of financial position and income statement is shown below:

Expandable text

The income statement may be presented in one of two ways.

(1) The **function of expenditure** or **cost of sales** method shows expenses classified under the headings: cost of sales, distribution costs and administrative expenditure.

(2) The **nature of expenditure** method analyses expenses according to their nature:

	$m	$m
Sales revenue		X
Other operating income		X
Changes in inventories of finished goods and work in progress	(X)	
Raw materials and consumables used	(X)	
Staff costs	(X)	
Depreciation and amortisation expense	(X)	
Other operating expenses	(X)	
		(X)
Profit from operations		X
Net interest cost (interest paid less interest received)		(X)
Profit before tax		X
Tax expense		(X)
Net profit for the period		X

Changes in inventories of finished goods and work in progress

This is simply the difference between the opening and closing amounts and could thus be a debit or a credit in the statement – if inventories have risen it will be a credit and if they have fallen a debit. Note that raw materials inventories are included below rather than here.

Raw materials and consumables used

This is purchases of raw materials adjusted for opening and closing inventories.

6 Statement of changes in equity

This statement is included within the accounts to provide further information on certain statement of financial position accounts, namely share capital and reserves.

Statement of changes in equity for XYZ Ltd

	Share capital $m	Share premium $m	Revaluation reserve $m	Accumulated profits $m	Total $m
Balance at 1 January	X	X	X	X	X
Equity shares issued	X	X			X
Revaluation surplus			X		X
Net profit				X	X
Dividends				(X)	(X)
	X	X	X	X	X

7 Share capital

A company is owned via shares.

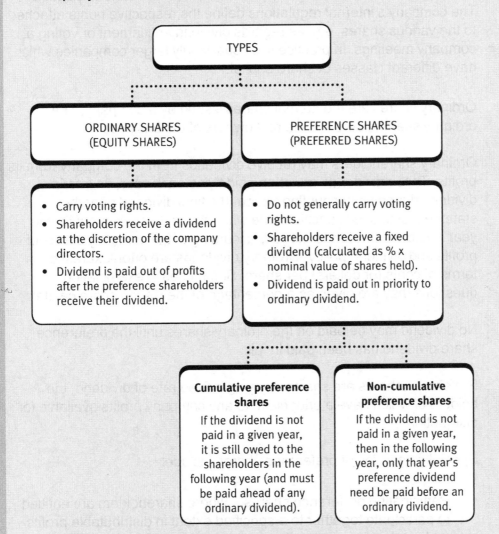

- Redeemable preference shares are preference shares which are repayable by the company at a specified future date. On this date the shares are cancelled and the shareholders repaid.

  These shares have the characteristics of debt. They are therefore classified as a liability on the statement of financial position.

- Irredeemable preference shares are preference shares which are not redeemable. They remain in existence indefinitely.

  These shares are classified as equity on the statement of financial position.

Expandable text

The share capital of a company may be divided into various classes. The company's internal regulations define the respective rights attached to the various shares, e.g. as regards dividend entitlement or voting at company meetings. In practice it is usually only larger companies which have different classes of share capital.

Ordinary shares are the normal shares issued by a company. The ordinary shareholders are the real owners of the business

Ordinary shareholders may receive dividends from the company from its profits. These dividends are often paid twice each year, an interim dividend during an accounting year and a final dividend after the statement of financial position date when the company's profit for the year is known. Dividends will vary according to the company's level of profits and dividend policy. Ordinary dividends are often expressed in terms of cents (or dollars) per share. Sometimes in examination questions they are given as a percentage of the issued share capital.

No dividend may be paid on the ordinary shares until the preference share dividend has been paid in full.

Preference shares are shares carrying a fixed rate of dividend, the holders of which have a prior claim to any company profits available for distribution.

Special categories of preference shares include:

- Participating preference shares – where shareholders are entitled to participate together to a specified extent in distributable profits and surpluses on liquidation

- Redeemable preference shares – the terms of issue specify that they are repayable by the company.

Share capital values

- Each share has a nominal or par value, often $1, 50c or 25c. This value is often used as a means of calculating dividends to shareholders (paid as a percentage of the nominal value).

- Shares are issued by the company at an issue price. This is at least equal to the nominal value of the share, but often exceeds it.

KAPLAN PUBLISHING

Expandable text

The market value of a share fluctuates according to the success and perceived expectations of a company. If a company is listed on the stock exchange, the value is determined by reference to recent transactions between buyers and sellers of shares. This value does not feature in the financial statements.

Share capital terminology

- **Authorised** share capital is the nominal value of the maximum number of shares that a company can have in issue at any particular point in time.

- **Issued** share capital is the share capital that has actually been issued to shareholders. The number of issued shares is used in the calculation of dividends.

- **Called-up** share capital is the amount of the nominal value paid by the shareholder plus any further amounts that they have agreed to pay in the future.

- **Paid up** share capital is the amount of the nominal value which has been paid at the current date.

Accounting for the issue of shares

A company will generally issue shares at above par (nominal) value.

The double entry to record an ordinary or irredeemable preference share issue is:

    Dr Cash   Issue price x no. shares

    Cr Share capital (SFP)   Nominal value x no. shares

    Cr Share premium   ß

Both the share capital and share premium accounts are shown on the statement of financial position within the 'Share Capital and Reserves' section.

The double entry to record a redeemable preference share issue is:

    Dr Cash   Issue price x no. shares

    Cr Liability   Issue price x no. of shares

Test your understanding 1

Bourbon issues 200,000 25c shares at a price of $1.75 each.

Show this transaction using ledger accounts.

8 Rights issues

A **rights issue** is:

the offer of new shares to existing shareholders in proportion to their existing shareholding at a stated price (normally below market values).

The **advantages** are:

*   A rights issue is the cheapest way for a company to raise finance through the issuing of further shares.

*   A rights issue to existing shareholders has a greater chance of success compared with a share issue to the public.

The **disadvantages** are:

*   A rights issue is more expensive than issuing debt.

*   It may not be successful in raising the finance required.

A rights issue is accounted for in the same way as a normal share issue.

Test your understanding 2

Upon incorporation in 20X4, The Jammy Dodger, a limited liability company, issues 1,000 50c shares at nominal value. Needing further funds, in 20X5 it makes a rights issue of 1 for 5 at $0.75. This offer is fully taken up.

What accounting entries are required in 20X4 and 20X5? Illustrate the relevant section of the statement of financial position at year end 20X5.

KAPLAN PUBLISHING

9 Bonus issues

A **bonus (or capitalisation or scrip)** issue is:

the issue of new shares to existing shareholders in proportion to their existing shareholding. No cash is received from a bonus issue.

The **advantages** are:

- Issued share capital is divided into a larger number of shares, thus making the market value of each one less, and so more marketable.

- Issued share capital is brought more into line with assets employed in the company.

The **disadvantages** are:

- the admin costs of making the bonus issue.

As no cash is received from a bonus issue, the issue must be funded from reserves. Any reserve can be used, though a non-distributable reserve such as the share premium account would be used in preference to reserves which can be distributed:

Dr Share premium   Nominal value

(or other reserve)

Cr Share capital   Nominal value

Test your understanding 3

Ginger Knut, a limited liability company, has 20,000 50c shares in issue (each issued for $1.25) and makes a 1 for 4 bonus issue, capitalising the share premium account.

What are the balances on the share capital and share premium accounts after this transaction?

	SC $	SP $
A	15,000	10,000
B	12,500	12,500
C	25,000	Nil
D	22,500	2,500

Test your understanding 4

Rich T is a limited liability company with 200,000 25c shares in issue. At 1 January the balance on the share premium account is $75,000. The following transactions occur in the year ended 31 December 20X6:

31 January There is a fully taken-up 2 for 5 rights issue. The issue price is $1.80.

12 August There is a 1 for 10 bonus issue made using the share premium account.

What are the balances on the share capital and share premium accounts on 31 December 20X6?

	SC $'000	SP $'000
A	308	111
B	77	84
C	154	93
D	77	192

10 Other reserves

Any balances representing profits or surpluses owed to the shareholders are called reserves.

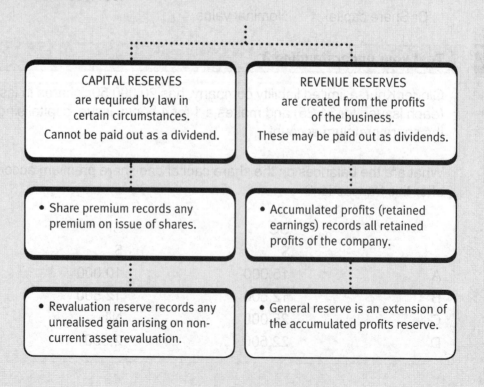

CAPITAL RESERVES
are required by law in certain circumstances.
Cannot be paid out as a dividend.

REVENUE RESERVES
are created from the profits of the business.
These may be paid out as dividends.

• Share premium records any premium on issue of shares.

• Accumulated profits (retained earnings) records all retained profits of the company.

• Revaluation reserve records any unrealised gain arising on non-current asset revaluation.

• General reserve is an extension of the accumulated profits reserve.

Expandable text

Accumulated profits (retained earnings) appear in the capital and reserves section of the statement of financial position in the same way that the profits of a sole trader are added to capital.

Retained profits are due (although generally not paid out) to the shareholders of the company. It follows that they should be presented as part of the liability to the shareholders.

11 Loan notes (loan stock)

- A limited company can raise funds by issuing loan notes .

- A loan note is a document that is evidence of a debt.

- A person will buy a loan note for a set nominal value, e.g. $100. He or she is effectively loaning $100 to the company.

- The nominal value of the loan note will be repayable after a certain number of years.

- In the meantime, the loan note-holder will receive an annual fixed amount of interest based on the nominal value.

- The interest incurred is included in 'finance cost' in the income statement.

Test your understanding 5

Custard Creameries is an incorporated business which needs to raise funds to purchase plant and machinery. On 1 March 20X5 it issues $150,000 10% loan notes, redeemable in 10 years' time. Interest is payable half yearly at the end of August and February.

What accounting entries are required in the year ended 31 December 20X5? Show relevant extracts from the statement of financial position.

12 Corporation tax

- Companies are charged corporation tax on their profits.

- Accounting for tax is initially based on estimates, since a company's tax bill is not finalised and paid until nine months after its year end.

- This means that a company will normally under– or overprovide for tax in any given year

- Tax will therefore appear in the year-end financial statements as:
  - A charge to profits in the income statement being
    - Current year estimated tax + previous year's underprovision; or
    - Current year estimated tax – previous year's overprovision.
- A year end liability in the statement of financial position being the current year's estimated tax.

Test your understanding 6

Garry Baldy commenced trade on 1 January 20X4 and estimates that the tax payable for the year ended 31 December 20X4 is $150,000.

In September 20X5, the accountant of Garry Baldy receives and pays a tax demand for $163,000 for the year ended 31 December 20X4. At 31 December 20X5 he estimates that the company owes $165,000 for corporation tax in relation to the year ended 31 December 20X5.

Draw up the tax charge and income tax payable accounts for the years ended 31 December 20X4 and 20X5 and detail the amounts shown in the statement of financial position and income statement in both years.

Test your understanding 7

Choccychip estimated last year's tax charge to be $230,000. As it happened, their tax advisor settled with the tax authorities at $222,000.

This year, Choccychip estimate their tax bill to be $265,000, but they are a little confused as to how this should be reflected in the financial statements. Which of the following is correct for the end of the current year?

	Statement of financial position liability ($)	Income statement tax charge ($)
A	257,000	265,000
B	273,000	265,000
C	265,000	257,000
D	265,000	273,000

13 Dividends

- Dividends are the share of profits paid out to shareholders.
- Dividends on preference shares are a fixed amount.
- Dividends on ordinary shares are expressed as an amount per share e.g 10c per share or 10% of nominal value

Preference dividends

In line with the statement of financial position presentation of preference shares:

- redeemable preference share dividends are classified as **finance costs**
- irredeemable preference share dividends are classified as **dividends**.

> **Expandable text**
>
> The return is calculated as a percentage of the nominal value of the preference share capital. If, at the year-end, the company has not paid all of the dividends due to preference share holders, the company will show the amount owing as a current liability on the statement of financial position under the heading 'proposed dividends' or 'interest accrual'.

Ordinary dividends

A company may pay a mid-year or interim dividend. The double entry is:

Dr Dividends – (statement of changes in equity) X

Cr Bank   X

At the end of the year companies may propose a dividend to the ordinary shareholders (i.e. tell the shareholders the amount of a dividend to be paid after the year end). This is a **final dividend**. It is not recorded unless it has been declared (or confirmed) prior to the year end. If this is the case, the double entry is:

Dr Dividends – (statement of changes in equity) X

Cr Dividends payable (SFP)   X

The balance on the dividends payable account is shown as a current liability on the statement of financial position

Test your understanding 8

Cracker, a company, has share capital as follows:

Ordinary share capital (50c shares) $200,000

8% Irredeemable Preference share capital $50,000

The company pays an interim dividend of 12.5c per share to its ordinary shareholders and pays the preference shareholders their fixed dividend. Before the year end the company declares a final dividend of 36.5c per share to its ordinary shareholders.

Calculate the amounts shown in the statement of changes in equity (SOCIE) and statement of financial position (SFP) in relation to dividends for the year.

	SOCIE	SFP
	$'000	$'000
A	200	150
B	54	nil
C	200	146
D	101	72

14 Preparation of company accounts

You will not be asked to produce a full set of accounts in the F3 examination, although you may be required to provide certain balances.

The following example will, however, help you to fully understand the preparation of company accounts.

Test your understanding 9

Preparation of company accounts

The trial balance of Penguin, a company as at 31 December 20X5 was as follows:

	Dr $	Cr $
Sales and purchases	20,000	50,000
Inventory	8,000	
Distribution costs	8,000	
Administration expenses	15,550	
Receivables and payables	10,000	20,000
Fundamental reorganisation costs	2,400	
Cash at bank	8,100	
Ordinary shares 50c		8,000
10% irredeemable preference shares $1		9,000
10% loan notes		8,000
Non-current assets at net book value	35,000	
Share premium		3,000
Accumulated profits at 1 January 20X5		3,000
Loan note Interest	400	
Preference dividend	450	
Interim ordinary dividend	1,600	
Tax		500
Suspense		8,000
	109,500	109,500

The following is to be taken into account.

(1) A building whose net book value is currently $5,000 is to be revalued to $11,000.

(2) A final ordinary dividend of 10c per share is to be proposed.

(3) The balance on the corporation tax account represents an overprovision of tax for the previous year. Tax for the current year is estimated at $3,000.

(4) Closing inventory is $12,000.

(5) The balance on the suspense account represents the proceeds from the issue of 4,000 ordinary shares.

Prepare the following statements for the year ended 31 December 20X5:

(1) statement of comprehensive income

(2) statement of financial position

(3) statement of changes in equity

(4) an income statement (hence ignoring the revaluation)

Chapter summary

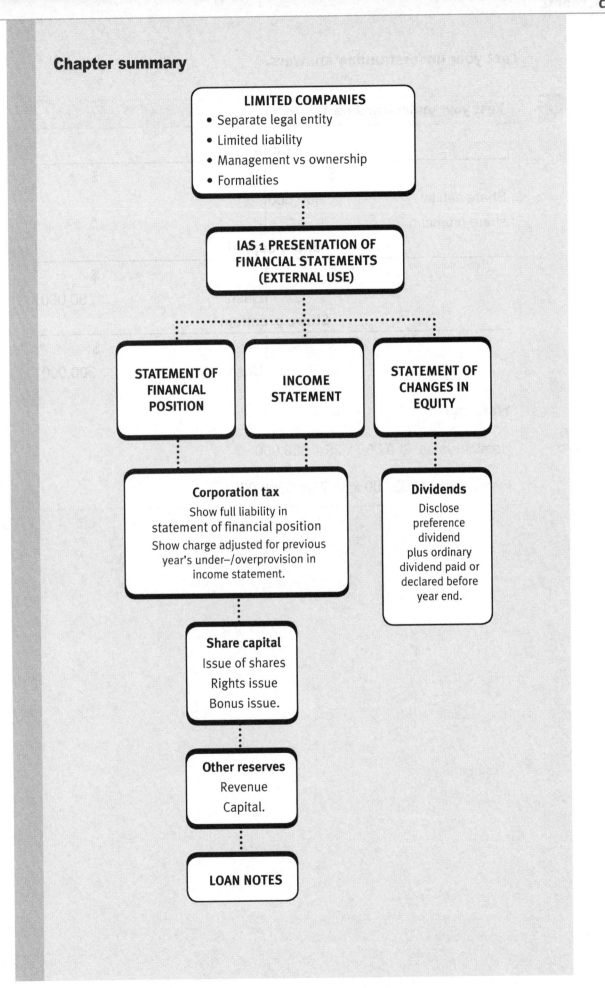

LIMITED COMPANIES
- Separate legal entity
- Limited liability
- Management vs ownership
- Formalities

IAS 1 PRESENTATION OF FINANCIAL STATEMENTS (EXTERNAL USE)

STATEMENT OF FINANCIAL POSITION

INCOME STATEMENT

STATEMENT OF CHANGES IN EQUITY

Corporation tax
Show full liability in statement of financial position
Show charge adjusted for previous year's under–/overprovision in income statement.

Dividends
Disclose preference dividend plus ordinary dividend paid or declared before year end.

Share capital
Issue of shares
Rights issue
Bonus issue.

Other reserves
Revenue
Capital.

LOAN NOTES

Test your understanding answers

Test your understanding 1

Cash

	$		$
Share capital / share premium	350,000		

Share capital

	$		$
		Cash	50,000

Share premium

	$		$
		Cash	300,000

Working:

Nominal value: 200,000 x 25 = $50,000

Funds raised: 200,000 x $1.75 = $350,000

Test your understanding 2

20X4 Dr Cash $500

    Cr Share capital $500

20X5 For every five shares a shareholder owns, he or she is are entitled to buy another one. The offer is fully taken up, meaning that 200 new shares are issued.

    Dr Cash (200 x 75c) $150

    Cr Share capital (200 x 50c) $100

    Cr Share premium $50

Statement of financial position

Capital and reserves:

	$
Share capital – 50c ordinary shares	600
Share premium	50
Accumulated profit	X

Test your understanding 3

The correct answer is B

- For every four shares held, a new share is issued.
- Therefore 5,000 new shares are issued

    Dr Share premium (5,000 x 50c) $2,500

    Cr Share capital $2,500

Statement of financial position

Capital and reserves:

	$
Share capital – 50c ordinary shares (20,000 x 50c) + $2,500	12,500
Share premium (20,000 x ($1.25 – $0.5)) – $2,500	12,500
Accumulated profit	X

Test your understanding 4

The correct answer is D

Share capital

	$		$
		Balance b/f	50,000
		Rights issue (cash)	20,000
Balance c/f	77,000	Bonus issue	7,000
	77,000		77,000
		Balance b/f	77,000

Share premium

	$		$
		Balance b/f	75,000
Bonus issue (SC)	7,000	Rights issue (cash)	124,000
Balance c/f	192,000		
	199,000		199,000
		Balance b/f	192,000

Statement of financial position

Capital and reserves:	$
Share capital – 25c ordinary shares	77,000
Share premium	192,000
Accumulated profit	X

Workings:

Rights issue: (200,000/5) x 2 = 80,000 new shares

   Proceeds: 80,000 x $1.80 = $144,000

   Nominal value: 80,000 x 25c =$20,000

Bonus issue: (280,000/10) x 1 = 28,000 new shares

Nominal value: 28,000 x 25c = $7,000

KAPLAN PUBLISHING

Test your understanding 5

1 March 20X5 Dr Cash	$150,000
Cr 10% Loan notes	$150,000
31 August 20X5 Dr Finance cost	$7,500
Cr Cash	$7,500

$150,000 x 10% x 6/12 = $7,500

| 31 December 20X5 Dr Finance cost | $5,000 |
| Cr Interest accrual | $5,000 |

$150,000 x 10% x 4/12 = $5,000

Statement of financial position

	$
Non-current liabilities	
10% Loan notes	150,000
Current liabilities	
Trade payables	X
Loan note interest payable	5,000

Test your understanding 6

Tax payable (statement of financial position)

	$		$
		20X4	
		income statement	150,000
September X5 Bank	163,000	Balance c/f	13,000
	163,000		163,000
Balance b/f (underprovision)	13,000	20X5 income	
Balance c/f	165,000	statement (ß)	178,000
	178,000		178,000
		Balance b/f	165,000

Tax charge (income statement)

	$		$
20X4 tax payable	150,000	Income statement	150,000
20X5 tax payable	178,000		178,000

The income statement tax charge in 20X5 is increased to reflect the underprovision made in 20X4.

Statement of financial position

	20X4 $000	20X5 $000
Corporation tax liability	150	165

Income statement

Tax expense	150	178

Test your understanding 7

The correct answer is C

- The liability in the statement of financial position= the estimated amount payable for the current year.

- The tax charge in the income statement = the estimated amount payable for the current year – last year's overprovision.

Test your understanding 8

The correct answer is C

No. of ordinary shares = $200,000/50c = 400,000

Ordinary dividend

Interim	400,000 x 12.5c	$50,000
Final	400,000 x 36.5c	$146,000
		$196,000

Preference dividend

50,000 x 8% = $4,000

Statement of changes in equity

	$
Retained earnings at start of year	X
dividends ($196,000 + $4,000)	(200,000)
At end of year	X

statement of financial position

Current liabilities	$
Proposed dividend	146,000

Test your understanding 9

Penguin

Statement of comprehensive income for the year ended 31 December 20X5

	$
Sales revenue	50,000
Cost of sales ($8,000+20,000 – 12,000)	(16,000)
Gross profit	34,000
Distribution costs	(8,000)
Administrative expenses	(15,550)
Operating profit	10,450
Fundamental reorganisation costs	(2,400)
	8,050
Interest payable (10% x 8,000)	(800)
Profit before taxation	7,250
Taxation (*3,000 – 500)	(2,500)
Profit after taxation	4,750
Other Comprehansive income	
Revaluation Gain	6,000
Total Comprehensive Income	10,750

Statement of financial position at 31 December 20X5		
	$	$
Tangible assets ($35,000 + 6,000)		41,000
Current assets		
Inventory	12,000	
Trade receivables	10,000	
Cash at bank and in hand	8,100	
	———	
		30,100
Total assets		———
		71,100
		———
Capital and reserves		
Ordinary share capital		10,000
($8,000 + 2,000)		
10% preference share capital		9,000
Share premium account		9,000
($3,000 + 6,000)		
Revaluation reserve		6,000
Accumulated profits		5,250
		———
		39,250
Non-current liabilities		
10% loan notes		8,000
Current liabilities		
Trade payables	20,000	
Proposed preference		
dividends (900 – 450)	450	
Taxation	3,000	
Loan note interest	400	
	———	
		23,850
		———
		71,100
		———

Income statement for the year ended 31 December 20X5

	$
Revenue	50,000
Cost of sales	(16,000)
Gross profit	34,000
Distribution costs	(8,000)
Administrative expenses	(15,550)
Profit from operations	10,450
Fundamental reorganisation costs	(2,400)
Finance costs	(800)
Profit before tax	7,250
tax expense	(2,500)
Net profit for the period	4,750

Statement of changes in equity
for the year ended 31 December 20X5

	Ordinary share capital	Share premium	Reval-uation Reserve	Accum profits	Total
	$	$	$	$	$
Balance at 1 Jan 20X5	8,000	3,000	–	3,000	14,000
Surplus on revaluation of building			6,000		6,000
Net gains and losses not recognised in the income statement			6,000		6,000
Net profit for the year				4,750	4,750
Dividends					
-Preference (10% x 9,000)				(900)	(900)
-Ordinary Interim				(1,600)	(1,600)
Issue of share capital (4000 shares = $8,000 thus issue price is $2 which is made up the nominal value of $0.50 and share premium of $1.50)	2,000	6,000			8,000
Balance at 31 December 20X5	10,000	9,000	6,000	5,250	30,250

Accounting standards

Chapter learning objectives

Upon completion of this chapter you will be able to:

- recognise the difference between tangible non-current assets and intangible non-current assets

- identify types of intangible non-current assets.

- define research and development

- explain the accounting treatment of research and development costs in accordance with IAS 38

- calculate the amounts to be capitalised as development expenditure or expensed from given information.

- explain the purpose of amortisation

- calculate the amortisation charge and account for it correctly

- define an event after the reporting period date.

- account for both adjusting and non-adjusting events correctly in the financial statements

- classify events as adjusting or non-adjusting.

- define provision, contingent liability and contingent asset.

- classify items as provision, contingent asset or contingent liability from information given

- account for provisions, contingent liabilities and contingent assets correctly

- calculate provisions and changes in provisions and account for these changes correctly

- report provisions in the final accounts

- explain what is meant by an accounting policy and the provisions of IAS 8 regarding changes in accounting policy

- identify the appropriate accounting treatment for a change in a material accounting policy according to IAS 8

- describe the provisions of IAS 8 which govern financial statements regarding material errors which result in prior period adjustments

- explain the requirements of IAS 18 governing revenue recognition.

Some other examples of intangible assets which you may come across are brands, quotas and patents.

1 Research and development (IAS 38)

Research can be defined as original and planned investigation undertaken with the prospect of gaining new scientific or technical knowledge and understanding.

Development can be defined as the application of research findings or other knowledge to a plan or design for the production of new or substantially improved materials, devices, products, processes, systems or services before the start of commercial production or use.

Test your understanding 1

Which of the following should be classified as development?

(1) Braynee Ltd has spent $300,000 investigating whether a particular substance, flubber, found in the Amazon rainforest is resistant to heat.

(2) Cleverclogs Ltd has incurred $120,000 expenses in the course of making a new waterproof and windproof material with the idea that it may be used for ski-wear.

(3) Ayplus Ltd has found that a chemical compound, known as XYX, is not harmful to the human body.

(4) Braynee Ltd has incurred a further $450,000 using flubber in creating prototypes of a new heat-resistant suit for stuntmen.

   A   All of them

   B   1 and 3

   C   2 and 4

   D   2 only

Accounting treatment of research and development

Where a company undertakes research and development, expenditure is being incurred with the intention of producing future benefits.

The accounting issue is therefore whether these costs should be expensed to the income statement or capitalised as an intangible asset on the statement of financial position to match to future benefits arising.

Research

- All research expenditure should be written off to the income statement as it is incurred. This is in compliance with the prudence concept.

- Research expenditure does not directly lead to future benefits and therefore it is not possible to follow the matching concept.

- Any capital expenditure on research equipment should be capitalised and depreciated as normal.

2.1 Development

- Development expenditure must be capitalised as an intangible asset provided that certain criteria are met:
  - **S**eparate project
  - **E**xpenditure identifiable and reliably measured
  - **C**ommercially viable
  - **T**echnically feasible
  - **O**verall profitable
  - **R**esources available to complete

- If the above criteria are not met, development expenditure must be written off to the income statement as it is incurred.

- Once expenditure has been treated as an expense, it cannot be reinstated as an asset.

Subsequent treatment of capitalised development expenditure

- The asset should be amortised over the period that is expected to benefit. This ensures that costs are matched to the revenue in the income statement.

- Amortisation should commence with commercial production. It should be charged over the period of benefit, and also in proportion to the revenue generated.

- Each project should be reviewed at the year end to ensure that the 'SECTOR' criteria are still met. If they are no longer met, the previously capitalised expenditure must be written off to the income statement immediately.

If a policy of capitalisation is adopted, it should be applied to all projects that meet the criteria.

Development

An intangible asset arising from development (or from the development phase of an internal project) should be recognised if, and only if, an enterprise can demonstrate all of the following:

- the technical feasibility of completing the intangible asset so that it will be available for use or sale

- its intention to complete the intangible asset and use or sell it

- its ability to use or sell the intangible asset

- how the intangible asset will generate probable future economic benefits. Among other things, the enterprise should demonstrate the existence of a market for the output of the intangible asset or the intangible asset itself or, if it is to be used internally, the usefulness of the intangible asset.

- the availability of adequate technical, financial and other resources to complete the development and to use or sell the intangible asset

- its ability to measure reliably the expenditure attributable to the intangible asset during its development.

The amount to be included is the cost of the development. Note that expenditure once treated as an expense cannot be reinstated as an asset.

Amortisation

If the useful life of an intangible asset is finite, its capitalised development costs must be amortised once commercial exploitation begins.

The amortisation method used should reflect the pattern in which the asset's economic benefits are consumed by the enterprise. If that pattern cannot be determined reliably, the straight-line method should be used.

An intangible asset with an indefinite useful life should not be amortised. An asset has an indefinite useful life if there is no foreseeable limit to the period over which the asset is expected to generate net cash inflows for the business.

Illustration – Accounting for development costs

Brightspark Ltd is developing a new product, the widget. This is expected to be sold over a three-year period starting in 20X6. The forecast data is as follows:

	20X5 $000	20X6 $000	20X7 $000	20X8 $000
Net revenue from other activities	400	500	450	400
Net revenue from widgets	–	450	600	400
Development costs	(900)	–	–	–

Show how the development costs should be treated if:

(a) the costs do not qualify for capitalisation

(b) the costs do qualify for capitalisation .

Expandable text

Solution

(a) Profit treating development costs as expenses when incurred

	20X5 $000	20X6 $000	20X7 $000	20X8 $000
Net revenue from other activities	400	500	450	400
Net revenue from widgets	–	450	600	400
Development costs	(900)	–	–	–
Net profit/(loss)	(500)	950	1,050	800

(b) Net profit amortising development costs over life of widgets

	20X5 $000	20X6 $000	20X7 $000	20X8 $000
Net revenue from other activities	400	500	450	400
Net revenue from widgets	–	450	600	400
Development costs of widgets	–			
(W)		(279.3)	(372.4)	(248.3)
Net profit	400	670.7	677.6	551.7

KAPLAN PUBLISHING

Amortisation working:

20X6: (450/1450) x $900,000 = $279,300

20X7: (600/1450) x $900,000 = $372,400

20X8: (400/1450) x $900,000 = $248,300

Test your understanding 2

This year, Deep Blue Sea Ltd has developed a new material from which the next generation of wetsuits will be made. This special material will ensure that swimmers are kept warmer than ever. The costs incurred meet the capitalisation criteria and by the 31 December 20X5 year end $250,000 has been capitalised.

The wetsuits are expected to generate revenue for five years from the date that commercial production commences on 1 January 20X6. What amount is charged to the income statement in the year ended 31 December 20X6?

A   nil

B $250,000

C $100,000

D $50,000

Expandable text

Disclosure

The financial statements should disclose the following for capitalised development costs:

- the amortisation method used and the expected period of amortisation

- a reconciliation of the carrying amounts at the beginning and end of the period, showing new expenditure incurred, amortisation and amounts written off because a project no longer qualifies for capitalisation

- amortisation during the period.

> In addition, the financial statements should also disclose the total amount of research and development expenditure recognised as an expense during the period.

2 Events after the reporting period date (IAS 10)

Events after the reporting period date can be defined as those material events which occur between the statement of financial position date and the date on which the financial statements are approved.

Adjusting and non-adjusting events

Expandable text

Adjusting events

These events provide additional evidence of conditions existing at the reporting date. For example, irrecoverable debts arising one or two months after the reporting date may help to quantify the allowance for receivables as at the reporting date. Adjusting events may, therefore, affect the amount at which items are stated in the reporting.

Examples of adjusting events

- The settlement after the reporting date of a court case which confirms a year end obligation.
- The receipt of information after the reporting date that indicates that an asset was impaired at the reporting date.
- The bankruptcy of a customer after the reporting date that confirms that a year-end debt is irrecoverable.
- The sale of inventories after the reporting period at a price lower than cost.
- The determination after the reporting date of the cost of assets purchased or proceeds from assets sold before the reporting date.
- The discovery of fraud or errors showing that the financial statements are incorrect.

Non-adjusting events

These are events arising after the reporting date but which do not concern conditions existing at the reporting date. Such events will not, therefore, have any effect on items in the reporting or income statement. However, in order to prevent the financial statements from presenting a misleading position, some form of additional disclosure is required if the events are material, by way of a note to the financial statements giving details of the event.

Examples of non-adjusting events

- Announcing a plan to discontinue an operation.
- Major purchases of assets.
- The destruction of assets after the reporting date by fire or flood.
- Entering into significant commitments or contingent liabilities (see section 4).
- Commencing a court case arising out of events after the reporting date.

Proposed dividends

It is not acceptable to include dividends declared after the reporting date as liabilities at the year end.

If dividends are declared before the year end, they must be shown in the statement of changes in equity and accrued for in the reporting period update.

Test your understanding 3

Which of the following are adjusting events for BigCo Ltd? The year end is 30 June 20X6 and the accounts are approved on 18 August 20X6.

(1) Sales of year end inventory on 2 July 20X6 at less than cost.

(2) The issue of new ordinary shares on 4 July 20X6.

(3) A fire in the main warehouse occurred on 8 July 20X6. All stock was destroyed.

(4) A major credit customer was declared bankrupt on 10 July 20X6

(5) All of the share capital of a competitor, TeenyCo Ltd was acquired on 21 July 20X6.

(6) On 1 August 20X6, $500,000 was received in respect of an insurance claim dated 13 February 20X6.

A   1,4 and 6

B   1,2,4 and 6

C   1,2,5 and 6

D   1,4,5 and 6

Disclosure

Where there are material non-adjusting events, a note to the financial statements should explain:

* the nature of the event

* an estimate of the financial effect.

Expandable text - Disclosure

In respect of each event after the reporting that must be disclosed as above, the following information should be stated by way of notes in the financial statements:

(1) (a) the nature of the event

(2) (b) an estimate of the financial effect, or a statement that such an estimate cannot be made.

The date on which the financial statements were authorised for issue, and who gave the authorisation, should be disclosed in the financial statements.

If the owners or others have the power to amend the financial statements after issue, that fact should be disclosed.

3 Provisions, contingent liabilities and assets (IAS 37)

A provision can be defined as a Liability of uncertain timing or amount.

Expandable text

A contingent liability is:

(1) a possible obligation that arises from past events and whose existence will be confirmed only by the occurrence or non-occurrence of one or more uncertain future events not wholly within the control of the enterprise; or

(2) a present obligation that arises from past events but is not recognised because:

  –   it is not probable that an outflow of resources embodying economic benefits will be required to settle the obligation; or

  –   the amount of the obligation cannot be measured with sufficient reliability.

A contingent asset is a possible asset that arises from past events and whose existence will be confirmed only by the occurrence or non-occurrence of one or more uncertain future events not wholly within the control of the enterprise.

Accounting for contingent liabilities and assets

The requirements of IAS 37 as regards contingent liabilities and assets are summarised in the following table:

Probability of Occurrence	Contingent liabilities	Contingent assets
Virtually certain	Provide	Recognise
Probable	Provide	Disclose in note
Possible	Disclose in note	Ignore
Remote	Ignore	Ignore

- Note that the standard gives no guidance as the meaning of the terms in the left-hand column. One possible interpretation is as follows:

  Virtually certain > 95%

  Probable 51% – 95%

  Possible 5% – 50%

  Remote < 5%

Expandable text

A provision is made where all of the following conditions are met:

- A present obligation (legal or constructive) exists as the result of a past event.
- There is a probable transfer of economic benefits.
- A reliable estimate of the amount can be made.

A legal present obligation is an obligation that derives from:

- the terms of a contract
- legislation
- any other operation of law.

A constructive obligation is an obligation that derives from an entity's actions where:

- The entity has in some way indicated that it will accept certain responsibilities.
- The entity has created an expectation on the part of other parties that it will meet those responsibilities.

Illustration

A retail store has a policy of refunding purchases by dissatisfied customers, even though it is under no legal obligation to do so. Its policy of making refunds is generally known.

Should a provision be made at the year end?

Expandable Text

The policy is well known and creates a valid expectation.

There is a constructive obligation.

It is probable some refunds will be made.

These can be measured using expected values.

Conclusion: A provision is required.

Test your understanding 4

The draft financial statements of Madras, a limited liability company, for the year ended 31 December 20X6 is currently under review. The following points have been raised:

(i) An ex-employee has started an action against the company for wrongful dismissal. The company's legal team have stated that the ex-employee is not likely to succeed. The following estimates have been given by the lawyers relating to the case:

   (a) Legal costs (to be incurred whether the claim is successful or not) $ 5,000

   (b) Settlement of claim if successful $15,000
   Total $ 20,000

   Currently no provision has been made by the company in the financial statements.

(ii) The company has a policy of refunding the cost of any goods returned by dissatisfied customers, even though it is under no legal obligation to do so. This policy of making refunds is generally known. At the year end returns totalling $4,800 have been made.

(iii) A claim has been made against a company for injury suffered by a pedestrian in connection with building work by the company. Legal advisers have confirmed that the company will probably have to pay damages of $100,000 but that a counterclaim made against the building subcontractors for $50,000 would probably be successful.

State with reasons what adjustments, if any, should be made by the company in the financial statements.

Accounting entries for provisions

A provision should initially be accounted for at the best estimate of the probable outflow:

   Dr relevant expense account

   Cr provision

Movement in provisions

Provisions should be reviewed at each statement of financial position date and adjusted to reflect the current best estimate.

Increase in provision: Dr Relevant expense account
                        Cr Provision

Decrease in provision: Dr Provision
                        Cr Relevant expense account

Expandable text

Reporting provisions in the final accounts

Provisions are reported as a liability.

They may be classed as current or non-current, depending upon the subject matter of the provision.

Disclosure

- Where the requirement is to provide for a contingent liability, the liability is reflected in the financial statements, but called a provision in order to highlight the uncertainty surrounding it

- The movement in this provision is recorded in the financial statements each year.

- When disclosure is made by note, the note should state:
  - the nature of the contingency
  - the uncertain factors that may affect the future outcome
  - an estimate of the financial effect, or a statement that such an estimate cannot be made.

4 Accounting policies, changes in accounting estimates and errors (IAS 8)

The main issues covered by this standard are:

- changes in accounting estimates
- changes in accounting policy
- correction of prior period errors.

Changes in accounting estimates

- These result in the adjustment of the carrying amount of an asset or liability, e.g revising the useful life of a non-current asset from five years to seven years.

- Any necessary change should be included in the current income statement under the same heading as the previous estimate, with a note giving details of the change if it has a material effect.

Changes in accounting policies

- Accounting policies are the specific principles, bases, conventions, rules and practices applied by an entity in preparing and presenting financial statements.

- The consistency theory means that a company's accounting policies will generally remain the same from year to year. There may, however, be circumstances where the policies do have to change:
  - If required by a standard or interpretation.
  - If the change will result in a more reliable and relevant presentation of events in financial statements.

- The change is applied retrospectively by adjusting the opening balance of accumulated profit; this is reflected in the statement of changes in equity. Comparative information for previous years is also restated.

A change in accounting policy occurs if there has been a change in:

- recognition, e.g. an expense is now recognised rather than an asset

- presentation, e.g. depreciation is now included in cost of sales rather than administrative expenses, or

- measurement basis, e.g. stating assets at replacement cost rather than historical cost.

Fundamental errors

- E.g. discovery of a major fraud which occurred last year

- If a fundamental error from a prior period is reflected in the accounts, this must be corrected.

- The correction involves adjusting the opening balance of accumulated profits; this is reflected in the statement of changes in equity. Comparative information for prior years should also be restated if practical.

5 Revenue (IAS 18)

IAS 18 Revenue defines when revenue from various sources may be recognised. It deals with revenue arising from three types of transaction or event:

- sale of goods
- rendering of services
- interest, royalties and dividends from the assets of the enterprise.

Sale of goods

Revenue from the sale of goods should be recognised when all the following conditions have been satisfied:

(a) All the significant risks and rewards of ownership have been transferred to the buyer.

(b) The seller retains no effective control over the goods sold.

(c) The amount of revenue can be reliably measured.

(d) The benefits to be derived from the transaction are likely to flow to the enterprise.

(e) The costs incurred or to be incurred for the transaction can be reliably measured.

Expandable Text

Conditions (a) and (b) are usually met at the time when legal ownership passes to the buyer, but there are four examples in IAS 18 where the seller retains significant risks:

- when the seller has an obligation for unsatisfactory performance beyond normal warranty provisions
- when the receipt of the cash for the sale is contingent upon the buyer selling the goods on and receiving cash
- when the goods are to be installed at the buyer's site and this has not yet been completed
- when the buyer has the right to cancel the contract.

Revenue and associated costs are recognised simultaneously in accordance with the matching concept.

Rendering of services

The provision of a service is likely to be spread over a period of time.

IAS 18 states that revenue from services may be recognised according to the stage of completion of the transaction at the statement of financial position date.

As with the sale of goods, conditions must be satisfied:

(a) The amount of the revenue can be measured reliably.

(b) The benefits from the transaction are likely to flow to the enterprise.

(c) The stage of completion of the work can be measured reliably.

(d) The costs incurred or to be incurred for the transaction can be reliably measured.

When a partly completed service is in its early stages, or the outcome of the transaction cannot be reliably estimated, revenue should be recognised only up to the amount of the costs incurred to date, and then only if it is probable that the enterprise will recover in revenue at least as much as the costs.

If it is probable that the costs of the transaction will not be recovered, no revenue is to be recognised.

Expandable text

Interest, royalties and dividends

Provided the amount of revenue can be reliably measured and the receipt of the income is reasonably assured, these items should be recognised as follows:

- Interest should be recognised on a time-proportion basis taking account of the yield on the asset.

- Royalties should be recognised on an accruals basis in accordance with the relevant agreement.

- Dividends should be recognised when the shareholder's right to receive payment has been established.

Disclosure

- The accounting policy for revenue recognition, including the methods used to determine the stage of completion of service transactions.

- The amount of revenue recognised for each of the five categories above.

- The amount, if material, in each category arising from exchanges of goods or services.

Chapter summary

```
                    ┌─────────────────────────────────────────┐
                    │  INTERNATIONAL ACCOUNTING STANDARDS       │
                    └─────────────────────────────────────────┘
```

IAS 38 INTANGIBLE ASSETS (RESEARCH AND DEVELOPMENT)	IAS 10 EVENTS AFTER THE REPORTING PERIOD	IAS 37 PROVISIONS, CONTINGENT LIABILITIES AND CONTINGENT ASSETS	IAS 8 ACCOUNTING POLICIES, CHANGES IN ACCOUNTING ESTIMATES AND ERRORS	IAS 18 REVENUE

Research: original and planned investigation to gain new scientific or technical knowledge and understanding.

Development: application of research findings or other knowledge to a plan or design for the production of new or substantially improved materials, devices, products, processes, systems or services before the start of commercial production or use.

Those material events which occur between the reporting date and the date on which the financial statements are approved.

Adjusting event: amend financial statements to reflect event.

Non-adjusting event: do not amend financial statements unless event impacts going concern. Disclose non-adjusting event if material.

Provision: a liability of uncertain timing or amount.

Contingent liability: a possible obligation that arises from past events.

Contingent asset: possible assets arising from past events.

Change to accounting policy applied retrospectively (i.e. financial statements altered to show the position as if the new policy had always been in place).

Change to accounting estimates accounted for prospectively (i.e. previous years' results not amended).

Adjust opening balances to correct fundamental **errors** of prior years.

- Sale of goods
- Rendering of services.
- Interest, royalties and dividends.

Recognition criteria depend on type of revenue.

Research costs expensed to income statement.

Development costs capitalised on balance sheet if SECTOR criteria met.

Development costs expensed to income statement if SECTOR criteria not met.

	Cont. liability	Cont. asset
Virtually certain	Provide	Recognise
Probable	Provide	Disclose
Possible	Disclose	Ignore
Remote	Ignore	Ignore

Test your understanding answers

Test your understanding 1

The correct answer is C

Both 1 and 3 involve researching materials, without any form of commercial production in mind.

Test your understanding 2

The correct answer is D

Amortisation will be charged for each of the five years that revenue is generated.

As there is no reliable pattern of this revenue, amortisation will be charged on the straight-line basis.

Therefore the amortisation charge for each of the years ended 31 December 20X6 – 20Y0 will be:

$250,000/5 years = $50,000

Test your understanding 3

The correct answer is A

(1) Sales of year end inventory at less than cost	Adjusting	Closing inventory must be valued at the lower of cost and net realisable value. The post-year-end sale provides evidence of the net realisable value. Therefore closing inventory must be adjusted to reflect the reduction in value.
(2) Share issue	Non-adjusting	
(3) Fire in warehouse	Non-adjusting	If this is BigCo's only or main warehouse and the fire affects going concern, the event will be reclassified as adjusting.
(4) Bankruptcy of major customer	Adjusting	The bankruptcy of the customer provides evidence of their inability to pay their debt at the year-end. The amount outstandinpg from the customer at 30 June 20X6 should therefore be written off in the year end accounts.
(5) Acquisition of TeenyCo Ltd	Non-adjusting	
(6) Receipt of insurance monies	Adjusting	The receipt of insurance monies provides evidence of a year-end asset. The amount subsequently received should be reflected as such in the year-end accounts.

KAPLAN PUBLISHING

Test your understanding 4

(i)   IAS 37 defines a contingency as an obligation or an asset that arises from past events whose existence will be confirmed only by the occurrence or non-occurrence of one or more uncertain future events not wholly within the control of the enterprise. A provision should be made if:

    (a) There is an obligation.

    (b) A transfer is probable.

    (c) There is a reliable estimate.

The legal costs of $5,000 should therefore be provided for since they will have to be paid whatever the outcome of the case. However, the claim is not likely to succeed and so no provision should be made. A disclosure note should be made for the potential loss of $15,000.

(ii) IAS 37 states that an obligation can be legal or constructive. In this case the policy of refunds has created a constructive obligation. A provision for $4,800 should therefore be made.

(iii) As the success of the claim for damages of $100,000 is probable, it constitutes a present obligation as a result of a past obligating event, and would therefore be accounted for as a provision. The success of the counterclaim for $50,000 is also considered probable and would therefore need to be disclosed as a contingent asset (reimbursement). Only if it were considered virtually certain would the counterclaim be recognised as an asset in the statement of financial position.

Statement of cash flows

Chapter learning objectives

Upon completion of this chapter you will be able to:

- explain the differences between profit and cash flows

- explain the need for management to control cash flows

- explain the value of a statement of cash flows to users of financial statements

- explain the inward and outward flows of cash in a typical company

- calculate cash flows from operating activities using the indirect method

- calculate cash flows from operating activities using the direct method

- calculate the cash flows from investing activities

- calculate the cash flows from financing activities

- prepare extracts from statement of cash flows from given information.

THE NEED FOR A CASH FLOW STATEMENT

FORMAT OF A CASH FLOW STATEMENT

PREPARATION OF CASH FLOW STATEMENT

INTERPRETATION USING A CASH FLOW STATEMENT

1 The need for a statement of cash flows

Profit and liquidity

The accounting concepts of accruals and matching are used to compute a profit figure which shows the additional wealth created for the owners of a business during an accounting period. However, it is important for a business to generate cash as well as to make profits. The two do not necessarily go hand in hand.

Expandable text

Profit represents the increase in net assets in a business during an accounting period. This increase can be in cash or it may be 'tied up' in other assets, for example:

- non-current assets may have been purchased

- there may be an increased amount of receivables

- there may be increased investment in inventory

- the liabilities of the business may have decreased, i.e. more cash has been spent this year in paying off suppliers more quickly than was the case last year.

KAPLAN PUBLISHING

The benefits of a statement of cash flows

A statement of cash flows is needed as a consequence of the above differences between profits and cash. It helps to:

- provide additional information on business activities

- assess the current liquidity of the business

- allow the user to see the major types of cash flows into and out of the business

- estimate future cash flows

- determine cash flows generated from trading transactions rather than other cash flows.

Expandable text

The drawbacks of a statement of cash flows

- The statement of cash flows is backward looking. Users of the accounts are particularly interested in the future.

- No interpretation of the statement of cash flows is provided within the accounts. Users are required to draw their own conclusions as to the relevance of the figures contained within it.

- Non-cash transactions, e.g. a bonus issue of shares are not highlighted on the face of the statement of cash flows (although they are disclosed elsewhere within the accounts). These are of interest to users as they will impact future cash flows.

2 Format of a statement of cash flows

IAS 7 Statement of cash flows requires companies to prepare a statement of cash flows within their financial statements. The cash flow must be presented using standard headings.

Statement of cash flows for the period ended ...

	$000	$000
Cash flows from operating activities		
Cash generated from operations	2,550	
Interest paid	(270)	
Dividends paid	(300)	
Income taxes paid	(420)	
Net cash from operating activities		1,560
Cash flows from investing activities		
Purchase of property, plant and equipment	(900)	
Proceeds of sale of equipment	20	
Interest received	200	
Dividends received	200	
Net cash used in investing activities		(480)
Cash flows from financing activities		
Proceeds of issue of shares	1,210	
Repayment of loans	(2,000)	
Net cash used in financing activities		(790)
Net increase in cash and cash equivalents		290
Cash and cash equivalents at the beginning of the period		120
Cash and cash equivalents at the end of the period		410

Expandable text

Key points:

- Operating activities are the principal revenue-producing activities of the business. This section of the statement begins with cash generated from operations. This figure can be calculated using either the direct or indirect method.

- Investing activities are cash spent on non-current assets, proceeds of sale of non-current assets and income from investments.

- Financing activities include the proceeds of issue of shares and long-term borrowings made or repaid.

- Net increase or decrease in cash and cash equivalents is the overall increase (or decrease) in cash and cash equivalents during the year. After adding the cash and cash equivalents at the beginning of the year, the final balance of cash and cash equivalents at the end of the year emerges.

- Cash means cash in hand and deposits available on demand.

- Cash equivalents means short-term highly liquid investments that are readily convertible to known amounts of cash and which are subject to an insignificant risk of changes in value. (Investments are thus not cash equivalents unless they have these two attributes of being readily convertible and with little or no risk of change in value.)

Expandable text

IAS 7 requires a note to the statement of cash flows giving details of the make-up of cash and cash equivalents:

Cash and cash equivalents

	At end of year $000	At beginning of year $000
Cash on hand and balance at banks	40	25
Short-term investments	370	95
	410	120

3 Cash generated from operations

There are two methods of calculating cash from operations – the direct or indirect method. The method used will depend upon the information provided within the question.

Direct method

This method uses information contained in the ledger accounts of the company to calculate the cash from operations figure as follows:

	$	$
Cash sales		X
Cash received from debtors		X
		___
		X
Less:		
Cash purchases	X	
Cash paid to credit suppliers	X	
Cash expenses	X	
	___	
		(X)
		___
Cash generated from operations		X

Expandable text

Example of calculations using direct method

The gross cash flows necessary for the direct method can be derived:

(1) from the accounting records of the entity by totalling the cash receipts and payments directly, or

(2) from the opening and closing statement of financial positions and income statement for the year by constructing summary control accounts for:

 – sales (to derive cash received from customers)

 – purchases (to derive cash payments to suppliers)

 – wages (to derive cash paid to and on behalf of employees).

Example using control accounts

The statement of financial positions of a business are:

	Last year $	This year $
Non-current assets	153,364	149,364
Inventories		
Receivables	265,840	346,000
Cash		165,166
	419,204	660,530

	Last year $	This year $
Share capital	200,000	200,000
Reserves		141,640
	200,000	341,640
Current liabilities	219,204	318,890
	4,19,204	6,60,530

Extracts from the income statement for the year are:

	$	$
Sales revenue		1,589,447
Cost of sales		
Purchases (no inventory)	1,105,830	
Wages and salaries	145,900	
		(1,251,730)
Administration		
Purchases	96,077	
Salaries	100,000	
		(196,077)
Operating profit and retained profit for the year		141,640

Additional information

(1) Payables consist of

	Last year $	This year $
Payables ledger		
Re non-current assets		46,000
Other	210,564	258,240
Wages accrued	8,640	14,650

(2) Purchase invoices relating to the acquisition of non-current assets totalling $80,000 have been posted to the payables ledger during the year.

Calculate the net cash flow from operating activities using the direct method.

Solution

	$
Operating activities	
Cash received from customers (W1)	1,509,287
Cash payments to suppliers (W2)	(1,154,231)
Cash paid to and on behalf of employees (W3)	(239,890)
Net cash inflow from operating activities	115,166

Workings

(W1)

Receivables ledger control account

	$		$
Balance b/f	265,840	Cash receipts (ß)	1,509,287
Sales revenue	1,589,447	Balance c/f	346,000
	1,855,287		1,855,287

(W2)

Payables ledger control account (excluding non-current asset purchases)

	$		$
Cash paid (ß)	1,154,231	Balance b/f	210,564
Balance c/f	258,240	Purchases	
		– Cost of sales	1,105,830
		– Administration	96,077
	1,412,471		1,328,471

Tutorial note: information relating to non-current assets is not included in the payables ledger control account above in order to compute cash paid to suppliers of operating costs.

(W3)

Wages control

	$		$
Net wages paid (ß)	239,890	Balance b/f	8,640
Balance c/f	14,650	Cost of sales	145,900
		Administration	100,000
	254,540		254,540

Indirect method

This method reconciles between profit before tax (as reported in the income statement) and cash generated from operations as follows:

	$
Profit before tax	X
Finance cost	X
Investment income	(X)
Depreciation charge	X
Loss/(profit) on disposal of non-current assets	X/(X)
(Increase)/decrease in inventories	(X)/X
(Increase)/decrease in trade receivables	(X)/X
Increase/(decrease) in trade payables	X/(X)
Cash generated from operations	X

This working begins with the profit before tax as shown in the income statement. The remaining figures are the adjustments necessary to convert the profit figure to the cash flow for the period.

Depreciation – Added back to profit because it is a non-cash expense

Interest expense – Added back because it is not part of cash generated from operations (the interest actually paid is deducted later)

Increase in trade receivables – Deducted because this is part of the profit not yet realised into cash but tied up in receivables

Decrease in inventories – Added on because the decrease in inventories liberates extra cash

Decrease in trade payables – Deducted because the reduction in payables must reduce cash

In order to prepare a statement of cash flows, information from the current and prior year statement of financial position and the current year income statement is used. The following financial statements provide the source data for the requirements of Test your understanding 1 throughout this chapter:

Test your understanding 1

Requirement 1

Statement of cash flows source data

Statement of financial position of Geronimo at 31 December

	20X6	20X5
	$000	$000
Non-current assets	1,048	750
Accumulated depreciation	(190)	(120)
	858	630
Current assets		
Inventory	98	105
Trade receivables	102	86
Dividend receivable	57	50
Cash	42	18
	299	259
Total assets	1,157	889

	20X6	20X5
	$000	$000
Capital and reserves		
Share capital	200	120
Share premium	106	80
Revaluation reserve	212	12
Accumulated profits	283	226
	801	438
Non-current liabilities		
Loan	200	300
Current liabilities		
Trade payables	47	52
Dividend payable	30	27
Interest accrual	3	5
Tax	76	67
	156	151
Total liabilities	1,157	889

Income statement of Geronimo at 31 December 20X6

	$000
Sales revenue	1,100
Cost of sales	(678)
Gross profit	422
Operating expenses	(309)
Operating profit	113
Investment income – interest	15
– dividends	57
Finance charge	(22)
Income tax	(71)
Net profit for year	92

> Operating expenses include a loss on disposal of non-current assets of $5,000.
>
> - During the year plant which originally cost $80,000 and with depreciation of $15,000 was disposed of.
>
> Calculate the cash generated from operations using the indirect method.

4 Cash from operating activities

Cash flows may include:

- interest paid
- dividends paid
- income taxes paid.

Calculation of interest/income taxes paid

The cash flow should be calculated by reference to:

- the charge to profits for the item (shown in the income statement); and
- any opening or closing payable balance shown on the statement of financial position.

A T account working may be useful:

e.g Interest payable

	$		$
		Interest accrual b/f	X
Cash paid (ß)	X	Income statement	
		Interest charge	X
Interest accrual c/f	X		
	X		X

If there is no change to the opening or closing then it should be the statement of financial position payable amount.

Calculation of dividends paid

The cash flow should again be calculated by reference to the charge to profits and the opening or closing dividend payable shown in the statement of financial position.

Note that the charge to profits for dividends is not shown in the income statement. It can, however, be derived using an accumulated profits T account working.

Test your understanding 2
Requirement 2 Identify and calculate the remaining amounts to be shown under the heading 'Cash flows from operating activities' within Geronimo's statement of cash flows.

5 Cash from investing activities

Cash inflows may include:

- interest received
- dividends received
- proceeds of sale of equipment.

Cash outflows may include:

- purchase of property, plant and equipment.

Calculation of interest and dividends received

Again, the calculation should take account of both the income receivable shown in the income statement and any relevant receivables balance from the opening and closing statement of financial positions.

A T account working may be useful:

e.g Interest receivable

	$		$
Interest receivable b/f	X		
Income statement interest receivable	X	Cash received (ß)	X
		Interest receivable c/f	X
	X		X

Test your understanding 3

Requirement 3

Identify and calculate the dividends and interest received to be shown under the heading ' cash flow from investing activities' within Geronimo's statement of cash flows .

Calculation of purchase of property, plant and equipment and proceeds of sale of equipment

These amounts are often the trickiest to calculate within a statement of cash flows. It is therefore recommended that T account workings are used.

The following T accounts will be required for each class of assets:

- cost account
- accumulated depreciation account
- disposals account (where relevant).

Data provided in the source financial statements should then be entered into these T accounts and the required cash flows found – often as balancing figures.

NB If there is evidence of a revaluation, remember to include the uplift in value on the debit side of the cost T account.

In some cases, insufficient detail is provided to produce separate cost and accumulated depreciation accounts. Instead, a net book value account should be used:

Net book value(NBV)

	$		$
NBV b/f	X		
Additions at NBV (= cash to purchase PPE)	X	Disposals at NBV	X
Revaluation	X	Depreciation charge for year	X
		Net book value c/f	X
	X		X

Test your understanding 4

Requirement 4

Identify and calculate the cash outflow to purchase property, plant and equipment and the proceeds from the sale of equipment to be shown under the heading 'Cash flows from investing activities' within Geronimo's statement of cash flows.

6 Cash from financing activities

Cash inflows may include:

- proceeds of issue of shares
- proceeds of issue of loans/debentures.

Cash outflows may include:

- repayment of loans/debentures.

Calculation of proceeds of issue of shares

This cash inflow is derived by comparison of the sum brought forward and sum carried forward balances on two accounts:

- share capital
- share premium.

Calculation of proceeds of issue of loans/repayment of loans

This cash flow is derived by simply subtracting the brought forward balance from the carried forward.

Test your understanding 5

Requirement 5

Identify and calculate each of the amounts to be shown under the heading 'Cash flows from financing activities' within Geronimo's statement of cash flows.

Test your understanding 6

Requirement 6

Complete the following proforma statement of cash flows for Geronimo using your answers to Test your understanding 1 requirements 1-5.

Statement of cash flows for Geronimo for year ended 31 December 20X6

	$000	$000
Cash flows from operating activities		
Cash generated from operations		
Interest paid		
Dividends paid		
Tax paid		
		————
Net cash from operating activities		
Cash flows from investing activities		
Proceeds of sale of equipment		
Purchase of property, plant and equipment		
Interest received		
Dividends received		
		————
Net cash used in investing activities		
Cash flows from financing activities		
Proceeds of issue of shares		
Repayment of loans		
		————
Net cash used in financing activities		
Net increase in cash and cash equivalents		
		————
Cash and cash equivalents at beginning of period		
		————
Cash and cash equivalents at end period		

Test your understanding 7

You are given below, in summarised form, the accounts of Algernon, a limited company, for 20X6 and 20X7.

	20X6 SFP			20X7 SFP		
	Cost	Dep'n	Net	Cost	Dep'n	Net
	$	$	$	$	$	$
Plant	10,000	4,000	6,000	11,000	5,000	6,000
Buildings	50,000	10,000	40,000	90,000	11,000	79,000
			46,000			85,000
Investments at cost			50,000			80,000
Land			43,000			63,000
Inventory			55,000			65,000
Receivables			40,000			50,000
Bank			3,000			
			237,000			343,000
Ordinary shares of $1 each			40,000			50,000
Share premium			12,000			14,000
Revaluation reserve (land)			–			20,000
Accumulated profit			45,000			45,000
10% Loan notes			100,000			150,000
Payables			40,000			60,000
Bank			–			4,000
			237,000			343,000

Income statement

	20X6	20X7
	$	$
Sales	200,000	200,000
Cost of sales	(100,000)	(120,000)
	100,000	80,000
Expenses	(50,000)	(47,000)
	50,000	33,000
Interest	(10,000)	(13,000)
Net profit for year	40,000	20,000

Notes:

A $20,000 dividend has been paid in the year.

(a) Prepare a statement of cash flows for Algernon for 20X7, to explain as far as possible the movement in the bank balance. The statement of cash flows should be prepared using the direct method.

(b) Using the summarised accounts given, and the statement you have just prepared, comment on the position, progress and direction of Algernon.

Test your understanding 8

Part of a company's statement of cash flows is shown below:

	$'000
Operating profit	1,255
Loss on disposal	(455)
Increase in receivables	(198)
Increase in payables	340

The following criticisms of the extract have been made:

(1) The loss on disposal should have been added, not deducted.

(2) Increase in receivables should have been added, not deducted.

(3) Increase in payables should have been deducted, not added.

Which of the criticisms is valid?

A   1, 2 and 3

B   1 only

C   2 and 3 only

D   none of them

Test your understanding 9

Which of the following could appear in a company's statement of cash flows?

(1) Proposed dividend

(2) Dividends received

(3) Bonus issue of shares

(4) Surplus on revaluation of non-current assets

A   1 and 2

B   1,2 and 3

C   2 only

D   2 and 3

Test your understanding 10

The following details are provided to the accountant of Caddyshack Ltd, which has an operating profit of $469,850 in the year ended 31 December 20X6:

(1) Depreciation of $37,400 has been charged to the income statement; this included an amount of $7,600 which was the loss on disposal of a non-current asset.

(2) The following extract of the statement of financial position at 31 December 20X5 and 20X6 have been provided:

	31 December 20X6	31 December 20X5
	$000	$000
Inventory	145	167
Trade receivables	202	203
Prepayments	27	16
Trade payables	196	212
Interest accrual	6	28

What is the cash generated from operations?

A $511,250

B $510,850

C $501,250

D $503,250

Chapter summary

The need for a statement of cash flows

- Helps to assess liquidity of a company.
- Helps to assess future cash flows.
- User can see cash flows in and out of the business.

Format of a statement of cash flows

IAS 7 requires the cash flow statement to have three headings:

- Operating activities
- Investing activities
- Financing activities.

Preparation of a statement of cash flows

The cash movement is simply the movement between the current and previous year's balance in the statement of financial position. Watch out for trickier areas such as taxation, and non-current assets where a working will need to be done.

Interpretation using a statement of cash flows

The cash flow provides useful information including:

- how a business spends and receives cash
- whether operating activities yield a positive cash flow
- whether the business has the ability to generate cash in the future.

Test your understanding answers

Test your understanding 1

Requirement 1

	$000
Net profit before taxation	163
Finance charge	22
Investment income	(72)
Depreciation (W1)	85
Loss on disposal of plant	5
Decrease in inventory	7
Increase in trade receivables	(16)
Decrease in trade payables	(5)
	————
Cash generated from operations	189
	————

(W1)

Accumulated depreciation			
	$000		$000
Disposals	15	balance b/f	120
Balance c/f	190	Depreciation charge (ß)	85
	————		————
	205		205
	————		————

Test your understanding 2

Requirement 2

Interest paid

Interest payable

	$000		$000
		Interest accrual b/f	5
Cash paid (ß)	24	Income statement	
Interest accrual c/f	3	finance charge	22
	___		___
	27		27
	___		___

Dividends paid

Accumulated profits

	$000		$000
		Balance b/f	226
Dividend (ß)	35	Retained profit shown in income statement	92
Balance c/f	283		
	___		___
	318		318
	___		___

Dividend payable

	$000		$000
		Dividend payable b/f	27
Cash paid (ß)	32	Dividend (accumulated profits)	35
Dividend payable c/f	30		
	___		___
	62		62
	___		___

Income tax payable

	$		$
		Tax payable b/f	67
Cash paid (ß)	62	Income statement tax charge	71
Tax payable c/f	76		
	138		138

Test your understanding 3

Requirement 3

There is no balance for interest receivable at the start or end of the year; therefore interest received must equal interest receivable in the income statement

Interest received $15,000

Dividends received

Dividends receivable

	$		$
Dividends receivable b/f	50	Cash received (ß)	50
Income statement dividends receivable	57	Dividends receivable c/f	57
	X		X

Test your understanding 4

Requirement 4

(see Solution to Requirement 1 for accumulated depreciation account.)

PPE Cost

	$000		$000
balance b/f	750		
Additions (= Cash to purchase PPE)	178	Disposals	80
Revaluation	200	Balance c/f	1,048
	1,128		1,128

Disposals

	$000		$000
Cost	80	Accumulated depreciation	15
		Loss on disposal	5
		Proceeds (ß)	60

Test your understanding 5

Requirement 5

	20X6	20X5	
	$000	$000	$000
Share capital	200	120	
Share premium	106	80	
	——	——	
	306	200	
	——		
Proceeds of share issue			106

Repayment of loan

- Balance on loan account was $300,000 in 20X5; in 20X6 it is $200,000.
- Therefore $100,000 has been repaid.

KAPLAN PUBLISHING

Test your understanding 6

Requirement 6

Statement of cash flows for Geronimo for year ended 31 December 20X6

	$000	$000
Cash flows from operating activities		
Cash generated from operations	189	
Interest paid	(24)	
Dividends paid	(32)	
Tax paid	(62)	
		71
Net cash from operating activities		
Cash flows from investing activities		
Proceeds of sale of equipment	60	
Purchase of property, plant and equipment	(178)	
Interest received	15	
Dividends received	50	
Net cash used in investing activities		(53)
Cash flows from financing activities		
Proceeds of issue of shares	106	
Repayment of loans	(100)	
Net cash used in financing activities		6
Net increase in cash and cash equivalents		24
Cash and cash equivalents at beginning of period		18
Cash and cash equivalents at end of period		42

Test your understanding 7

Statement of Cashflows for Algernon for year ended 31 December 2007

	$	$
Cash flows from operating activities		
Cash receipts from customers (W1)	190,000	
Cash paid to suppliers and employees (W2)	(155,000)	
	————	
Cash generated from operations	35,000	
Interest paid	(13,000)	
Dividends paid	(20,000)	–
Net cash from operating activities		2,000
Cash flows from investing activities		
Purchase of tangible non-current assets (1,000 + 40,000)	(41,000)	
Purchase of investments	(30,000)	
Net cash used for investing activities		(71,000)
Cash flows from financing activities		
Issue of shares (10,000 + 2,000)	12,000	
Loan notes	50,000	
	————	
Net cash from financing activities		62,000
Net decrease in cash and cash equivalents		(7,000)
Cash and cash equivalents at 1 January 20X7		3,000
		————
Cash and cash equivalents at 31 December 20X7		(4,000)
		————

	31 December	
	20X6	20X7
	$	$
Balance at bank	3,000	(4,000)
	————	————

KAPLAN PUBLISHING

Workings

(W1) Receipts from sales

Receivables control

	$		$
Balance b/f	40,000	Cash receipts (ß)	190,000
Sales revenue	200,000	Balance c/f	50,000
	240,000		240,000

(W2) Payables and wages control

Payable and wages control

	$		$
Cash paid (ß)	155,000	Balance b/f	40,000
Depreciation	2,000	Purchases re cost of sales (W3)	130,000
Balance c/f	60,000		
		Expenses	47,000
	217,000		217,000

(W3) Cost of sales

Cost of sales

	$		$
Opening inventory	55,000	Cost of sales	120,000
Purchases and wages (ß)	130,000	Closing inventory	65,000
	185,000		185,000

Tutorial note Little information has been given as to the nature of the costs of the company; for example, no information is supplied on wages and salaries. The payments figure thus includes all cash outflows relating to trading activities. Depreciation would have been charged in either cost of sales or expenses and this needs to be adjusted for. It does not matter whether the adjustment is shown in the payables control or the cost of sales accounts.

(b) Algernon has invested substantially in buildings, investments, inventory and receivables in the year. The finance has come from new share capital in part but mainly from loans. The equity to assets ratio of the company has thus decreased. The working capital has been financed by an equal increase in trade payables.

The profits have been fully distributed as dividends despite the halving of profits from last year. It might have been wiser to cut back on dividends in the period of expansion until the benefits of the expansion are seen in the form of higher profits.

Test your understanding 8

The correct answer is B

A loss on disposal should be added back to profit as it is a non-cash expense.

Test your understanding 9

The correct answer is C

Dividends received involve a cash receipt. The other transactions do not involve a movement of cash.

Test your understanding 10

The correct answer is D

	$
Operating profit	469,850
Depreciation and loss on disposal	37,400
Decrease in inventory	22,000
Decrease in trade receivables	1,000
Increase in prepayments	(11,000)
Decrease in trade payables	(16,000)
	503,250

Note that the movement in the interest accrual is not part of the reconciliation as this is dealt with within the Interest paid line of the statement of cash flows.

The regulatory and conceptual framework

Chapter learning objectives

Upon completion of this chapter you will be able to:

- explain the regulatory system:
  - International Accounting Standards Committee (IASC) Foundation
  - International Accounting Standards Board (IASB),
  - the Standards Advisory Council (SAC) and
  - the International Financial Reporting Interpretations Committee (IFRIC)

- explain how International Financial Reporting Standards (IFRSs) affect the financial reporting process

- explain the meaning of the qualitative characteristics of financial reporting and define and apply each of the following:
  - relevance (including materiality)
  - reliability (including faithful representation, substance over form, neutrality, prudence and completeness)
  - comparability
  - understandability

- illustrate the problems of achieving a balance between the qualitative characteristics

- explain the meaning of accounting concepts and define and apply each of the following:
    - going concern
    - accruals
    - consistency
    - materiality
    - substance over form
    - prudence
- explain the advantages and disadvantages of historical cost accounting (HCA) in times of changing prices
- explain in principle the main alternatives to HCA:
    - replacement cost
    - net realisable value
    - economic value.

1 The regulatory framework

The need for regulation

- Regulation ensures that accounts are sufficiently reliable and useful, and prepared without unnecessary delay.

- Financial accounts are used as the starting point for calculating taxable profits.

- The annual report and accounts is the main document used for reporting to shareholders on the condition and performance of a company.

- The stock markets rely on the financial statements published by companies.

- International investors prefer information to be presented in a similar and comparable way, no matter where the company is based.

The role of international accounting standards

- International accounting standards are the rules that govern accounting for transactions.

- They don't have the force of law. They are effective only if adopted by the national regulatory bodies.

2 The role and structure of the IASB

The **IASC Foundation** is the supervisory body. Its objective is to:

- develop, in the public interest, a single set of high-quality accounting standards

- promote the use and rigorous application of those standards

- bring about the convergence of national accounting standards and international accounting standards.

- The **IASB** is responsible for issuing new International Financial Reporting Standards (IFRSs).

- The **IFRIC** issue rapid guidance where there are differing interpretations of IASs/IFRSs.

- The **SAC** advises the IASB in developing new accounting standards.

Expandable text

The regulatory framework

The main source of regulations for the purpose of the ACCA's Preparing Financial Statements examination is the International Accounting Standards Board (IASB) which has issued a number of authoritative IASs and IFRSs.

Structure of the International Accounting Standards Board

International Financial Reporting Interpretations Committee (IFRIC)

The IFRIC's main task is to interpret the application of IASs and IFRSs if difficulties arise. They may issue Draft Interpretations for public comment before finalising an Interpretation. They report to the IASB and must obtain Board approval for their Interpretations before issue.

Standards Advisory Council

The SAC exists to provide the IASB with advice on major standard-setting projects and other matters. It has about 50 members, including representatives of national standard setters and other interested parties.

Benchmark and allowed alternative treatments

An IAS sometimes contains more than one permitted accounting treatment for a transaction or event. One of them may be designated the benchmark treatment. The other treatments, if acceptable, are classified as allowed alternative treatments. The IASB tries to limit the number of alternative treatments allowed in an IAS, and thus tries to minimise the number of Standards containing allowed alternative treatments.

Generally accepted accounting practice (GAAP)

You may come across the expression generally accepted accounting practice (GAAP). This means the set of accounting practices applied in a given country or context. For an individual country, GAAP is a combination of legislation, accounting standards, stock exchange requirements and, in areas where detailed rules do not exist, other acceptable accounting practices. Thus one may speak of 'UK GAAP' or 'US GAAP'. In an international context, 'GAAP' means accounting practice as defined in IASs, with each country adding its own local requirements and practices.

3 The conceptual framework

The framework for the preparation and presentation of financial statements sets out the concepts that underlie financial statements for external users. It is designed to:

- assist the Board of the IASB in developing new standards and reviewing existing ones

- assist in harmonising accounting standards and procedures

- assist national standard-setting bodies in developing national standards

- assist preparers of financial statements in applying IASs/IFRSs and in dealing with topics not yet covered by IASs/IFRSs

- assist auditors in forming an opinion as to whether financial statements conform with IASs/IFRSs

- assist users of financial statements in interpreting financial statements

- provide those interested in the work of the IASB with information about its approach to the formulation of IFRSs.

The scope of the framework

The framework deals with:

- the objective of financial statements
- the qualitative characteristics that determine the usefulness of information in financial statements
- the definition, recognition and measurement of the elements from which financial statements are constructed (not examinable at this level).
- concepts of capital and capital maintenance (not examinable at this level).

Underlying assumptions of the framework

The framework identifies two underlying assumptions:

(1) the accruals basis of accounting

The accruals basis of accounting means that the effects of transactions and other events are recognised as they occur and not as cash or its equivalent is received or paid.

(2) the going concern basis.

The going concern basis assumes that the entity has neither the need nor the intention to liquidate or curtail materially the scale of its operations.

These also appear in IAS 1.

Faithful representation

There is no absolute definition of fair presentation (known as the true and fair view in the UK). It is felt that its meaning evolves over time and with changes in generally accepted accounting practice (GAAP).

When do financial statements show fair presentation?

Financial statements will generally show a fair presentation when:

they conform with accounting standards
they conform with the any relevant legal requirements
they have applied the qualitative characteristics from the Framework.

True and fair override

IAS 1 states that an entity whose financial statements comply with IFRSs should disclose that fact.

However in extremely rare circumstances management may conclude that compliance with an IFRS or interpretation would be misleading.

In this case an entity should depart from the requirement of the standard provided the relevant regulatory framework permits such departure.

4 Objectives of financial statements

The objective of financial statements is to provide information about:

- the financial position of an entity (provided mainly in the statement of financial position)
- the financial performance (provided mainly in the statement of comprehensive income) and
- changes in the financial position of an entity (provided in the statement of changes in equity and statement of cash flows)

that is useful to a wide range of users in making economic decisions.

Expandable text

User groups

- equity investors (existing and potential)
- existing lenders and potential lenders
- employees
- stock market analysts and advisers
- business contacts including customers,
- suppliers and competitors
- the government, including the tax authorities
- the general public.

5 Qualitative characteristics of financial statements

The qualitative characteristics of financial statements are a set of attributes which together make the information in the financial statements useful to users.

```
            QUALITATIVE CHARACTERISTICS OF
             USEFUL FINANCIAL INFORMATION
```

RELEVANT	RELIABLE	COMPARABLE	UNDERSTANDABLE
• To the needs of users to assist in evaluating performance.	• Can be relied upon • Free from material error • Neutral • Complete • Prudent.	• With other businesses • With the previous periods' results.	• Must be presented so it is understandable to users.

Expandable Text

Problems of achieving a balance between the qualitative characteristics

At any given point in time it is unlikely that all of the qualitative characteristics can be satisfied, and therefore there will be conflicts between them. Examples are as follows:

- **Relevance and timeliness**

  If financial statements are to be tailored to the needs of each individual user, then they will take longer to prepare.

- **Understandability and completeness**

  If all aspects of the business are to be shown, this may make the financial statements less comprehensible.

- **Relevance and reliability** – sometimes the information that is most relevant is not the most reliable or vice versa. In such conflicts, the information that is most relevant of the information that is reliable should be used.

KAPLAN PUBLISHING

This conflict might also arise over the timeliness of information, e.g. a delay in providing information can make it out of date and so affect its relevance, but reporting on transactions before uncertainties are resolved may affect the reliability of the information. Information should not be provided until it is reliable.

- **Neutrality and prudence** – neutrality requires information to be free of deliberate or systematic bias while prudence is a potentially biased concept towards not overstating gains or assets or understating losses or liabilities. Neutrality and prudence are reconciled by finding a balance that ensures that the deliberate and systematic overstatement of assets and gains and understatement of losses and liabilities do not occur.

6 Other accounting principles

These generally recognised principles underlie accounting and financial statements.

Going concern	The assumption that the business will c ontinue in operation for the foreseeable future without significantly curtailing its activity.
Accruals/Matching	To calculate the profit for the period, one must include all the revenue and expenditure relating to the period, whether or not the cash has been received or paid. This concept also states that income and expenses should be matched against each other within an accounting period as far as possible.
Consistency	Items should be treated in the same way year on year. This will enable valid comparisons to be made. However, if circumstances change then a business is allowed to change policies to give a fairer representation of the financial statements.
Materiality	Materiality is a threshold quality that is demanded of all information given in the financial statements, i.e. information that is material should be given in the financial statements but information that is not material need not be given. Information is material if its omission or misstatement might reasonably be expected to influence the economic decisions of users. Whether or not information is material will depend on the size and nature of the item and the size of the business.

Substance overform	The economic substance of a transaction should be recorded rather than simply its legal form. E.g. A non-current asset acquired under a hire purchase agreement should be accounted for as an owned asset. This is the commercial substance of such a situation, even though it is not the case legally.
Prudence	Prudence is the inclusion of a degree of caution when making estimates under conditions of uncertainty. It ensures that assets and income are not overstated and liabilities or expenses are not understated.

Test your understanding 1

Which of the following statements are correct?

(1) Materiality means that only tangible items may be recognised as assets.

(2) Substance over form means that the commercial effect of a transaction must always be shown in the financial statements even if this differs from legal form.

(3) A business may only change an accounting policy to achieve a fairer representation.

A   2 and 3 only.

B   All of them.

C   1 and 2 only.

D   1 and 3 only.

7 Historical cost

The limitations of historical cost accounting

Under historical cost accounting, assets are recorded at the amount of cash or cash equivalents paid, or the fair value of the consideration given for them.

Liabilities are recorded at the amount of proceeds received in exchange for the obligation. This method of accounting has advantages, but it also has serious disadvantages.

Expandable text

The limitations of historical cost accounting

Introduction

Virtually everything you have studied so far in this book has been based on historical cost accounting. Under historical cost accounting, assets are recorded at the amount of cash or cash equivalents paid, or the fair value of the consideration given for them.

Liabilities are recorded at the amount of proceeds received in exchange for the obligation. This method of accounting has advantages, but it also has serious disadvantages.

Advantages of historical cost accounting

(1) Records are based on objectively verifiable amounts (actual cost of assets, etc.).

(2) It is simple and cheap.

(3) The profit concept is well understood.

(4) Within limits, historical cost figures provide a basis for comparison with the results of other companies for the same period or similar periods, with the results of the same company for previous periods and with budgets.

(5) Lack of acceptable alternatives.

Disadvantages of historical cost accounting

(1) It overstates profits when prices are rising through inflation. Several factors contribute to this. For example, if assets are retained at their original cost, depreciation is based on that cost. As inflation pushes prices up, the true value to the enterprise of the use of the asset becomes progressively more than the depreciation charge.

   This disadvantage can be overcome by revaluing non-current assets. IAS 16 then requires depreciation to be based on the revalued amount.

(2)   It maintains financial capital but does not maintain physical capital.

If an enterprise makes a profit it must necessarily have more net assets. If the whole of that profit is distributed as dividend by a company, or withdrawn by a sole trader, the enterprise has the same capital at the end of the year as it had at the beginning. In other words, it has maintained its financial capital. However, it will not have maintained its physical capital if prices have risen through inflation during the year, because the financial capital will not buy the same inventory and other assets to enable the enterprise to continue operating at the same level.

(3)   The statement of financial position does not show the value of the enterprise. A statement of financial position summarises the assets and liabilities of the enterprise, but there are several reasons why it does not represent the true value of the enterprise. One reason for this could be that the use of historical cost accounting means that assets are included at cost less depreciation based on that cost rather than at current value. (Another reason is, of course, that not all the assets are included in the statement of financial position– internally generated goodwill does not appear.)

(4)   It provides a poor basis for assessing performance. The profit is overstated as explained in (1), while assets are understated as discussed in (3) above. The result is that return on capital employed is doubly distorted and exaggerated.

(5)   It does not recognise the loss suffered through holding monetary assets while prices are rising. An enterprise holding cash or receivables through a period of inflation suffers a loss as their purchasing power declines.

The impact of changing prices

When prices are not changing, historical cost accounting (HCA) does accurately and fairly show profits made by the enterprise and the value of the assets less liabilities to the enterprise. When prices are changing, however, there are problems.

Depreciation

Under a system of HCA, the purpose of depreciation is simply to allocate the original cost (less estimated residual value) of a non-current asset over its estimated useful life. If depreciation is charged in the income statement, then by reducing the amount which can be paid out as a dividend, funds are retained within the company rather than paid to the shareholders. When the time comes to replace the asset, management must ensure that those funds are available in a sufficiently liquid form.

When inflation is taken into account, we can note that:

(1) The depreciation charge is based on the original cost of the asset measured in terms of historical $s, whereas the revenues against which depreciation is matched are measured in terms of current $s. The profit figure we calculate is not meaningful as it ignores price changes which have taken place since the asset was purchased.

(2) Although the concept of depreciation ensures that the capital of the enterprise is maintained intact in money terms, it does not ensure that the capital of the enterprise is maintained intact in real terms (see examples below).

The accumulated depreciation at the end of the asset's useful life will fall short of its replacement cost.

Example 1

An enterprise starts off with $1,000 cash and buys two machines at a cost of $500 each. All profits are distributed to the owners. At the end of ten years the company has no machines and $1,000 cash. Thus the capital of the enterprise has been maintained intact in money terms. Suppose at the end of ten years the current replacement cost of one machine is $1,000. Therefore the $1,000 cash at the end of the ten years will buy only one machine. In real terms, the capital at the end of the period is half that at the beginning of the period.

Profit has been over-distributed. If profit is a true surplus, the owners should be able to withdraw all the profit and be in exactly the same position as before in real terms.

Inventory and cost of sales

Assume a company values inventory on a historical cost basis using the FIFO method. During a period of inflation the effect of this method is to overstate the real profit of the enterprise, since sales (in current terms) are matched with cost of sales (in historical terms). If the company distributed the whole of its historical cost profit, it would not be maintaining the capital of the enterprise intact in real terms.

Example 2

An enterprise starts off on 1 January 20X7 with $1,000 cash (contributed by the proprietor). On the same day it purchases 500 motors at $2 each. These are sold on 31 March 20X7 for proceeds of $1,650. At this date the replacement cost of an identical motor is $2.20.

Under HCA the profit for the three months is $650 ($1,650 – $1,000). If the proprietor withdraws this profit, the closing statement of financial position at 31 March would show capital account $1,000 represented by cash of $1,000.

Although capital has been maintained intact in money terms (it was $1,000 at 1 January), it has not been maintained intact in real terms. At 31 March $1,000 cash will buy only 455 (approximately!) motors.

Comparability of data over time

Example 3

We saw earlier a need for users of accounts to be able to compare the results of the enterprise over a number of years so that trends could be identified. Thus, if sales were $100,000 four years ago and $130,000 in the current year, we could conclude that sales have increased by 30%. However, in real terms the increase may not be this amount, as price levels may have changed in the previous four years. If price levels have risen by 40% in the last four years, then the sales should be $140,000 in the current year in order to maintain the real value of sales. There has therefore been a real decline.

Expandable text

Alternatives to historical cost accounting

- Replacement cost involves recording assets at the cost of replacing them. An advantage is that the replacement cost is more up to date than the historical cost.

- Net realisable value assets and liabilities are carried at the amount which could currently be obtained by an orderly disposal. Assets are recorded at the amount after deducting the actual/expected disposal costs. Liabilities are recorded at their settlement values.

- Economic value involves recording assets at the value of keeping them in the business. i.e. not disposing of them. Assets recorded in this way are normally carried at the present value of the future discounted net cash flows. Liabilities are recorded at their discounted net present values.

KAPLAN PUBLISHING

Test your understanding 2

In a time of rising prices, what effect does the use of the historical cost concept have on an entity's profit and asset values?

A   Both profit and asset values are understated.

B   Profit is understated and asset values overstated.

C   Profit is overstated and asset values understated.

D   Both profit and asset values are overstated.

Chapter summary

REGULATORY AND CONCEPTUAL FRAMEWORK

The regulatory framework

- IASB produce accounting standards.
- SAC and IFRIC assist in standard-setting process.

The conceptual framework

- The framework for the preparation and presentation of accounts.

Other accounting principles

- Going concern
- Accruals
- Consistency
- Materiality
- Substance over form
- Prudence.

Objective of financial statements

- Aim to provide information about financial position and performance of an entity.

Historical Cost Accounting

- Advantages
- Disadvantages
- Alternatives.

Qualitative characteristics

- Relevant
- Reliable
- Comparable
- Understandable.

Test your understanding answers

Test your understanding 1

The correct answer is A

Test your understanding 2

The correct answer is C

KAPLAN PUBLISHING

Questions

MULTIPLE CHOICE QUESTIONS

Chapter 2: Statement of financial position and income statement

Q 1 Which of the following is the accounting equation

A Assets – Liabilities – Capital = Drawings + Profit

B Assets = Liabilities – Capital + Profit – Drawings

C Assets – Liabilities – Capital = Profit – Drawings

D Assets + Liabilities = Capital + Profit – Drawings

(1 mark)

Q 2 Which of the following statements is true?

A The income statement illustrates a business' financial position.

B The income statement includes dividends paid.

C The income statement illustrates the business' financial performance.

D The income statement has to show the results for one year.

(1 mark)

Q 3 What is included in the statement of financial position of a business?

A Capital, drawings, assets and liabilities.

B Capital, dividends paid, sales and assets.

C Assets, liabilities, profit on disposals of non-current assets and introduced capital.

D Dividends paid, assets, discounts and liabilities.

(1 mark)

Q 4 Which of the following is incorrect?

A The statement of financial position and income statement form part of the financial statements of a business.

B The statement of financial position illustrates the accounting equation.

C The income statement illustrates the accounting equation.

D The statement of financial position and income statement illustrate the financial position and performance of the business.

(1 mark)

Q 5 **Which statement is not true?**

A Inventory is shown on the income statement and in the statement of financial position.

B Expenses should be included on the income statement.

C Inventory should be included on the statement of financial position only.

D Receivables are included in current assets on the statement of financial position.

(1 mark)

Chapter 3: Double entry bookkeeping

Q 6 **Which of the following is correct?**

A A debit entry will increase non-current assets.
A debit entry will increase drawings.
A debit entry will increase profit.

B A credit entry will increase a bank overdraft.
A debit entry will increase payables.
A credit entry will increase receivables.

C A debit entry will increase profit.
A debit entry will increase receivables.
A debit entry will decrease payables.

D A debit entry will increase receivables.
A credit entry will decrease non-current assets.
A credit entry will increase profit.

(1 mark)

Q 7 **A credit balance on a ledger account indicates:**

A an asset or an expense

B a liability or an expense

C an amount owing to the organisation

D a liability or revenue

(1 mark)

Q 8 **The double entry system of bookkeeping normally results in which of the following balances on the ledger accounts?**

Debit balances	Credit balances
A Assets and revenues	Liabilities, capital and expenses
B Revenues, capital and liabilities	Assets and expenses
C Assets and expenses	Liabilities, capital and revenues
D Assets, expenses and capital	Liabilities and revenues

(1 mark)

Q 9 The main aim of accounting is to:

A maintain ledger accounts for every asset and liability

B provide financial information to users of such information

C produce a trial balance

D record every financial transaction individually

(1 mark)

Q 10 A Debit entry could lead to:

A an increase in assets or a decrease in expenses

B an increase in sales or an increase in liabilities

C a decrease in sales or a decrease in assets

D a decrease in liabilities or an increase in expenses

(1 mark)

Q 11 A credit entry could lead to:

A an increase in assets or increase in liabilities

B an increase in expense or an increase in share capital

C an increase in liabilities or an increase in share capital

D an increase in liabilities and a decrease in sales

(1 mark)

Chapter 4: Inventory

Q 12 Tracey's business sells three products – A, B and C. The following information was available at the year end:

	A $ per unit	B $ per unit	C $ per unit
Original cost	7	10	19
Estimated selling price	15	13	20
Selling and distribution costs	2	5	6
Units of inventory	20	25	15

The value of inventory at the year end should be:

A $675

B $670

C $795

D $550

(2 marks)

Q **13** An inventory record card shows the following details:

January 1   50 units in inventory at a cost of $10 per unit

4   90 units purchased at a cost of $15 per unit

10   65 units sold

20   30 units purchased at a cost of $20 per unit

26   40 units sold

What is the value of inventory at 31 January using the FIFO method?

A $1,125

B $725

C $975

D $1,000

(2 marks)

Q **14** **What would be the effect on a business' profit, which has been calculated including inventory at cost, of discovering that one of its inventory items which cost $7,500 has a net realisable value of $8,500?**

A an increase of $8,500

B an increase of $1,000

C no effect at all

D a decrease of $1,000

(1 mark)

Q **15** According to IAS 2 Inventories, which of the following costs should be included in valuing the inventories of a manufacturing company?

1) Carriage outwards

2) Depreciation of factory plant

3) Carriage inwards

4) General administrative overheads

A All four items

B 1, 3 and 4 only

C 1 and 2 only

D 2 and 3 only

(1 mark)

Q 16 The closing inventory of X amounted to $116,400 excluding the following two inventory lines:

- 400 items which had cost $4 each. All were sold after the statement of financial position date for $3 each, with selling expenses of $200 for the batch.
- 200 different items which had cost $30 each. These items were found to be defective at the statement of financial position date. Rectification work after the statement of financial position amounted to $1,200, after which they were sold for $35 each, with selling expenses totalling $300.

Which of the following total figures should appear in the statement of financial position of X for inventory?

A $122,300

B $121,900

C $122,900

D $123,300

(2 marks)

Chapter 5: Sales tax

Q 17 All the sales of Gail, a retailer, were made at a price inclusive of sales tax at the standard rate of 17.5% and all purchases and expenses bore sales tax at the standard rate. For the three months ended 31 March 2005 gross sales were $23,500, purchases were $12,000 (net) and expenses $800 (net).

How much is due to the tax authority for the quarter?

A $1,260

B $1,400

C $1,594

D $1,873

(2 marks)

Q 18 The sales account is:

A credited with the total of sales made, including sales tax

B credited with the total of sales made, excluding sales tax

C debited with the total of sales made, including sales tax

D debited with the total of sales made, excluding sales tax

(1 mark)

Q 19 If sales (including sales tax) amounted to $27,612.50 and purchases (excluding sales tax) amounted to $18,000, the balance on the sales tax account, assuming all items are subject to sales tax at 17.5%, would be:

A $962.50 debit

B $962.50 credit

C $1,682.10 debit

D $1,682.10 credit

(2 marks)

Q 20 A business commenced with capital in cash of $1,000. Inventory costing $800 net of sales tax at 17.5% is purchased on credit. Half of this inventory is then sold for $1,000 plus sales tax, the customer paying promptly in cash.

The accounting equation after these transactions would show:

A assets $1,775 less liabilities $175 equals capital $1,600

B assets $2,775 less liabilities $975 equals capital $1,200

C assets $2,575 less liabilities $800 equals capital $1,775

D assets $2,575 less liabilities $975 equals capital $1,600

(2 marks)

Chapter 6: Accruals and prepayments

Q 21 The electricity account for the year ended 30 April 2005 was as follows:

	$
Electricity accrued at 1 May 2004	250
Payments made during the year in relation to:	
Quarter ending 30 June 2004	400
Quarter ending 30 September 2004	350
Quarter ending 31 December 2004	425
Quarter ending 31 March 2005	450

Which of the following is the appropriate entry for electricity?

	Accrued at 30 April 2005	Charge to income statement for year ended 30 April 2005
A	$Nil	$1,375
B	$150	$1,525
C	$300	$1,675
D	$450	$1,825

(2 marks)

Q 22 The year end of Lansdown is 31 December. The company pays for its electricity by a standing order of $100 per month. On 1 January 2005 the statement from the electricity supplier showed that the company had overpaid by $25. Lansdown received electricity bills for the four quarters starting on 1 January 2005 and ending on 31 December 2005 for $350, $375, $275 and $300 respectively.

Which of the following is the correct entry for electricity in Lansdown's income statement and statement of financial position for the year ending 31 December 2005?

IS	SFP
A $1,300	$75 accrual
B $1,300	$75 prepayment
C $1,200	$125 accrual
D $1,200	$125 prepayment

(2 marks)

Q 23 At 1 January 2005, Michael had a prepayment of $200 in respect of rent. He paid $1,200 on 1 March 2005 in respect of the year ended 28 February 2006

What is the charge to the income statement in respect of rent for the year ended 31 December 2005?

A $1,400

B $1,200

C $1,100

D $1,300

(1 mark)

Q 24 At 31 December 2003, Tony had accrued $240 in respect of light and heat for the quarter ending 31 December 2003. In January 2004 he discovered that he had under-accrued by $10.

The bills for the next four quarters were as follows (q.e. = quarter ended):

Amount	Relating to	Date paid
$260	q.e. 31 March 2004	15 April 2004
$220	q.e. 30 June 2004	17 July 2004
$210	q.e. 30 September 2004	14 October 2004
$230	q.e. 31 December 2004	19 January 2005

Tony always accrues for expenses based on the last bill.

What is the charge to the income statement in respect of light and heat for the 15-month period ended 31 March 2005?

A $1,160

B $1,150

C $930

D $920

(2 marks)

Q 25 Stationery paid for during the year amounted to $1,350. At the beginning of the year there was an inventory of stationery on hand of $165 and an outstanding stationery invoice for $80. At the end of the year there was an inventory of stationery on hand of $140 and an outstanding stationery invoice for $70. **The stationery figure to be shown in the income statement for the year is:**

A $1,195

B $1,335

C $1,365

D $1,505

(1 mark)

Chapter 7: Irrecoverable debts and allowances for receivables

Q 26 At 30 April 2005, Gareth has a receivables balance of $50,000 and an allowance for receivables of $800. Following a review of receivables, Gareth wishes to write off an irrecoverable debt of $1,000 and adjust his allowance to 5% of receivables.

What will be the adjusted balance of the allowance for receivables?

A $1,650

B $2,450

C $2,500

D $3,450

(1 mark)

Q 27 As at 31 March, Phil had receivables of $82,500. Following a review of receivables, Phil has decided to write off the following irrecoverable debts:

John	$1,000
Beatrice	$500
Peter	$3,250

Phil would like to provide against a specific debt of $250 and based on past experience, make a general allowance at 2% of receivables. The current balance on the allowance for receivables account is $2,000. Phil also received $300 from a debt that had been previously been written off.

What is the charge to the income statement in respect of irrecoverable debt expense and the entry on the statement of financial position for net receivables at 31 March?

	Income statement charge	Statement of financial position
A	$4,250	$75,950
B	$4,450	$77,750
C	$4,450	$75,950
D	$4,250	$77,750

(2 marks)

Q 28 At the start of the year Joe had an allowance of $700 against receivables. During the year $450 of this amount went bad and $150 was received; the balance remained unpaid at the year end. Another amount of $170 went bad. At the year end it was decided to provide for a new debt of $240.

What was the total irrecoverable debt expense for the year?

A $170

B $260

C $410

D $710

(2 marks)

Q 29 Doris currently has a receivables balance of $47,800 and an allowance for receivables of $1,250. She has received $150 in respect of half of a debt that she had provided against. She now believes the other half of the debt to be bad and wishes to write it off. She also wishes to maintain her allowance at 2% receivables.

KAPLAN PUBLISHING

What is the total charge to the income statement in respect of these items?

A $150 debit

B $150 credit

C $300 debit

D $300 credit

(2 marks)

Q 30 At the year end, Harold has a receivables balance of $100,000 and an allowance for receivables of $5,000. He has not yet accounted for a receipt of $500 in respect of a debt which he had previously provided against or a receipt of $1,000 in respect of a debt which had been written off in the previous year. Harold wishes to maintain his allowance for receivables at 7% of receivables.

What balances will be shown in his statement of financial position at the year end for receivables and the allowance for receivables?

	Receivables	Allowance
A	$98,500	$6,465
B	$99,500	$6,465
C	$98,500	$6,965
D	$99,500	$6,965

(2 marks)

Q 31 James has been advised that one of his customers has ceased trading and that it is almost certain that he will not recover the balance of $720 owed by this customer.

What entry should James make in his general ledger?

A Dr Receivables $720

   Cr Irrecoverable debts $720

   Being write off of irrecoverable debt

B Dr Irrecoverable debts $720

   Cr Receivables $720

   Being write off of irrecoverable debt

C Dr Receivables $720

   Cr Bank $720

   Being write off of irrecoverable debt

D Dr Bank $720

   Cr Receivables $720

   Being write off of irrecoverable debt.

(1 mark)

Q **32** Gordon's receivables owe a total of $80,000 at the year end. These include $900 of long-overdue debts that might still be recoverable, but for which Gordon has created an allowance for receivables. Gordon has also provided an allowance of $1,582, which is the equivalent of 2% of the other receivables' balances.

What best describes Gordon's allowance for receivables as at his year end?

A a specific allowance of $900 and an additional allowance of $1,582 based on past history

B a specific allowance of $1,582 and an additional allowance of $900 based on past history

C a specific allowance of $2,482

D a general allowance of $2,482

(1 mark)

Chapter 8: Non-current assets

Q **33** At 1 January 2005, Mary has motor vehicles which cost $15,000. On 31 August 2005 she sells a motor vehicle for $5,000 which had originally cost $8,000 and which had a NBV of $4,000 at the date of disposal. She purchased a new motor vehicle which cost $10,000 on 30 November 2005.

Her policy is to depreciate motor vehicles at a rate of 25% pa on the straight-line basis, based on the number of months' ownership.

What is the depreciation charge for the year ended 31 December 2005?

A $3,750

B $3,291

C $4,250

D $3,500

(2 marks)

Q **34** **Which of the following best explains what is meant by 'capital expenditure'?**

A expenditure on non-current assets, including repairs and maintenance

B expenditure on expensive assets

C expenditure relating to the issue of share capital

D expenditure relating to the acquisition or improvement of non-current assets

(1 mark)

Q **35** A non-current asset was purchased at the beginning of Year 1 for $2,400 and depreciated by 20% pa by the reducing-balance method. At the beginning of Year 4 it was sold for $1,200. The result of this was:

A a loss on disposal of $240.00

B a loss on disposal of $28.80

C a profit on disposal of $28.80

D a profit on disposal of $240.00

(2 marks)

Q **36** Giles bought a new machine from abroad. The machine cost $100,000 and delivery and installation costs were $7,000. Testing it amounted to $5,000. Training employees on how to use the machine cost of $1,000.

What should be the cost of the machine in the company's statement of financial position?

A $100,000

B $107,000

C $112,000

D $113,000

(1 mark)

Q **37** Joseph's machinery cost account showed a balance of $5,000 at 1 January 2005. During the year he had the following transactions:

28 February	Disposed of machine costing $300
31 March	Acquired machine costing $1,000
1 November	Disposed of machine costing $600

Joseph depreciates machines at a rate of 10% pa on the straight-line basis based on the number of months' ownership.

What is the depreciation charge in respect of machinery for the year ended 31 December 2005?

A $545

B $540

C $510

D $630

(2 marks)

Q **38** B acquired a lorry on 1 May 20X0 at a cost of $30,000. The lorry has an estimated useful life of four years, and an estimated resale value at the end of that time of $6,000. B charges depreciation on the straight-line basis, with a proportionate charge in the period of acquisition.

What will the depreciation charge for the lorry be in B's ten-month accounting period to 30 September 20X0?

A $3,000

B $2,500

C $2,000

D $5,000

(1 mark)

Chapter 9: From trial balance to financial statements

The following is the extract of Jessie's trial balance as at 31 December 2005:

	Dr	Cr
	$	$
Buildings	580,000	
Buildings accumulated depreciation		116,000
Plant and machinery	50,000	
Plant and machinery accumulated depreciation		12,500
Receivables	25,800	
Allowance for receivables		1,900
Rent	34,000	
Insurance	30,000	
Irrecoverable debts	1,800	

The following notes are provided:

(i)   Buildings are depreciated at 2% pa on a straight-line basis.

(ii) Plant and machinery is depreciated at 25% pa on a reducing-balance basis.

(iii) Additional irrecoverable debts of $3,200 were discovered at the year end. It has been decided to make an allowance for receivables of 5% on the adjusted receivables at the year end.

(iv) The monthly rental charge is $3,000.

(v) The insurance charge for the year is $24,000.

Using the above information attempt the following questions.

(2 marks)

Q 39 The depreciation charge for buildings for the year and the net book value (NBV) at the year end will be:

	Depreciation charge $	NBV $
A	11,600	568,400
B	9,280	464,000
C	11,600	452,400
D	11,600	464,000

(2 marks)

Q 40 The depreciation charge for plant and machinery for the year and the NBV at the year end will be:

	Depreciation charge $	NBV $
A	9,375	37,500
B	12,500	25,000
C	9,375	40,625
D	9,375	28,125

(2 marks)

Q 41 The total irrecoverable debt expense for the year and the closing net receivable balance will be:

	Irrecoverable debt expense $	Receivables $
A	4,230	21,470
B	5,000	21,470
C	5,770	21,830
D	2,430	19,670

(2 marks)

Q 42 **What is the charge for rent and insurance for the year and the closing accrual and prepayment?**

	Charge for the year		Closing accrual/prepayment	
		$		$
A	Rent	30,000	Rent accrual	3,000
	Insurance	24,000	Insurance prepayment	6,000
B	Rent	36,000	Rent accrual	2,000
	Insurance	24,000	Insurance prepayment	6,000
C	Rent	36,000	Rent accrual	3,000
	Insurance	24,000	Insurance prepayment	6,000
D	Rent	30,000	Rent accrual	3,000
	Insurance	30,000	Insurance prepayment	6,000

(2 marks)

Chapter 10: Books of prime entry and control accounts

Q 43 **Which of the following is not the purpose of a receivables ledger control account?**

A A receivables ledger control account provides a check on the arithmetic accuracy of the personal ledger.

B A receivables ledger control account helps to locate errors in the trial balance.

C A receivables ledger control account ensures that there are no errors in the personal ledger.

D Control accounts deter fraud.

(1 mark)

Q 44 **Which one of the following is a book of prime entry and part of the double-entry system?**

A the journal

B the petty cash book

C the sales day book

D the purchase ledger

(1 mark)

Q 45 On 1 January 2005 the balance of receivables was $22,000. Calculate the closing receivables after taking the following into consideration:

	$
Sales	120,000
Bank receipts	115,000
Discount allowed	1,000
Discount received	3,000
Dishonoured cheque	9,000
Contra – Set off	5,000

A $30,000

B $23,000

C $12,000

D $28,000

(1 mark)

Chapter 11: Control account reconciliations

Q 46 A receivables ledger control account had a closing balance of $8,500. It contained a contra to the purchase ledger of $400, but this had been entered on the wrong side of the control account.

The correct balance on the control account should be:

A $7,700 debit

B $8,100 debit

C $8,400 debit

D $8,900 debit

(1 mark)

Q 47 The receivables ledger control account at 1 May had balances of $32,750 debit and $1,275 credit. During May sales of $125,000 were made on credit. Receipts from receivables amounted to $122,500 and cash discounts of $550 were allowed. Refunds of $1,300 were made to customers. The closing credit balance is $2,000.

The closing debit balances at 31 May should be:

A $35,175

B $35,675

C $36,725

D $34,725

(1 mark)

Q **48** A supplier sends you a statement showing a balance outstanding of $14,350. Your own records show a balance outstanding of $14,500.

The reason for this difference could be that:

A The supplier sent an invoice for $150 which you have not yet received.

B The supplier has allowed you $150 cash discount which you had omitted to enter in your ledgers.

C You have paid the supplier $150 which he has not yet accounted for.

D You have returned goods worth $150 which the supplier has not yet accounted for.

(1 mark)

Q **49** **A credit balance of $917 brought forward on Y's account in the books of X means that:**

A X owes Y $917

B Y owes X $917

C X has paid Y $917

D X is owed $917 by Y

(1 mark)

Q **50** **In a receivables ledger control account, which of the following lists is composed only of items which would appear on the credit side of the account?**

A Cash received from customers, sales returns, irrecoverable debts written off, contras against amounts due to suppliers in the accounts payable ledger

B Sales, cash refunds to customers, irrecoverable debts written off, discounts allowed

C Cash received from customers, discounts allowed, interest charged on overdue accounts, irrecoverable debts written off

D Sales, cash refunds to customers, interest charged on overdue accounts, contras against amounts due to suppliers in the accounts payable ledger.

(1 mark)

Chapter 12: Bank reconciliations

Q **51** **The following information relates to a bank reconciliation.**

(i) The bank balance in the cash book before taking the items below into account was $5,670 overdrawn.

(ii) Bank charges of $250 on the bank statement have not been entered in the cash book.

(iii) The bank has credited the account in error with $40 which belongs to another customer.

(iv) Cheque payments totalling $325 have been correctly entered in the cash book but have not been presented for payment.

(v) Cheques totalling $545 have been correctly entered on the debit side of the cash book but have not been paid in at the bank.

What was the balance as shown by the bank statement before taking the items above into account?

A $5,670 overdrawn

B $5,600 overdrawn

C $5,740 overdrawn

D $6,100 overdrawn

(2 marks)

Q **52** At 31 August 2005 the balance on the company's cash book was $3,600 credit. Examination of the bank statements revealed the following:

– Standing orders amounting to $180 had not been recorded in the cash book.

– Cheques paid to suppliers of $1,420 did not appear on the bank statements.

What was the balance on the bank statement at 31 August 2005?

A $5,200 overdrawn

B $5,020 overdrawn

C $2,360 overdrawn

D $3,780 overdrawn

(1 mark)

Q 53 An organisation's cash book has an operating balance of $485 credit. The following transactions then took place:
- cash sales $1,450 including sales tax of $150
- receipts from customers of debts of $2,400
- payments to payables of debts of $1,800 less 5% cash discount
- dishonoured cheques from customers amounting to $250.

The resulting balance in the bank column of the cash book should be:

A $1,255 debit

B $1,405 debit

C $1,905 credit

D $2,375 credit

(2 marks)

Q 54 The cash book shows a bank balance of $5,675 overdrawn at 31 March 2005. It is subsequently discovered that a standing order for $125 has been entered twice and that a dishonoured cheque for $450 has been debited in the cash book instead of credited.

The correct bank balance should be:

A $5,100 overdrawn

B $6,000 overdrawn

C $6,250 overdrawn

D $6,450 overdrawn

(1 mark)

Q 55 **The attempt below at a bank reconciliation statement has been prepared by Q Limited. Assuming the bank statement balance of $38,600 to be correct, what should the cash book balance be?**

A $76,500 overdrawn, as stated

B $5,900 overdrawn

C $700 overdrawn

D $5,900 cash at bank

	$
Overdraft per bank statement	38,600
Add: deposits not credited	41,200
	79,800
Less: outstanding cheques	3,300
Overdraft per cash book	76,500

(1 mark)

KAPLAN PUBLISHING

Q **56** After checking a business cash book against the bank statement, which of the following items could require an entry in the cash book?

1 Bank charges

2 A cheque from a customer which was dishonoured

3 Cheque not presented

4 Deposits not credited

5 Credit transfer entered in bank statement

6 Standing order entered in bank statement.

A 1, 2, 5 and 6

B 3 and 4

C 1, 3, 4 and 6

D 3, 4, 5 and 6

(1 mark)

Chapter 13: Correction of errors and suspense accounts

Q **57** Faulty goods costing $210 were returned to a supplier but this was recorded as $120 in the ledger accounts.

What is the journal entry necessary to correct the error?

	Dr		Cr	
A	Suspense	90	Purchases returns	90
B	Purchases	90	Payables	90
C	Payables	90	Suspense	90
D	Payables	90	Purchases returns	90

(1 mark)

Q **58** A suspense account was opened when a trial balance failed to agree. The following errors were later discovered:

- a gas bill of $420 had been recorded in the gas account as $240

- discount of $50 given to a customer had been credited to discounts received

- interest received of $70 had been entered in the bank account only.

The original balance on the suspense account was:

A debit $210

B credit $210

C debit $160

D credit $160

(2 marks)

Q 59 Molly starts up in business as a florist on 1 April 2004. For the first six months, she has a draft profit of $12,355.

On investigation you discover the following:

- Rent paid for the 12 months ending 31 March 2005 of $800 has not been recorded in the accounts.
- Closing inventory in the accounts at a cost of $1,000 has a net realisable value of $800.

What is the adjusted profit for the period?

A $11,355

B $11,755

C $12,155

D $12,555

(1 mark)

Q 60 **In an accounting system where individual receivables and payables ledger accounts are maintained as an integral part of the double entry, which of the following errors will not be identified by a trial balance?**

A overcasting of the sales day book

B undercasting of the analysed cash book

C failure to transfer a non-current asset to the disposal account when sold

D transposition error in an individual receivables account

(1 mark)

Q 61 A trial balance has been extracted and a suspense account opened. One error relates to the misposting of an amount of $400, being discount received from suppliers, which was posted to the wrong side of the discount received account

What is the correcting journal entry?

		Dr	Cr
A	Discount received	$400	
	Suspense		$400
B	Suspense	$400	
	Discount received		$400
C	Discount received	$800	
	Suspense		$800
D	Suspense	$800	
	Discount received		$800

(1 mark)

KAPLAN PUBLISHING

Q **62** A company, Y, purchased some plant on 1 January 20X0 for $38,000. The payment for the plant was correctly entered in the cash book but was entered on the debit side of plant repairs account.

Y charges depreciation on the straight-line basis at 20% pa, with a proportionate charge in the year of acquisition and assuming no scrap value at the end of the life of the asset.

How will Y's profit for the year ended 31 March 20X0 be affected by the error?

A Understated by $30,400

B Understated by $36,100

C Understated by $38,000

D Overstated by $1,900

(2 marks)

Q **63 The trial balance of Z failed to agree, the totals being:**

Debit $836,200

Credit $819,700

A suspense account was opened for the amount of the difference and the following errors were found and corrected:

1 The totals of the cash discount columns in the cash book had not been posted to the discount accounts. The figures were discount allowed $3,900 and discount received $5,100.

2 A cheque for $19,000 received from a customer was correctly entered in the cash book but was posted to the customer's account as $9,100.

What will the remaining balance on the suspense account be after the correction of these errors?

A $25,300 credit

B $7,700 credit

C $27,700 credit

D $5,400 credit

(2 marks)

Q 64 The trial balance of C did not agree, and a suspense account was opened for the difference. Checking in the bookkeeping system revealed a number of errors.

1 $4,600 paid for motor van repairs was correctly treated in the cash book but was credited to motor vehicles asset account.

2 $360 received from B, a customer, was credited in error to the account of BB.

3 $9,500 paid for rent was debited to the rent account as $5,900.

4 The total of the discount allowed column in the cash book had been debited in error to the discounts received account.

5 No entries had been made to record a cash sale of $100.

Which of the errors above would require an entry to the suspense account as part of the process of correcting them?

A 3 and 4

B 1 and 3

C 2 and 5

D 2 and 3

(2 marks)

Chapter 14: Applications of IT

Q 65 Which of the following is not a quality of information?

A Accuracy

B Colourfulness

C Cost effectiveness

D Timeliness

(1 mark)

Q 66 Match the different types of input device listed in column 1 with the relevant applications listed in column 2.

Column 1

Optical mark reader

Bar code reader

Scanner

Optical character recognition

Column 2

Cheque processing

Examination answer sheets

Capturing images

Point of sale systems

(1 mark)

Q 67 'User friendly' is an expression which is used to describe functionality which has been designed specifically to make the system easier to use for those who are not IT-trained. Both hardware and software features can be considered.

Which of the following is an example of hardware user friendliness (the others are examples of software)?

A Icon

B Touch screen

C Pull down list

D Default value

(1 mark)

Chapter 15: Incomplete records

Q 68 **Ashley started a business on 1 January 2005. He acquired the following assets:**

Van	$2,000
Inventory	$1,000
Receivables	$500
Prepaid insurance for inventory	$100

He also opened a business bank account and paid in $4,000. At the end of the first year of trading, he had the following:

Van	$1,800
Fixtures	$500
Inventory	$840
Receivables	$600
Payables	$400
Cash	$3,400

He had drawn $1,000 in cash during the period.

What was Ashley's profit or loss for the year?

A $140 loss

B $140 profit

C $1,860 loss

D $1,860 profit

(2 marks)

Q 69 George started a business by investing $10,000 into a business bank account. At the end of his first year's trading he had earned a profit of $5,000 and had the following assets and liabilities:

Non-current assets	$20,000
Current assets	$15,000
Current liabilities	$8,000

During the year he had withdrawn $2,000 from the business.

How much further capital had he introduced in the year?

A $20,000

B $24,000

C $10,000

D $14,000

(1 mark)

Q 70 **If Harry's mark-up on cost of sales is 15%, what is his gross profit margin?**

A 12.5%

B 13.04%

C 15%

D 17.65%

(1 mark)

Q 71 A sole trader had opening capital of $10,000 and closing capital of $4,500. During the period the owner introduced capital of $4,000 and withdrew $8,000 for her own use.

Her profit or loss during the period was:

A $9,500 loss

B $1,500 loss

C $7,500 profit

D $17,500 profit

(1 mark)

Q 72 From the following information, calculate the value of purchases:

	$
Opening payables	142,600
Cash paid	542,300
Discounts received	13,200
Goods returned	27,500
Closing payables	137,800

A $302,600

B $506,400

C $523,200

D $578,200

(2 marks)

Q 73 Carol owns a shop. The only information available for the year ended 31 December 2005 is as follows:

Inventory at 1 January 2005	$3,500
Inventory at 31 December 2005	$1,350
Sales	$17,000
Gross profit margin	25%

What were the purchases of the shop for the year?

A $11,450

B $12,750

C $14,900

D $10,600

(1 mark)

Q 74 The following information is relevant to the calculation of the sales figure for Alpha, a sole trader who does not keep proper accounting records:

	$
Opening receivables	29,100
Cash received from credit customers and paid into the bank	381,600
Expenses paid out of cash received from credit customers before banking	6,800
Irrecoverable debts written off	7,200
Refunds to credit customers	2,100
Discounts allowed to credit customers	9,400
Cash sales	112,900
Closing receivables	38,600

The figure which should appear in Alpha's income statement for sales is:

A $525,300

B $511,700

C $529,500

D $510,900

(2 marks)

Q **75** A sole trader who does not keep full accounting records wishes to calculate her sales revenue for the year.

The information available is:

1	Opening inventory	$17,000
2	Closing inventory	$24,000
3	Purchases	$91,000
4	Standard gross profit percentage	40% on sales revenue

Which of the following is the sales revenue figure for the year calculated from these figures?

A $117,600

B $108,000

C $210,000

D $140,000

(1 mark)

Q **76** A business compiling its accounts for the year to 31 January each year pays rent quarterly in advance on 1 January, 1 April, 1 July and 1 October each year. After remaining unchanged for some years, the rent was increased from $24,000 per year to $30,000 per year as from 1 July 20X0.

Which of the following figures is the rent expense which should appear in the income statement for the year ended 31 January 20X1?

A $27,500

B $29,500

C $28,000

D $29,000

(1 mark)

Q **77** On 31 December 20X0 the inventory of V was completely destroyed by fire. The following information is available:

1 Inventory at 1 December 20X0 at cost $28,400.

2 Purchases for December 20X0 $49,600.

3 Sales for December 20X0 $64,800.

4 Standard gross profit percentage on sales revenue 30%.

Based on this information, which of the following is the amount of inventory destroyed?

A $45,360

B $32,640

C $40,971

D $19,440

(2 marks)

Chapter 16 : Partnerships

Q **78** Alf, Ben, Connie and Dora are in partnership. The capital they have invested in the partnership is $45,000, $30,000, $20,000 and $15,000 respectively. Their partnership agreement states the following terms:

– Interest is to be allowed on capital at a rate of 10% pa.
– Connie and Dora are to receive salaries of $5,000 each.
– Any remaining profits are to be shared in the ratio 4:3:2:1 respectively.

In the year ended 31 December 2005, the partnership earned profits of $56,000.

What is the total share of the profits each partner is entitled to in the year ended 31 December 2005?

	Alf	Ben	Connie	Dora
A	$14,000	$14,000	$14,000	$14,000
B	$22,400	$16,800	$11,200	$5,600
C	$22,500	$16,500	$11,000	$6,000
D	$18,500	$13,500	$14,000	$10,000

(2 marks)

Q 79 Warren, Hall and Oates are in partnership. In the year ended 31 December 2005 the partners received the following shares of the profits:

	Warren	Hall	Oates
Interest on capital	$5,200	$4,940	$4,550
Remaining share of profits	$12,656	$9,492	$3,164
Total	$17,856	$14,432	$7,714

The capital accounts of Warren, Hall and Oates were $40,000, $38,000 and $35,000 respectively.

Which of the following best describes the terms for appropriating profits in the partnership?

A Interest on capital at 13%, PSR of 4:3:1

B Interest on capital at 10%, PSR of 4:3:1

C Interest on capital at 13%, PSR of 3:2:1

D Interest on capital at 10%, PSR of 3:2:1

(2 marks)

Q 80 Alpha, Beta and Gamma are in partnership. The profits of the partnership for the year ended 30 June 2005 have currently been appropriated as follows:

Alpha $30,000

Beta $10,000

Gamma $8,000

The partnership agreement states that Beta is entitled to a guaranteed minimum profit share (GMPS) of $14,000. The profit sharing ratio is 3:2:1.

What share of the profits is each partner entitled to in the year ended 30 June 2005?

	Alpha	Beta	Gamma
A	$30,000	$14,000	$8,000
B	$27,000	$14,000	$7,000
C	$26,000	$14,000	$8,000
D	$28,000	$14,000	$6,000

(2 marks)

Q **81** D, E and F are in partnership, sharing profits in the ratio 5:3:2 respectively, after charging salaries for E and F of $24,000 each per year.

On 1 July 20X0 they agreed to change the profit-sharing ratio to 3:1:1 and increase E's salary to $36,000 per year, F's salary continuing unchanged.

For the year ended 31 December 20X0 the partnership profit amounted to $480,000.

Which of the following correctly states the partners' total profit shares for the year?

	D	E	F
A	$234,000	$136,800	$109,200
B	$213,000	$157,800	$109,200
C	$186,000	$171,600	$122,400
D	$237,600	$132,000	$110,400

(2 marks)

Q **82** J and K are in partnership sharing profits and losses in the ratio of 4:1. They decide to admit L to the partnership. The new partnership ratio is to be 4:3:3. At the time of admission of L goodwill is valued at $80,000. It has been decided not to maintain a goodwill account.

What is the overall net double entry in the capital accounts of the partners for the adjustment of goodwill after admission of L is taken into account?

A Dr Capital a/c – J $32,000
   Cr Capital a/c – K $8,000
   Cr Capital a/c – L $24,000

B Dr Capital a/c – K $8,000
   Dr Capital a/c – L $24,000
   Cr Capital a/c – J $32,000

C Dr Capital a/c – K $8,000
   Dr Capital a/c – L $24,000
   Cr Capital a/c – J $32,000

D Dr Capital a/c – K $8,000
   Dr Capital a/c – L $24,000
   Cr Capital a/c – J $32,000

(2 marks)

Chapter 17: Company accounts

Q **83** Geese's trial balance shows an overprovision in respect of income tax for the year ended 31 December 2004 of $5,000. Geese estimates that tax liability in respect of the year ended 31 December 2005 will be $23,000.

What is the tax charge in Geese's income statement and the statement of financial position entry for the year ended 31 December 2005?

	Income statement charge	Statement of financial position
A	$5,000	$18,000
B	$23,000	$18,000
C	$18,000	$23,000
D	$28,000	$23,000

(1 mark)

Q **84** **The correct journal entry to record the issue of 100,000 50c shares (fully paid) at an issue price of $2.50 a share is:**

			$	$
A	Dr	Bank	250,000	
	Cr	Share capital		100,000
	Cr	Share premium		150,000
B	Dr	Bank	250,000	
	Cr	Share capital		50,000
	Cr	Share premium		200,000
C	Dr	Bank	50,000	
	Cr	Share premium		50,000
D	Dr	Share capital	100,000	
	Dr	Share premium	150,000	
	Cr	Bank		250,000

(1 mark)

Q **85** **A company has the following share capital:**

	Authorised	Issued
	$000	$000
25c ordinary shares	8,000	4,000
6% 50c preference shares	2,000	1,000

In addition to providing for the year's preference dividend, an ordinary dividend of 2c per share is to be paid.

Q   What are total dividends for the year?

   A $140,000

   B $380,000

   C $440,000

   D $760,000

(1 mark)

Q   86   Revenue reserves are:

   A accumulated and undistributed profits of a company

   B amounts which cannot be distributed as dividends

   C amounts set aside out of profits to replace
      revenue items

   D amounts set aside out of profits for a specific purpose

(1 mark)

Q   87   On 1 April 2004 the balance on B's accumulated profit account was $50,000 credit. The balance on 31 March 2005 was $100,000 credit. On 10 March 2005 dividends of $50,000 were declared in respect of the year ended 31 March 2005, payable on 31 May 2005.

   Based on this information, profit after tax (but before dividends) for the year ended 31 March 2005 was:

   A Nil

   B $50,000

   C $100,000

   D $150,000

(1 mark)

Chapter 18: Accounting standards

88   Jackson's year end is 31 December 2005. In February 2006 a major credit customer went into liquidation and the directors believe that they will not be able to recover the $450,000 owed to them.

   How should this item be treated in the financial statements of Jackson for the year ended 31 December 2005?

   A The irrecoverable debt should be disclosed by note.

   B The financial statements are not affected.

   C The debt should be provided against.

   D The financial statements should be adjusted to reflect the irrecoverable debt.

(1 mark)

Q **89** A former employee is claiming compensation of $50,000 from Harriot, a limited liability company. The company's solicitors have stated that they believe that the claim is unlikely to succeed. The legal costs relating to the claim are likely to be in the region of $5,000 and will be incurred regardless of whether or not the claim is successful.

How should these items be treated in the financial statements of Harriot Ltd?

A Provision should be made for $55,000.

B Provision should be made for $50,000 and the legal costs should be disclosed by note.

C Provision should be made for $5,000 and the compensation of $50,000 should be disclosed by note.

D No provisions should be made but both items should be disclosed by note.

(1 mark)

Q **90** Cowper has spent $20,000 researching new cleaning chemicals in the year ended 31 December 2005. It has also spent $40,000 developing a new cleaning product which will not go into commercial production until next year. The development project meets the criteria laid down in IAS 38.

How should these costs be treated in the financial statements of Cowper for the year ended 31 December 2005?

A $60,000 should be capitalised as an intangible asset on the statement of financial position.

B $40,000 should be capitalised as an intangible asset and should be amortised; $20,000 should be written off to the income statement.

C $40,000 should be capitalised as an intangible asset and should not be amortised; $20,000 should be written off to the income statement.

D $60,000 should be written off to the income statement.

(1 mark)

Q **91** The directors of ABC estimated that inventory which had cost $50,000 had a net realisable value of $40,000 at 30 June 2005 and recorded it in the financial statements for the year ended 30 June 2005 at this lower value in accordance with IAS 2. They have since found out that the net realisable value of the inventory is only likely to be $30,000.

What adjustments, if any, should be made in the financial statements in respect of this inventory?

A No adjustments required.

B Increase the value of inventory by $10,000.

C Decrease the value of inventory by $10,000.

D Decrease the value of inventory by $20,000.

(1 mark)

Q 92 Which of the following items are non-adjusting items per IAS 10?

(a) the issue of new share or loan capital

(b) financial consequences of losses of non-current assets or inventory as a result of fires or floods

(c) information regarding the value of inventory sold at less than cost thus resulting in a reduction in the value of inventory

(d) mergers and acquisitions

(e) bankruptcy of a credit customer

A (a), (b) and (d)

B (c) and (e)

C (a), (d) and (e)

D (b), (c) and (e)

(1 mark)

Q 93 Which of the following correctly describes how research and development expenditure should be treated in accordance with IAS 38?

A Research and development expenditure must be written off to the income statement as incurred.

B Research and development expenditure should be capitalised as an intangible asset on the statement of financial position.

C Research expenditure should be written off to the income statement; development expenditure must be capitalised as an intangible asset provided that certain criteria are met.

D Research expenditure should be capitalised as an intangible asset provided that certain criteria are met; development expenditure should be written off to the income statement.

(1 mark)

Q 94 **Who issues International Financial Reporting Standards?**

A The Auditing Practices Board

B The Stock Exchange

C The International Accounting Standards Board

D The government

(1 mark)

Q 95 **Which of the following statements concerning the accounting treatment of research and development expenditure are true, according to IAS 38 Intangible Assets?**

1 If certain criteria are met, research expenditure may be recognised as an asset.

2 Research expenditure, other than capital expenditure on research facilities, should be recognised as an expense as incurred.

3 In deciding whether development expenditure qualifies to be recognised as an asset, it is necessary to consider whether there will be adequate finance available to complete the project.

4 Development expenditure recognised as an asset must be amortised over a period not exceeding five years.

5 The financial statements should disclose the total amount of research and development expenditure recognised as an expense during the period.

A 1, 4 and 5

B 2, 4 and 5

C 2, 3 and 4

D 2, 3 and 5

(2 marks)

KAPLAN PUBLISHING

Q **96** IAS10 Events after the reporting period regulates the extent to which events after the reporting period date should be reflected in financial statements.

Which of the following lists of such events consists only of items that, according to IAS10 should normally be classified as non-adjusting?

A Insolvency of a debtor whose account receivable was outstanding at the statement of financial position date, issue of shares or loan notes, a major merger with another company.

B Issue of shares or loan notes, changes in foreign exchange rates, major purchases of non-current assets.

C A major merger with another company, destruction of a major non-current asset by fire, discovery of fraud or error which shows that the financial statements were incorrect.

D Sale of inventory giving evidence about its value at the statement of financial position date, issue of shares or loan notes, destruction of a major non-current asset by fire.

(2 marks)

Chapter 19: Statement of cash flows

Q **97** In the year ended 31 December 2005, Lamb bought new vehicles from Warwick Motors with a list price of $100,000 for $70,000 cash and an allowance against old motor vehicles of $30,000. The value of the vehicles taken in part exchange was $27,000.

Lamb sold other vehicles with a net book value of $12,000 for $15,000 cash.

In Lamb's statement of cash flow for the year ended 31 December 2005, how would the above transactions be presented under the heading 'Investing activities'?

	Cash inflow	Cash outflow
A	–	$76,000
B	$45,000	$100,000
C	$15,000	$70,000
D	$15,000	$100,000

(2 marks)

Q 98 Baldrick has the following balances in its statement of financial position as at 30 June 2004 and 30 June 2005:

	30 June 2005 $	30 June 2004 $
Current liabilities		
Taxation payable	600	400
Dividends (declared before the year end)	3,300	2,500
Non-current liabilities		
8% Loan notes	50,000	40,000
Capital and reserves		
Accumulated profits	65,500	45,500

In the year ended 30 June 2005 taxation of $550 was paid. The additional loan notes were issued on 30 June 2005.

What is the operating profit of Baldrick for the year ended 30 June 2005?

A $27,250

B $26,450

C $28,050

D $27,100

(2 marks)

Q 99 At 31 December 2004, Topaz had provided $50,000 in respect of income tax. At 31 December 2005, the company estimated that its income tax bill in respect of the year would be $57,000. The amount charged in the income statement for the year ended 31 December 2005 in respect of income tax was $60,000.

How much will appear in the statement of cash flows for the year ended 31 December 2005 in respect of income tax?

A $50,000

B $53,000

C $57,000

D $60,000

(1 mark)

Q 100 Evans had the following balances in its statement of financial positions as at 30 June 2004 and 2005:

	2004	2005
10% Loan notes	$150,000	$130,000
Share capital	$100,000	$120,000
Share premium	$35,000	$45,000

How much will appear in the cash flow statement for the year ended 30 June 2005 under the heading of 'Financing activities'?

A $nil

B $10,000 inflow

C $30,000 inflow

D $40,000 inflow

(1 mark)

The following information relates to Questions 101 and 102.

Scents had the following balances in its statement of financial positions as at 30 September 2004 and 2005:

	2004	2005
Loan interest accrual	$5,000	$3,000
Proposed ordinary dividends	$20,000	$25,000
10% Loan notes	$100,000	$100,000
Ordinary share capital	$150,000	$150,000
8% Preference share capital	$50,000	$50,000

Q 101 How much will appear in the statement of cash flowst for the year ended 30 September 2005 for the loan interest and preference dividend paid?

A $10,000

B $12,000

C $16,000

D $32,000

(2 marks)

Q 102 How much will appear in the statement of cash flows for the year ended 30 September 2005 for the ordinary dividend paid?

A $20,000

B $24,000

C $25,000

D $29,000

(1 mark)

Q 103 IAS 7 Statement of cash flows requires the statement of cash flows prepared using the indirect method to include the calculation of net cash from operating activities.

Which of the following lists consists only of items which could appear in such a calculation?

A Depreciation, increase in receivables, decrease in payables, proceeds of sale of plant.

B Increase in payables, decrease in inventories, profit on sale of plant, depreciation.

C Increase in payables, depreciation, decrease in receivables, proceeds of sale of plant.

D Depreciation, interest paid, equity dividends paid, purchase of plant.

(1 mark)

Chapter 20: The regulatory and conceptual framework

Q 104 **When preparing financial statements under historic cost accounting in periods of inflation, directors:**

A must reduce asset values

B must increase asset values

C must reduce dividends

D need make no adjustments

(1 mark)

Q 105 **If the owner of a business takes goods from inventory for his own personal use, the accounting concept to be considered is the:**

A relevance concept

B capitalisation concept

C money measurement concept

D separate entity concept

(1 mark)

Q 106 **A 'true and fair view' is one which:**

A presents the accounts in such a way as to exclude errors which would affect the actions of those reading them

B occurs when the accounts have been audited

C shows the accounts of an organisation in an understandable format

D shows the assets on the statement of financial position at their current market price

(1 mark)

Q **107** **Which concept is followed when a business records the cost of a non-current asset even though it does not legally own it?**

A substance over form

B prudence

C accruals

D going concern

(1 mark)

Q **108** The IASB Framework for the Preparation and Presentation of Financial Statements gives five characteristics that make financial information **reliable**.

These five characteristics are:

A prudence, consistency, understandability, faithful representation, substance over form

B accruals basis, going concern concept, consistency, prudence, true and fair view

C faithful representation, neutrality, substance over form, completeness, consistency, faithful and free

D free from material error, prudence, faithful representation, neutrality, completeness

(1 mark)

Q **109** **The accounting concept or convention which, in times of rising prices, tends to understate asset values and overstate profits, is the:**

A going concern concept

B prudence concept

C realisation concept

D historical cost concept

(1 mark)

KAPLAN PUBLISHING

Answers

MULTIPLE CHOICE ANSWERS

Chapter 2: Statement of financial position and income statement

A 1 C

A 2 C

A 3 A

A 4 C

A 5 C

Chapter 3: Double entry bookkeeping

A 6 D

A 7 D

A 8 C

A 9 B

A 10 D

A 11 C

Chapter 4: Inventory

A 12 D

	A $	B $	C $	Total $
Cost	7	10	19	
NRV	13	8	14	
Lower of cost or NRV	7	8	14	
x Number of units	20	25	15	
Valuation	140	200	210	550

A **13 A**

$(35 \times \$15) + (30 \times \$20) = \$1,125$

A **14 C**

A **15 The correct answer is D**

A **16 The correct answer is C**

400 items		$
Cost	400 x $4	1,600
NRV	(400 x $3) – $200	1,000

Therefore use NRV.

200 items		$
Cost	200 x $30	6,000
NRV	(200 x $35) – $1,200 – $300	5,500

Therefore use NRV.

Total inventory figure = $116,400 + $1,000 + $5,500
= $122,900.

Chapter 5: Sales tax

A **17 A**

Sales tax

	$		$
Purchases	2,100	Sales	3,500
(17.5 % x 12,000)		23,500 x 17.5/117.5	
Expenses	140		
(17.5% x 800)			
Bal c/f	1,260		
	3,500		3,500
		Bal b/f	1,260

A **18 B**

A **19 B**

Sales tax

	$		$
Purchases	3,150.00	Sales	4,112.50
(17.5 % x 18,000)		27,612.50 x 17.5/117.5	
Bal c/f	962.50		
	4,112.50		4,112.50
		Bal b/f	962.50

A **20 D**

Assets		$	$
	Cash (1,000 + 1,175)		2,175
	Inventory		400
			2,575
Liabilities	Payables (800 x 1.175)	940	
	Sales tax (175 – 140)	35	
			(975)
			1,600
Capital	Capital		1,000
	Profit (1,000 – 400)		600
			1,600

Chapter 6: Accruals and prepayments

A **21 B**

Electricity

	$		$
Bank	400	Bal b/f	250
Bank	350		
Bank	425	Income statement	1,525
Bank	450		
Bal c/f (ß)	150		
	1,775		1,775
		Bal b/f (450/3)	150

A **22 A**

Electricity

	$		$
Bal b/f	25		
Bank (12 x 100)	1,200		
		Income statement	1,300
		(350 + 375 + 275 + 300)	
Bal c/f (ß)	75		
	1,300		1,300
		Bal b/f	75

A **23 B**

Rent

	$		$
Bal b/f	200		
Bank	1,200	Income statement (ß)	1,200
		Bal c/f	200
	1,400		1,400
Bal b/f (2/12 x 1,200)	200		

A **24 A**

Light and heat

	$		$
Bank (240 + 10)	250	Bal b/f	240
Bank	260		
Bank	220		
Bank	210	Income statement (ß)	1,160
Bank	230		
Bal c/f	230		
	1,400		1,400
		Bal b/f	230
		(last quarter's bill)	

A **25 C**

Stationery payable

	$		$
		Bal b/f	80
Bank	1,350	Purchases of stationery (ß)	1,340
Bal c/f	70		
	1,420		1,420
		Bal b/f	70

Opening inventory + Purchases − Closing inventory = $165 + $1,340 − $140 = $1,365

Chapter 7: Irrecoverable debts and allowances for receivables

A **26 B**

5% x (50,000 − 1,000) = $2,450

A 27 A

Receivables

	$		$
Bal b/f	82,500	Irrecoverable debts	4,750
		Bal c/f	77,750
	82,800		82,800
Bal b/f	77,750		

Irrecoverable debts

	$		$
Receivables	4,750	Decrease in allowance	200
(1000 + 500 + 3250)		Cash receipt from debt	300
		previously written off	
		Income statement account	4,250
	4,750		4,750

Allowance at 31 March	$
Specific allowance	250
General allowance	1,550
(2% x (77,750 – 250))	1,800
Current allowance balance	2,000
Movement in allowance balance	200 decrease

Net receivables = $77,750 – $1,800 = $75,950

A 28 B

Allowance for receivables

	$		$
		Bal b/f	700
Irrecoverable debts (ß)	360		
Bal c/f	340		
	700		700
		Bal b/f	340

Irrecoverable debts

	$		$
Receivables	450	Decrease in allowance	360
Receivables	170	Income statement account	260
	620		620

Allowance required at end of year = $700 – $450 – $150 + $240 = $340

A **29 B**

Receivables

	$		$
Bal b/f	47,800	Bank	150
		Irrecoverable debts	150
		Bal c/f	47,500
	47,800		47,800
Bal b/f	47,500		

Irrecoverable debt expense

	$		$
		Decrease in allowance	300
Receivables	150		
Income statement	150		
	300		300

A **30 D**

Receivables

	$		$
Bal b/f	100,000	Bank	500
		Bal c/f	99,500
	101,000		101,000
Bal b/f	99,500		

Allowance for receivables

	$		$
		Bal b/f	5,000
		Income statement (ß)	1,965
Bal c/f	6,965		
	6,965		6,965
		Bal b/f (7% x 99,500)	6,965

A **31 B**

This is an example of an irrecoverable debt being written off. Credit the receivables account in order to clear the debt and debit the irrecoverable debts account with the amount of the debt written off.

A **32 A**

There is a specific allowance for the debt of $900 which has still not been written off as irrecoverable, and an additional allowance equivalent to 2% of the remaining balance based on past history.

Chapter 8: Non-current assets

A **33 B**

	$
Assets held all year ($15,000 – 8,000) x 25%	1,750
Asset disposed of $8,000 x 25% x 8/12	1,333
Asset acquired $10,000 x 25% x 1/12	208
Total depreciation	3,291

A **34 D**

A **35 B**

	$
Proceeds of sale	1,200.00
NBV at disposal (2,400 – 480 – 384 – 307.20)	(1,228.80)
Loss on disposal	(28.80)

Depreciation to disposal

Yr 1: $2,400 x 20% = $480
Yr 2: $(2,400 – 480) x 20% = $384
Yr 3: $(2,400 – 480 – 384) x 20% = $307.20

A **36 C**

$100,000 + $7,000 + $5,000 = $112,000

A **37 B**

	$
Assets held all year (5,000 – 300 – 600) x 10%	410
Disposals	
$300 x 10% x 2/12	5
$600 x 10% x 10/12	50
Acquisition $1,000 x 10% x 9/12	75
Total depreciation	540

A **38 B**

$$\frac{\$30,000 - \$6,000}{4} \times {}^{5}/_{12} = \$2,500$$

KAPLAN PUBLISHING

Chapter 9: From trial balance to financial statements

A 39 C

Depreciation charge = $11,600 (2% x $580,000)

NBV = $452,400 [$580,000 – ($116,000 + $11,600)]

A 40 D

Depreciation charge = $9,375 [25% x $37,500 ($50,000 – $12,500)]

Net book value = $28,125 [$50,000 – ($12,500 + $9,375)]

A 41 A

	$
Irrecoverable debts $1,800 + 3,200 =	5,000
Decrease in allowance for receivables	(770)
Total irrecoverable debt expense	**4,230**
Receivables ($25,800 – 3,200)	22,600
Less: Closing allowance for receivables	(1,130)
Net closing receivables	**21,470**

	$
Closing allowance for receivables [5% x ($25,800 – 3,200)]	1,130
Opening allowance for receivables	1,900
Decrease in allowance for receivables	770

A 42 B

	Charge for the year $			Closing $
Rent	**36,000** (12 x $3,000)	**Rent accrual**		**2,000**
		Due	36,000	
		Paid	34,000	
		Accrual	2,000	
Insurance	**24,000**	**Insurance prepayment**		**6,000**
		Paid	30,000	
		Due	24,000	
		Prepayment	6,000	

Chapter 10: Books of prime entry and control accounts

A 43 C

A 44 B

A 45 A

Receivables

	$		$
Bal b/f	22,000	Bank	115,000
Sales	120,000		
		Discounts allowed	1,000
Dishonoured cheque	9,000	Contra	5,000
		Bal c/f	30,000
	151,000		151,000
Bal b/f	30,000		

Chapter 11: Control account reconciliations

A 46 A

$8,500 – ($400 x 2) = $7,700

A 47 C

Receivables ledger control account

	$		$
Bal b/f	32,750	Bal b/f	1,275
Sales	125,000	Bank	122,500
Refunds	1,300	Discounts allowed	550
Bal c/f	2,000	Bal c/f	36,725
	161,050		161,050
Bal b/f	36,725	Bal b/f	2,000

A 48 B

A 49 A

A 50 A

The other three lists all contain one item which should appear on the debit side of the account.

Chapter 12: Bank reconciliations

A **51 D**

Bank – cash book

	$		$
		Bal b/f (i)	5,670
		Bank charges (ii)	250
Bal c/f	5,920		
	5,920		5,920
		Bal b/f	5,920

	$
Balance per bank statement (ß)	(6,100)
Add: Error (iii)	(40)
Add: Outstanding cheques (iv)	(325)
Less: Outstanding lodgements(v)	545
Balance per cash book	(5,920)

A **52 C**

Balance per bank statement (ß)	($2,360) o/d
Add: Outstanding cheques	($1,420)
Balance per cash book (3,600 + 180)	($3,780) o/d

A **53 B**

Bank – cash book

	$		$
Sales	1,450	Bal b/f	485
Receivables	2,400	Payables (0.95 x 1,800)	1,710
		Dishonoured cheques	250
		Bal c/f	1,405
	3,850		3,850
Bal b/f	1,405		

A **54 D**

Bank – cash book

	$		$
Standing order	125	Bal b/f	5,675
		Dishonoured cheque	900
		($450 x 2)	
Bal c/f	6,450		
	6,575		6,575
		Bal b/f	6,450

A 55 C

The bank reconciliation should have been calculated as follows:

	$
Overdraft per bank statement	(38,600)
Add deposits not yet credited	41,200
	2,600
Less outstanding cheques	(3,300)
Overdraft per cash book	(700)

A 56 A

Items 3 and 4 relate to timing differences only and would appear in the bank reconciliation.

Chapter 13: Correction of errors and suspense accounts

A 57 D

A 58 A

Suspense			
	$		$
Bal b/f (ß)	210	Gas (420 – 240)	180
Interest receivable	70	Discounts (50 x 2)	100
	280		280

A 59 B

Draft profit for the period	$12,355
Six months' rent 6/12 x 800	($400)
Closing Inventory adjustment (1,000 – 800)	($200)
	$11,755

A 60 C

A 61 D

A **62 B**

The profit will be understated by the following amount:

	$
Amount charged in error to the repairs account	38,000
Less depreciation chargeable on the plant (3/12 x 20% x $38,000)	(1,900)
	$36,100

A **63 D**

	$	
Opening balance on suspense account ($836,200 – $819,700)	16,500	Cr
Difference remaining after postings to the discount accounts ($5,100 – $3,900)	(1,200)	
Difference from cheque incorrectly posted ($19,000 – $9,100)	(9,900)	
	$5,400	Cr

A **64 B**

Items 1 and 3 would result in an imbalance in the trial balance and therefore require an entry to the suspense account. Items 2, 4 and 5 do not affect the balancing of the accounts.

Chapter 14: Applications of IT

A **65 B**

All of the other options are vital for the information to be understood by the user. Although colour might make the information to easier to understand, it often only improves the presentation.

A **66**

Input device	Application
Optical mark reader	Examination answer sheets
Bar code reader	Point of sale systems
Scanner	Capturing images
Optical character recognition	Cheque processing

A **67 B**

Touch screen is an example of hardware which can be installed and used for a number of applications such as purchasing a ticket, ATM (Automatic Teller Machines) and flight check in. All of the other examples (icon, pull down list and default values) are functions of the software.

Chapter 15: Incomplete records

A 68 B

Closing net assets – Opening net assets = Capital Introduced + Profit for year – Drawings

$6,740 – $7,600 = 0 + Profit for year – 1,000

Profit for year = $140

A 69 D

Closing net assets – Opening net assets = Capital Introduced + Profit for year – Drawings in year

$27,000 – $10,000 = Capital Introduced + $5,000 – $2,000

Capital Introduced = $14,000

A 70 B

	%
Sales	115
Cost of Sales	100
Gross profit	15

15/115 = 13.04%

A 71 B

Closing net assets – Opening net assets = Capital Introduced + Profit for year – Drawings

$4,500 – $10,000 = $4,000 + Profit/(loss) – $8,000

Loss for year = $1,500

A 72 D

Payables

	$		$
Bank	542,300	Bal b/f	142,600
Discounts received	13,200		
Returns outwards	27,500	Purchases (ß)	578,200
Bal c/f	137,800		
	720,800		720,800
		Bal b/f	137,800

KAPLAN PUBLISHING

A 73 D

Cost of Sales = 75% x $17,000 = $12,750

Purchases = $12,750 + $1,350 – $3,500 = $10,600

A 74 A

Credit sales can be calculated as a balancing figure on the Receivables ledger control account.

Receivables ledger control account

	$		$
Balance b/f	29,100	Bank takings	381,600
Bank – refunds	2,100	Expenses	6,800
Credit sales	412,400	Irrecoverable debts	7,200
(balance)		Discounts allowed	9,400
		Balance c/f	38,600
	443,600		443,600

Credit sales = $412,400, cash sales = $112,900, total sales = $525,300

A 75 D

	$
Opening inventory	17,000
Purchases	91,000
Closing inventory	(24,000)
Cost of sales	84,000

Sales = $84,000 x 100/60 = $140,000

A 76 A

The rent expense for the year should be:

(5/12 x $24,000) + (7/12 x $30,000) = $27,500

A 77 B

Cost of sales = 70% x $64,800 =	$45,360
	$
Opening inventory	28,400
Purchases	49,600
Cost of sales	(45,360)
Loss of inventory	32,640

Chapter 16 : Partnerships

A 78 D

	Alf $	Ben $	Connie $	Dora $	Total $
Profit					56,000
Salaries			5,000	5,000	(10,000)
Interest on capital	4,500	3,000	2,000	1,500	(11,000)
					35,000
PSR 4:3:2:1	14,000	10,500	7,000	3,500	(35,000)
Total	18,500	13,500	14,000	10,000	

A 79 A

$5,200/$40,000 = 13%

$12,656/$3,164 = 4

$9,492/$3,164 = 3

A 80 B

	Alpha $	Beta $	Gamma $
Appropriated	30,000	10,000	8,000
GMPS	(3,000)	4,000	(1,000)
Total	27,000	14,000	7,000

A 81 A

	D $000	E $000	F $000	Total $000
First 6 months' profit				240
Salaries		12	12	(24)
Balance in PSR (5:3:2)	108	64.8	43.2	216
Second 6 months' profit				240
Salaries		18	12	(30)
Balance in PSR (3:1:1)	126	42	42	210
Total profit shares	234	136.8	109.2	

KAPLAN PUBLISHING

A **82 B**

(i) Before admission of L record goodwill as follows:

Dr	Goodwill	$80,000
Cr	Capital a/c – J	$64,000
Cr	Capital a/c – K	$16,000

Credit old partners in their old profit share ratio (4:1)

(ii) After admission of L write off goodwill as follows:

Dr	Capital a/c – J	$32,000
Dr	Capital a/c – K	$24,000
Dr	Capital a/c – L	$24,000
Cr	Goodwill	$80,000

Debit new partners in their new profit share ratio (4:3:3)

(iii) Net double entry is (i) less (ii)

Dr	Capital a/c – K	$8,000
Dr	Capital a/c – L	$24,000
Cr	Capital a/c – J	$32,000

Chapter 17: Company accounts

A **83 C**

Income statement charge	$
2005 estimate	23,000
Overprovision 2004	(5,000)
	18,000
Tax liability	23,000

A **84 B**

A **85 B**

	$
Preference dividends (6% x 1,000,000) =	60,000
Ordinary dividends (16,000,000 x 0.02) =	320,000
Total dividend =	380,000

A **86 A**

A 87 C

	$
Profit after tax (balancing figure)	100,000
Dividends	(50,000)
Profit for year	50,000
Accumulated profit b/f	50,000
Accumulated profit c/f	100,000

Chapter 18: Accounting standards

A 88 D

A 89 C

A 90 C

A 91 C

A 92 A

A 93 C

A 94 C

A 95 D

Statements 2, 3 and 5 are correct

A 96 B

The other lists contain adjusting items

Chapter 19: Statements of cash flow

A 97 C

A **98 A**

	$
Retained profit for the year $(65,500 − 45,500)	20,000
Dividends	3,300
Taxation $(600 + 550 − 400)	750
Interest payable (8% x $40,000)	3,200
Operating profit	27,250

A **99 B**

Income tax

	$		$
		Bal b/f	50,000
Bank (ß)	53,000		
		Income statement	60,000
Bal c/f	57,000		
	110,000		110,000
		Bal b/f	57,000

A **100 B**

	$
Issue of share capital $(20,000+10,000)	30,000 inflow
Repayment of loan notes	20,000 outflow
	10,000 inflow

A **101 C**

Loan interest payable

	$		$
		Bal b/f	5,000
Bank (ß)	12,000	Income statement	10,000
		(100,000 x 10%)	
Bal c/f	3,000		
	15,000		15,000
		Bal b/f	3,000

Preference dividends 8% x $50,000 = $4,000
Total payments = $12,000 + $4,000 = $16,000

A **102 A**

A **103 B**

All other lists contain one or more items that would not appear in the calculation of net cash from operating activities

Chapter 20: The regulatory and conceptual framework

A **104 D**

A **105 D**

A **106 A**

A **107 A**

A **108 D**

The other three contain items which are not considered to contribute towards reliability.

A **109 D**

Index

Index

Index

Index

KAPLAN PUBLISHING

Index

Index

KAPLAN PUBLISHING